# Generalized Linear Mode

MW00843988

Actuaries should have the tools they need. Generalized linear models are used in the insurance industry to support critical decisions. Yet no text introduces GLMs in this context and addresses problems specific to insurance data. Until now.

Practical and rigorous, this books treats GLMs, covers all standard exponential family distributions, extends the methodology to correlated data structures, and discusses other techniques of interest and how they contrast with GLMs. The focus is on issues which are specific to insurance data and all techniques are illustrated on data sets relevant to insurance.

Exercises and data-based practicals help readers to consolidate their skills, with solutions and data sets given on the companion website. Although the book is package-independent, SAS code and output examples feature in an appendix and on the website. In addition, R code and output for all examples are provided on the website.

## International Series on Actuarial Science

Mark Davis, Imperial College London
John Hylands, Standard Life
John McCutcheon, Heriot-Watt University
Ragnar Norberg, London School of Economics
H. Panjer, Waterloo University
Andrew Wilson, Watson Wyatt

The International Series on Actuarial Science, published by Cambridge University Press in conjunction with the Institute of Actuaries and the Faculty of Actuaries, will contain textbooks for students taking courses in or related to actuarial science, as well as more advanced works designed for continuing professional development or for describing and synthesizing research. The series will be a vehicle for publishing books that reflect changes and developments in the curriculum, that encourage the introduction of courses on actuarial science in universities, and that show how actuarial science can be used in all areas where there is long-term financial risk.

# GENERALIZED LINEAR MODELS FOR INSURANCE DATA

PIET DE JONG

*Department of Actuarial Studies, Macquarie University, Sydney*

GILLIAN Z. HELLER

*Department of Statistics, Macquarie University, Sydney*

CAMBRIDGE
UNIVERSITY PRESS

# CAMBRIDGE
## UNIVERSITY PRESS

University Printing House, Cambridge CB2 8BS, United Kingdom

Published in the United States of America by Cambridge University Press, New York

Cambridge University Press is part of the University of Cambridge.

It furthers the University's mission by disseminating knowledge in the pursuit of education, learning and research at the highest international levels of excellence.

www.cambridge.org
Information on this title: www.cambridge.org/9780521879149
http://www.afas.mq.edu.au/research/books/glms_for_insurance_data

© P. de Jong and G. Z. Heller 2008

First published 2008
5th printing 2013

A catalogue record for this publication is available from the British Library

ISBN 978-0-521-87914-9 Hardback

# Contents

# Preface

The motivation for this book arose out of our many years of teaching actuarial students and analyzing insurance data. Generalized linear models are ideally suited to the analysis of non-normal data which insurance analysts typically encounter. However the acceptance, uptake and understanding of this methodology has been slow in insurance compared to other disciplines. Part of the reason may be the lack of a suitable textbook geared towards an actuarial audience. This book seeks to address that need.

We have tried to make the book as practical as possible. Analyses are based on real data. All but one of the data sets are available on the companion website to this book:

`http://www.afas.mq.edu.au/research/books/glms_for_`
`insurance_data`.

Computer code and output for all examples is given in Appendix 1.

The SAS software is widely used in the insurance industry. Hence computations in this text are illustrated using SAS. The statistical language R is used where computations are not conveniently performed in SAS. In addition, R code and output for all the examples is provided on the companion website. Exercises are given at the end of chapters, and fully worked solutions are available on the website.

The body of the text is independent of software or software "runs." In most cases, fitting results are displayed in tabular form. Remarks on computer implementation are confined to paragraphs headed "SAS notes" and "Implementation" and these notes can be skipped without loss of continuity.

Readers are assumed to be familiar with the following statistical concepts: discrete and continuous random variables, probability distributions, estimation, hypothesis testing, and linear regression (the normal model). Relevant basics of probability and estimation are covered in Chapters 2 and 3, but familiarity with these concepts is assumed. Normal linear regression is covered in Chapter 4: again it is expected readers have previously encountered the material. This chapter sets the scene for the rest of the book and discuss concepts that are applicable to regression models in general.

Excessive notation is avoided. The meanings of symbols will be clear from the context. For example a response variable is denoted by $y$, and there is no notational distinction between the random variable and its realization. The vector of outcomes is also denoted by $y$. Derivatives are denoted using the dot notation: $\dot{f}(y)$ and double dots denote second derivatives. This avoids confusion with the notation for matrix transposition $X'$, frequently required in the same mathematical expressions. Tedious and generally uninformative subscripting is avoided. For example, the expression $y = x'\beta$ used in this text can be written as $y_i = x_i'\beta$, or even more explicitly and laboriously as $y_i = \beta_0 + \beta_1 x_{i1} + \ldots + \beta_p x_{ip}$ . Generally such laboring is avoided. Usually $x$ denotes the vector $(1, x_1, \ldots, x_p)'$ and $\beta$ denotes $(\beta_0, \ldots, \beta_p)'$. The equivalence symbol "$\equiv$" is used when a quantity is defined. The symbol "$\sim$" denotes "distributed as," either exactly or approximately.

Both authors contributed equally to this book, and authorship order was determined by the alphabetical convention. Much of the book was written while GH was on sabbatical leave at CSIRO Mathematical and Information Sciences, Sydney, whom she thanks for their hospitality. We thank Christine Lu for her assistance. And to our families Dana, Doryon, Michelle and Dean, and Steven, Ilana and Monique, our heartfelt thanks for putting up with the many hours that we spent on this text.

Piet de Jong
Gillian Heller

Sydney, 2007

# 1

# Insurance data

Generalized linear modeling is a methodology for modeling relationships between variables. It generalizes the classical normal linear model, by relaxing some of its restrictive assumptions, and provides methods for the analysis of non-normal data. The tools date back to the original article by Nelder and Wedderburn (1972) and have since become part of mainstream statistics, used in many diverse areas of application.

This text presents the generalized linear model (GLM) methodology, with applications oriented to data that actuarial analysts are likely to encounter, and the analyses that they are likely required to perform.

With the GLM, the variability in one variable is explained by the changes in one or more other variables. The variable being explained is called the "dependent" or "response" variable, while the variables that are doing the explaining are the "explanatory" variables. In some contexts these are called "risk factors" or "drivers of risk." The model explains the connection between the response and the explanatory variables.

Statistical modeling in general and generalized linear modeling in particular is the art or science of designing, fitting and interpreting a model. A statistical model helps in answering the following types of questions:

- Which explanatory variables are predictive of the response, and what is the appropriate scale for their inclusion in the model?
- Is the variability in the response well explained by the variability in the explanatory variables?
- What is the prediction of the response for given values of the explanatory variables, and what is the precision associated with this prediction?

A statistical model is only as good as the data underlying it. Consequently a good understanding of the data is an essential starting point for modeling. A significant amount of time is spent on cleaning and exploring the data. This chapter discusses different types of insurance data. Methods for

1

the display, exploration and transformation of the data are demonstrated and biases typically encountered are highlighted.

## 1.1 Introduction

Figure 1.1 displays summaries of insurance data relating to $n = 22\,036$ settled personal injury insurance claims, described on page 14. These claims were reported during the period from July 1989 through to the end of 1999. Claims settled with zero payment are excluded.

The top left panel of Figure 1.1 displays a histogram of the dollar values of the claims. The top right indicates the proportion of cases which are legally represented. The bottom left indicates the proportion of various injury codes as discussed in Section 1.2 below. The bottom right panel is a histogram of settlement delay.

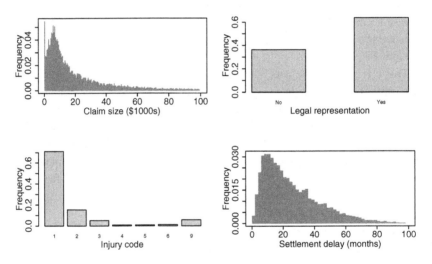

Fig. 1.1. Graphical representation of personal injury insurance data

This data set is typical of those amenable to generalized linear modeling. The aim of statistical modeling is usually to address questions of the following nature:

- What is the relationship between settlement delay and the finalized claim amount?
- Does legal representation have any effect on the dollar value of the claim?
- What is the impact on the dollar value of claims of the level of injury?
- Given a claim has already dragged on for some time and given the level of injury and the fact that it is legally represented, what is the likely outcome of the claim?

Answering such questions is subject to pitfalls and problems. This book aims to point these out and outline useful tools that have been developed to aid in providing answers.

Modeling is not an end in itself, rather the aim is to provide a framework for answering questions of interest. Different models can, and often are, applied to the same data depending on the question of interest. This stresses that modeling is a pragmatic activity and there is no such thing as the "true" model.

Models connect variables, and the art of connecting variables requires an understanding of the nature of the variables. Variables come in different forms: discrete or continuous, nominal, ordinal, categorical, and so on. It is important to distinguish between different types of variables, as the way that they can reasonably enter a model depends on their type. Variables can, and often are, transformed. Part of modeling requires one to consider the appropriate transformations of variables.

## 1.2 Types of variables

Insurance data is usually organized in a two-way array according to cases and variables. Cases can be policies, claims, individuals or accidents. Variables can be level of injury, sex, dollar cost, whether there is legal representation, and so on. Cases and variables are flexible constructs: a variable in one study forms the cases in another. Variables can be quantitative or qualitative. The data displayed in Figure 1.1 provide an illustration of types of variables often encountered in insurance:

- *Claim amount* is an example of what is commonly regarded as continuous variable even though, practically speaking, it is confined to an integer number of dollars. In this case the variable is skewed to the right. Not indicated on the graphs are a small number of very large claims in excess of $100 000. The largest claim is around $4.5 million dollars. Continuous variables are also called "interval" variables to indicate they can take on values anywhere in an interval of the real line.
- *Legal representation* is a categorical variable with two levels "no" or "yes." Variables taking on just two possible values are often coded "0" and "1" and are also called binary, indicator or Bernoulli variables. Binary variables indicate the presence or absence of an attribute, or occurrence or non-occurrence of an event of interest such as a claim or fatality.
- *Injury code* is a categorical variable, also called qualitative. The variable has seven values corresponding to different levels of physical injury: 1–6 and 9. Level 1 indicates the lowest level of injury, 2 the next level and so on up to level 5 which is a catastrophic level of injury, while level 6 indicates death. Level 9 corresponds to an "unknown" or unrecorded level of injury

and hence probably indicates no physical injury. The injury code variable is thus partially ordered, although there are no levels 7 and 8 and level 9 does not conform to the ordering. Categorical variables generally take on one of a discrete set of values which are nominal in nature and need not be ordered. Other types of categorical variables are the type of crash: (non-injury, injury, fatality); or claim type on household insurance: (burglary, storm, other types). When there is a natural ordering in the categories, such as (none, mild, moderate, severe), then the variable is called ordinal.

- The distribution of *settlement delay* is in the final panel. This is another example of a continuous variable, which in practical terms is confined to an integer number of months or days.

Data are often converted to counts or frequencies. Examples of count variables are: number of claims on a class of policy in a year, number of traffic accidents at an intersection in a week, number of children in a family, number of deaths in a population. Count variables are by their nature non-negative integers. They are sometimes expressed as relative frequencies or proportions.

### 1.3 Data transformations

The panels in Figure 1.2 indicate alternative transformations and displays of the personal injury data:

- **Histogram of log claim size.** The top left panel displays the histogram of log claim size. Compared to the histogram in Figure 1.1 of actual claim size, the logarithm is roughly symmetric and indeed almost normal. Historically normal variables have been easier to model. However generalized linear modeling has been at least partially developed to deal with data that are not normally distributed.
- **Claim size versus settlement delay.** The top right panel does not reveal a clear picture of the relationship between claim sizes and settlement delay. It is expected that larger claims are associated with longer delays since larger claims are often more contentious and difficult to quantify. Whatever the relationship, it is masked by noise.
- **Claim size versus operational time.** The bottom left panel displays claim size versus the percentile rank of the settlement delay. The percentile rank is the percentage of cases that settle faster than the given case. In insurance data analysis the settlement delay percentile rank is called operational time. Thus a claim with operational time 23% means that 23% of claims in the group are settled faster than the given case. Note that both the mean and variability of claim size appear to increase with operational time.
- **Log claim size versus operational time.** The bottom right panel of Figure 1.2 plots log claim size versus operational time. The relationship

between claim and settlement delay is now apparent: log claim size increases virtually linearly with operational time. The log transform has "stabilized the variance." Thus whereas in the bottom left panel the variance appears to increase with the mean and operational time, in the bottom right panel the variance is approximately constant. Variance-stabilizing transformations are further discussed in Section 4.9.

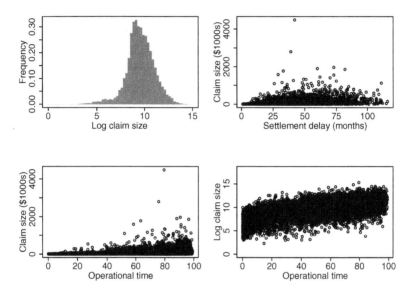

Fig. 1.2. Relationships between variables in personal injury insurance data set

The above examples illustrate ways of transforming a variable. The aim of transformations is to make variables more easily amenable to statistical analysis, and to tease out trends and effects. Commonly used transformations include:

- **Logarithms.** The log transform applies to positive variables. Logs are usually "natural" logs (to the base e $\approx$ 2.718 and denoted $\ln y$). If $x = \log_b(y)$ then $x = \ln(y)/\ln(b)$ and hence logs to different bases are multiples of each other.
- **Powers.** The power transform of a variable $y$ is $y^p$. For mathematical convenience this is rewritten as $y^{1-p/2}$ for $p \neq 2$ and interpreted as $\ln y$ if $p = 2$. This is known as the "Box–Cox" transform. The case $p = 0$ corresponds to the identity transform, $p = 1$ the square root and $p = 4$ the reciprocal. The transform is often used to stabilize the variance – see Section 4.9.
- **Percentile ranks and quantiles.** The percentile rank of a case is the percentage of cases having a value less than the given case. Thus the percentile

rank depends on the value of the given case as well as all other case values. Percentile ranks are uniformly distributed from 0 to 100. The quantile of a case is the value associated with a given percentile rank. For example the 75% quantile is the value of the case which has percentile rank 75. Quantiles are often called percentiles.

- **z-score.** Given a variable $y$, the z-score of a case is the number of standard deviations the value of $y$ for the given case is away from the mean. Both the mean and standard deviation are computed from all cases and hence, similar to percentile ranks, z-scores depend on all cases.
- **Logits.** If $y$ is between 0 and 1 then the logit of $y$ is $\ln\{y/(1-y)\}$. Logits lie between minus and plus infinity, and are used to transform a variable in the $(0,1)$ interval to one over the whole real line.

## 1.4 Data exploration

Data exploration using appropriate graphical displays and tabulations is a first step in model building. It makes for an overall understanding of relationships between variables, and it permits basic checks of the validity and appropriateness of individual data values, the likely direction of relationships and the likely size of model parameters. Data exploration is also used to examine:

  (i) relationships between the response and potential explanatory variables; and
 (ii) relationships between potential explanatory variables.

The findings of (i) suggest variables or risk factors for the model, and their likely effects on the response. The second point highlights which explanatory variables are associated. This understanding is essential for sensible model building. Strongly related explanatory variables are included in a model with care.

Data displays differ fundamentally, depending on whether the variables are continuous or categorical.

**Continuous by continuous.** The relationship between two continuous variables is explored with a scatterplot. A scatterplot is sometimes enhanced with the inclusion of a third, categorical, variable using color and/or different symbols. This is illustrated in Figure 1.3, an enhanced version of the bottom right panel of Figure 1.2. Here legal representation is indicated by the color of the plotted points. It is clear that the lower claim sizes tend to be the faster-settled claims without legal representation.

Scatterplot smoothers are useful for uncovering relationships between variables. These are similar in spirit to weighted moving average curves, albeit more sophisticated. Splines are commonly used scatterplot smoothers. They

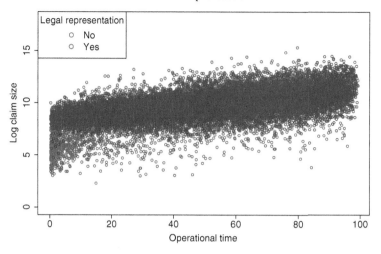

Fig. 1.3. Scatterplot for personal injury data

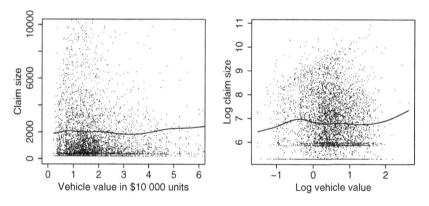

Fig. 1.4. Scatterplots with splines for vehicle insurance data

have a tuning parameter controlling the smoothness of the curve. The point of a
scatterplot smoother is to reveal the shape of a possibly nonlinear relationship.
The left panel of Figure 1.4 displays claim size plotted against vehicle value,
in the vehicle insurance data (described on page 15), with a spline curve superimposed. The right panel shows the scatterplot and spline with both variables
log-transformed. Both plots suggest that the relationship between claim size
and value is nonlinear. These displays do not indicate the strength or statistical
significance of the relationships.

Table 1.1. *Claim by driver's age in vehicle insurance*

| Claim | Driver's age category | | | | | | |
| | 1 | 2 | 3 | 4 | 5 | 6 | Total |
|---|---|---|---|---|---|---|---|
| Yes | 496 | 932 | 1 113 | 1 104 | 614 | 365 | 4 624 |
| | 8.6% | 7.2% | 7.1% | 6.8% | 5.7% | 5.6% | 6.8% |
| No | 5 246 | 11 943 | 14 654 | 15 085 | 10 122 | 6 182 | 63 232 |
| | 91.4% | 92.8% | 92.9% | 93.2% | 94.3% | 94.4% | 93.2% |
| Total | 5 742 | 12 875 | 15 767 | 16 189 | 10 736 | 6 547 | 67 856 |

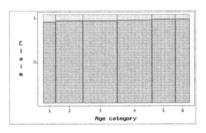
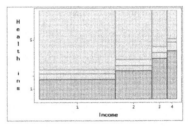

Vehicle insurance                 Private health insurance

Fig. 1.5. Mosaic plots

**Categorical by categorical.** A frequency table is the usual means of display when examining the relationship between two categorical variables. Mosaic plots are also useful. A simple example is given in Table 1.1, displaying the occurrence of a claim in the vehicle insurance data tabulated by driver's age category. Column percentages are also shown. The overall percentage of no claims is 93.2%. This percentage increases monotonically from 91.4% for the youngest drivers to 94.4% for the oldest drivers. The effect is shown graphically in the mosaic plot in the left panel of Figure 1.5. The areas of the rectangles are proportional to the frequencies in the corresponding cells in the table, and the column widths are proportional to the square roots of the column frequencies. The relationship of claim occurrence with age is clearly visible.

A more substantial example is the relationship of type of private health insurance with personal income, in the National Health Survey data, described on page 17. The tabulation and mosaic plot are shown in Table 1.2 and the right panel of Figure 1.5, respectively. "Hospital and ancillary" insurance is coded as 1, and is indicated as the red cells on the mosaic plot. The trend for increasing uptake of hospital and ancillary insurance with increasing income level is apparent in the plot.

Table 1.2. *Private health insurance type by income*

| Private health insurance type | | <$20 000 1 | Income $20 000 –$35 000 2 | $35 000 –$50 000 3 | >$50 000 4 | Total |
|---|---|---|---|---|---|---|
| Hospital and ancillary | 1 | 2 178 22.6% | 1 534 32.3% | 875 45.9% | 693 54.8% | 5 280 30.1% |
| Hospital only | 2 | 611 6.3% | 269 5.7% | 132 6.9% | 120 9.5% | 1 132 6.5% |
| Ancillary only | 3 | 397 4.1% | 306 6.5% | 119 6.2% | 46 3.6% | 868 4.9% |
| None | 5 | 6 458 67.0% | 2 638 55.6% | 780 40.9% | 405 32.0% | 10 281 58.5% |
| Total | | 9 644 | 4 747 | 1 906 | 1 264 | 17 561 |

Mosaic plots are less effective when the number of categories is large. In this case, judicious collapsing of categories is helpful. A reference for mosaic plots and other visual displays is Friendly (2000).

**Continuous by categorical.** Boxplots are appropriate for examining a continuous variable against a categorical variable. The boxplots in Figure 1.6 display claim size against injury code and legal representation for the personal injury data. The left plots are of raw claim sizes: the extreme skewness blurs the relationships. The right plots are of log claim size: the log transform clarifies the effect of injury code. The effect of legal representation is not as obvious, but there is a suggestion that larger claim sizes are associated with legal representation.

Scatterplot smoothers are useful when a binary variable is plotted against a continuous variable. Consider the occurrence of a claim versus vehicle value, in the vehicle insurance data. In Figure 1.7, boxplots of vehicle value (top) and log vehicle value (bottom), by claim occurrence, are on the left. On the right, occurrence of a claim ($1 =$ yes, $0 =$ no) is plotted on the vertical axis, against vehicle value on the horizontal axis, with a scatterplot smoother. Raw vehicle values are used in the top plot and log-transformed values in the bottom plot. In the boxplots, the only discernible difference between vehicle values of those policies which had a claim and those which did not, is that policies with a claim have a smaller variation in vehicle value. The plots on the right are more informative. They show that the probability of a claim is nonlinear, possibly quadratic, with the maximum probability occurring for vehicles valued

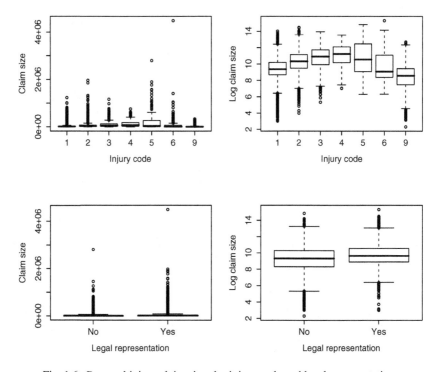

Fig. 1.6. Personal injury claim sizes by injury code and legal representation

around $40 000. This information is important for formulating a model for the probability of a claim. This is discussed in Section 7.3.

## 1.5 Grouping and runoff triangles

Cases are often grouped according to one or more categorical variables. For example, the personal injury insurance data may be grouped according to injury code and whether or not there is legal representation. Table 1.3 displays the average log claim sizes for such different groups.

An important form of grouping occurs when claims data is classified according to year of accident and settlement delay. Years are often replaced by months or quarters and the variable of interest is the total number of claims or total amount for each combination. If $i$ denotes the accident year and $j$ the settlement delay, then the matrix with $(i, j)$ entry equal to the total number or amount is called a runoff triangle. Table 1.4 displays the runoff triangle corresponding to the personal injury data. Runoff triangles have a triangular structure since $i + j > n$ is not yet observed, where $n$ is current time.

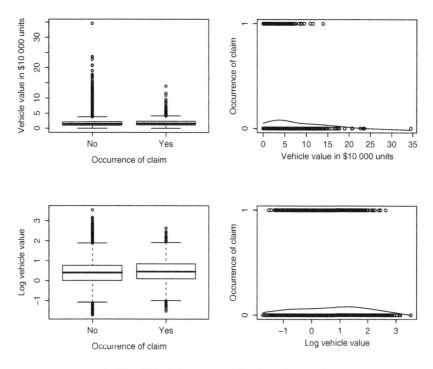

Fig. 1.7. Vehicle insurance claims by vehicle value

Table 1.3. *Personal injury average log claim sizes*

| Legal representation | Injury code | | | | | | |
|---|---|---|---|---|---|---|---|
| | 1 | 2 | 3 | 4 | 5 | 6 | 9 |
| No | 9.05 | 10.06 | 10.42 | 11.16 | 10.17 | 9.36 | 7.69 |
| Yes | 9.54 | 10.46 | 10.88 | 11.00 | 11.25 | 9.97 | 9.07 |

This runoff triangle also has the feature of zeroes in the top left, which occurs because data collection on settlements did not commence until the fourth year.

Accident years, corresponding to each row, show how claims "runoff." Settlement delay, corresponding to the columns, is often called the "development" year. Each calendar year leads to another diagonal of entries. For this triangle the final diagonal corresponds to a partial year, explaining the low totals. Runoff triangles are often standardized on the number of policies written in each year. The above triangle suggests this number is increasing over time.

Runoff triangles are usually more regular than the one displayed in Table 1.4, with a smooth and consistent progression of settlement amounts either in the development year direction or in the accident year direction.

Table 1.4. *Runoff triangle of amounts*

| Accident | Development year | | | | | | | | | |
|---|---|---|---|---|---|---|---|---|---|---|
| year | 0 | 1 | 2 | 3 | 4 | 5 | 6 | 7 | 8 | 9 |
| 1 | 0 | 0 | 0 | 6215 | 23050 | 20852 | 16946 | 10583 | 7340 | 3535 |
| 2 | 0 | 0 | 9765 | 23228 | 28464 | 21046 | 16672 | 13443 | 1882 | |
| 3 | 0 | 7719 | 21545 | 22191 | 23229 | 22947 | 13181 | 2713 | | |
| 4 | 2482 | 13474 | 26993 | 22446 | 26411 | 22718 | 5008 | | | |
| 5 | 4953 | 18546 | 29960 | 32750 | 29390 | 11388 | | | | |
| 6 | 7357 | 20054 | 39780 | 48431 | 9855 | | | | | |
| 7 | 6271 | 24084 | 39474 | 12684 | | | | | | |
| 8 | 6987 | 35430 | 12434 | | | | | | | |
| 9 | 9988 | 8858 | | | | | | | | |
| 10 | 707 | | | | | | | | | |

Runoff triangles are often the basis for forecasting incurred but not yet settled liabilities, corresponding to the lower triangular entries. One approach to
forecasting these liabilities is to use generalized linear modeling, discussed in
Section 8.1.

## 1.6 Assessing distributions

Statistical modeling, including generalized linear modeling, usually makes
assumptions about the random process generating the data. For example it
may be assumed that the logarithm of a variable is approximately normally
distributed. Distributional assumptions are checked by comparing empirical
percentile ranks to those computed on the basis of the assumed distribution.
For example suppose a variable is assumed normal. To check this, the observed
percentile ranks of the variable values are first computed. If the sample size
is $n$ then the smallest value has percentile rank $100/n$, the second smallest
$200/n$, and so on. These sample percentile ranks are compared to the theoretical percentile ranks of the sample values, based on the normal with the same
mean and standard deviation as the given sample. The "pp-plot" is a graphical means of assessing the agreement between these two sets of ranks. The
sample and theoretical percentile ranks are plotted against one another. Points
falling near the $45°$ line indicate the normal model fits the data well. A similar
procedure is used for testing distributions other than the normal.

The two panels in Figure 1.8 illustrate pp-plots for assessing the distribution of the size of claims for the personal injury insurance data. The left panel
compares the log of claim size against the normal, assessing whether the data
is lognormally distributed. The slight hump above the $45°$ line indicates for
example that the theoretical 20% percentile rank cuts out less than 20% in the
empirical distribution and hence the distribution has more skew than expected
with the lognormal. Thus while there is a small departure from normality in

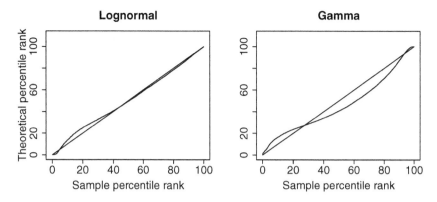

Fig. 1.8. pp-plots for personal injury claim sizes

the left tail, the overall fit of the lognormal distribution appears reasonable. The right panel indicates the gamma is a worse fit.

## 1.7 Data issues and biases

Insurance data sets are typically very large, of the order of tens of thousands up to millions of cases. Problems such as missing values (often indicated by a blank or zero or, in the case of a date, 1 January 1900) and inconsistent or invalid recording must be resolved before statistical modelling. Exploratory plots as discussed above can reveal the most blatant recording errors.

Problems often arise because those who collect or enter information may not appreciate the statistical uses (as opposed to the accounting uses) to which the data will be put. They may not be aware of the need for consistent recording across all records. Designers of the data recording system may not be aware of the myriad of cases which need be accommodated.

A statistical analysis is, ideally, "unbiased." Roughly speaking, this means results do not favor one or other conclusion. Biases arise in many ways:

- Outcomes are often censored. For example when studying the average lifetime of those born in 1950, deaths from this cohort have only arisen for the younger ages: no observations have as yet been made about lifetimes of the survivors. This is a crude and obvious example of censoring. A more subtle example is displayed in Figure 1.9. For the personal injury data, the mean (higher curve) and standard deviation (lower curve) of log claim amounts are plotted against accident month, that is the month in which the accident occurred. It appears that the average log claim amount is falling with time; however, this appearance is deceptive. The later accident months have many

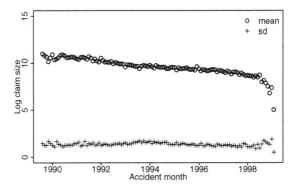

Fig. 1.9. Mean and standard deviation by accident month of log claim sizes

outstanding claims, which are typically outstanding because they involve bigger amounts and are more contentious. Thus the feature of falling claim amounts over time is a consequence of biased sampling, with larger claims having been censored from the sample. Any model for these data is likely to be misleading unless this sampling bias is dealt with.

- Cases are sometimes not independent. For example many accidents involve two or more cars, but each car may constitute a distinct claim.

- The significance of a claim is different for policies which have been in force only a short period of time, compared with those that have been exposed to risk for the entire period of observation. Exposure difference must be adjusted for in the statistical model.

- Length bias sampling occurs, for example, if on a particular day one considers all the non-settled claims on the books of an insurance company. The sample drawn on this day will be overrepresented with the more slowly settling claims.

### 1.8  Data sets used

**Personal injury insurance.** This data set contains information on 22 036 settled personal injury insurance claims. These claims arose from accidents occurring from July 1989 through to January 1999. Claims settled with zero payment are not included. The data set contains the variables listed in Table 1.5. A histogram of the claim sizes is shown in the left panel of Figure 1.10. For clarity, 1825 claims over $100 000 have been omitted from the display.

Table 1.5. *Personal injury settlements*

| Variable | Range |
|----------|-------|
| Settled amount | $10–$4490 000 |
| Injury code | 1 (no injury), 2, 3, 4, 5, 6 (fatal), 9 (not recorded) |
| Accident month | coded 1 (July 1989) through to 120 (June 1999) |
| Reporting month | coded as accident month |
| Finalization month | coded as accident month |
| Legal representation | 0 (no), 1 (yes) |

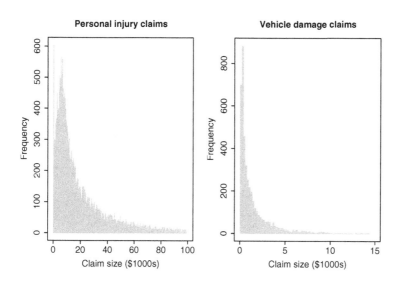

Fig. 1.10. Histograms of personal injury and vehicle claim sizes

**Vehicle insurance.** This data set is based on one-year vehicle insurance policies taken out in 2004 or 2005. There are 67 856 policies of which 4624 (6.8%) had at least one claim. The variables in this data set are listed in Table 1.6. A histogram of the (positive) claim costs is given in the right panel of Figure 1.10. For clarity the horizontal axis is truncated at $15 000. A total of 65 claims between $15 000 and $57 000 are omitted from this display.

**Number of children.** This data set contains the number of children for each of 141 pregnant women. The age of each mother or mother-to-be is also recorded (Leader 1994). Figure 1.11 plots the number of children versus mother's age. Since both variables are integers, the points fall on a grid. To facilitate the display, a small amount of randomness is added to each data point,

Table 1.6. *Vehicle insurance*

| Variable | Range |
| --- | --- |
| Age band of policy holder | 1 (youngest), 2, 3, 4, 5, 6 |
| Gender | male, female |
| Area of residence | A, B, C, D, E, F |
| Vehicle value | $0–$350 000 |
| Vehicle age | 1 (new), 2, 3, 4 |
| Vehicle body type | bus, convertible, coupe, hatchback, hardtop, motorized caravan/combi, minibus, panel van, roadster, sedan, station wagon, truck, utility |
| Exposure | 0–1 |
| Claim occurrence | 0 (no), 1 (yes) |
| Claim size | $0–$57 000 ($0 if no claim) |

a process called jittering. As the mother's age increases there is a tendency for more children. However it is not clear whether the relationship is linear or curvilinear.

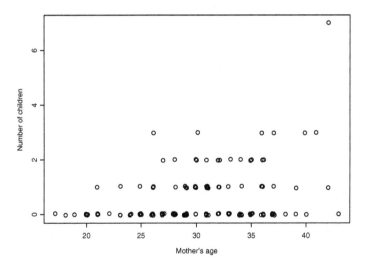

Fig. 1.11. Number of children

**Diabetes deaths.** The number of deaths due to diabetes in New South Wales, Australia in 2002 were provided by the Australian Institute of Health and Welfare, from their mortality database. The age by gender breakdown is given in Table 1.7.

Table 1.7. *Diabetes deaths*

| Gender | Age | Deaths | Population | Rate per 100 000 |
|--------|-----|--------|-----------|------------------|
| Male | <25 | 3 | 1141 100 | 0.26 |
| | 25–34 | 0 | 485 571 | 0.00 |
| | 35–44 | 12 | 504 312 | 2.38 |
| | 45–54 | 25 | 447 315 | 5.59 |
| | 55–64 | 61 | 330 902 | 18.43 |
| | 65–74 | 130 | 226 403 | 57.42 |
| | 75–84 | 192 | 130 527 | 147.10 |
| | 85+ | 102 | 29 785 | 342.45 |
| Female | <25 | 2 | 1086 408 | 0.18 |
| | 25–34 | 1 | 489 948 | 0.20 |
| | 35–44 | 3 | 504 030 | 0.60 |
| | 45–54 | 11 | 445 763 | 2.47 |
| | 55–64 | 30 | 323 669 | 9.27 |
| | 65–74 | 63 | 241 488 | 26.09 |
| | 75–84 | 174 | 179 686 | 96.84 |
| | 85+ | 159 | 67 203 | 236.60 |

**Swedish mortality data.** The Human Mortality Database (2007) provides mortality data for countries across periods of time. Recorded are the number of live births, deaths, and population at risk classified according to age and sex. From these are calculated such quantities as death rates and expectations of life. This text uses data for Sweden from 1951 through to 2005.

**Third party claims.** Third party insurance is a compulsory insurance for vehicle owners in Australia. It insures vehicle owners against injury caused to other drivers, passengers or pedestrians, as a result of an accident.

This data set records the number of third party claims in a twelve-month period between 1984 and 1986 in each of 176 geographical areas (local government areas) in New South Wales, Australia. Areas are grouped into 13 statistical divisions. Other recorded variables are the number of accidents, the number of people killed or injured and population.

**National Health Survey data.** The Australian National Health Survey (Australian Bureau of Statistics 1996) collects information on a range of health-related issues. The 1995 National Health Survey is based on 53 828 interviews. Approximately 1000 health-related variables are recorded. This text uses the variables listed in Table 1.8.

Age and gross personal annual income are grouped into broader bands than those reported in the survey. The "SEIFA quintile" is the quintile of the Socio-Economic Index For Area where each respondent lives. The *Type of insurance* variable has the four listed possibilities.

Table 1.8. *National Health Survey variables*

| Variable | Frequency | Percent |
|---|---|---|
| Type of insurance | | |
| Hospital and ancillary | 6636 | 12.3 |
| Hospital only | 1405 | 2.6 |
| Ancillary only | 988 | 1.8 |
| Without private insurance | 11 824 | 22.0 |
| Not applicable/don't know | 32 975 | 61.3 |
| | | |
| Age (years) | | |
| <20 | 16 182 | 30.1 |
| 20–34 | 12 534 | 23.3 |
| 35–49 | 12 266 | 22.8 |
| 50–64 | 7215 | 13.4 |
| ≥65 | 5631 | 10.5 |
| | | |
| Sex | | |
| Male | 26 452 | 49.1 |
| Female | 27 376 | 50.9 |
| | | |
| Employment status | | |
| Employed | 24 800 | 46.1 |
| Unemployed (looking for work) | 1820 | 3.4 |
| Not in labor force | 9183 | 17.1 |
| Not applicable | 18 025 | 33.5 |
| | | |
| SEIFA quintile | | |
| First | 9274 | 17.2 |
| Second | 9707 | 18.0 |
| Third | 9785 | 18.2 |
| Fourth | 11 666 | 21.7 |
| Fifth | 13 250 | 24.6 |
| Not known | 146 | 0.3 |
| | | |
| Gross personal annual income | | |
| <$20 000 | 18 996 | 35.3 |
| $20 000–$35 000 | 9493 | 17.6 |
| $35 000–$50 000 | 3821 | 7.1 |
| >$50 000 | 2604 | 4.8 |
| Not applicable/don't know/not stated | 18 914 | 35.1 |

**Degree of vehicle crash.** This data set consists of all drivers involved in a crash in 2004 in New South Wales, Australia (Roads and Traffic Authority 2004). Variables in the data set include those listed in Table 1.9. There are a total of 82 659 drivers in the data set. Drivers with unknown age, age less than 17 years, or road user class "Other" are omitted, leaving 76 341 cases.

**Enterprise Miner data.** The Enterprise Miner data set is supplied by SAS. It consists of claims data on a class of auto insurance policies and includes

Table 1.9. *Vehicle crash variables*

| Variable | Frequency | Percent |
|---|---|---|
| Degree of crash | | |
| Non-casualty | 44 296 | 58.0 |
| Injury | 31 369 | 41.1 |
| Fatal | 676 | 0.9 |
| | | |
| Age (years) | | |
| 17–20 | 10 954 | 14.4 |
| 21–25 | 11 141 | 14.6 |
| 26–29 | 7264 | 9.5 |
| 30–39 | 16 385 | 21.5 |
| 40–49 | 13 685 | 17.9 |
| 50–59 | 9151 | 12.0 |
| ≥60 | 7761 | 10.2 |
| | | |
| Sex | | |
| Male | 49 503 | 64.8 |
| Female | 26 838 | 35.2 |
| | | |
| Driver class | | |
| Car | 64 290 | 84.2 |
| Light truck | 6510 | 8.5 |
| Bus/heavy rigid truck/articulated truck | 3357 | 4.4 |
| Motorcycle | 2184 | 2.9 |

policies on which there were no claims. Numerous risk factors are given. This data set is used in exercises.

## 1.9 Outline of rest of book

Chapters 2–4 provide the necessary statistical background for the development of the GLM. Chapter 2 covers the response distributions encountered in generalized linear modeling, and Chapter 3 covers the exponential family of distributions and maximum likelihood estimation. Chapter 4 provides an introduction to the classical normal linear model. Regression concepts which carry across to the GLM, such as collinearity and interaction, are covered in this chapter. Readers familiar with this material may skip these chapters. Chapter 5 contains the theoretical development of the GLM, and provides the basis for the rest of the book. Chapters 6–8 cover the GLM methodology as applied to responses which are counts, categorical and continuous, respectively. Chapter 9 treats models for correlated observations. Finally Chapter 10 gives an overview of more recent developments of various models which have their origins in GLMs, but are not GLMs. Computer code and output for all the examples is given in Appendix 1.

# 2

# Response distributions

This chapter introduces the common statistical distributions used in insurance data analysis and generalized linear modeling. This sets the stage for the development and understanding of the generalized linear model. In statistical analysis, an outcome such as the size of a claim is regarded as at least partially determined by chance. This setup is formalized by the introduction of random variables.

## 2.1 Discrete and continuous random variables

A random variable $y$ is a real number determined by chance. This chance mechanism may arise naturally, from random sampling or may be a useful hypothetical construct. The set of values that $y$ can take on is called the sample space, denoted $\Omega$.

(i) **Discrete random variables.** In this case $\Omega$ is a finite or countable set of real numbers, for example the non-negative integers $\{0, 1, 2, \ldots\}$. Associated with the random variable is a probability function $f(y)$ indicating for each $y$ in $\Omega$ (written $y \in \Omega$) the probability the random variable takes on the value $y$. The function $f(y)$ is only non-negative on values in $\Omega$: $f(y) > 0$ if $y \in \Omega$ and 0 otherwise. Further

$$\sum_{y \in \Omega} f(y) = 1 .$$

The expected value and variance of a discrete random variable $y$ are defined as:

$$\mu = \mathrm{E}(y) \equiv \sum_{y \in \Omega} y\, f(y) , \quad \mathrm{Var}(y) \equiv \mathrm{E}\{(y-\mu)^2\} = \sum_{y \in \Omega} (y-\mu)^2 f(y) .$$

If $y$ is the number of events, usually within a fixed period of time and/or in a fixed area, then it is a count random variable. Counts are by their nature non-negative integers. Examples are given in Section 1.2. Distributions widely used to model counts include the binomial, Poisson and the negative binomial. These are discussed below.

(ii) **Continuous random variables.** In this case $\Omega$ is an interval of the real line. Probabilities are specified using a probability density function $f(y)$ with $f(y) \geq 0$ for $y \in \Omega$ and 0 otherwise. Areas under $f(y)$ correspond to probabilities:

$$P(a \leq y \leq b) = \int_a^b f(y)\,dy\;.$$

Hence the probability of $y$ taking on any given value is zero and

$$\int_{-\infty}^{\infty} f(y)dy = 1\;.$$

Analogous to the discrete case, the mean and variance of a continuous random variable $y$ are defined as

$$\mu = \mathrm{E}(y) \equiv \int_{-\infty}^{\infty} yf(y)dy\;, \qquad \mathrm{Var}(y) \equiv \int_{-\infty}^{\infty} (y-\mu)^2 f(y)dy\;.$$

Probability functions are a mathematical tool to describe uncertain situations or where outcomes are subject to chance. To simplify discussion the notation $f(y)$ is used for the probability function, for both discrete and continuous random variables. No notational distinction is made between probability density functions, which belong to continuous random variables, and probability (mass) functions, which belong to discrete random variables. It is understood that when integrating $f(y)$ for a discrete random variable $y$, the appropriate operation is summation.

## 2.2 Bernoulli

The Bernoulli distribution admits only two possible outcomes, usually coded as 0 or 1 and hence $\Omega = \{0, 1\}$. The event $y = 1$ is often called a "success," the other, $y = 0$, a "failure." Further $f(1) = \pi$ and $f(0) = 1 - \pi$ where $0 < \pi < 1$. Insurance examples are a claim or no claim on a policy in a given year, or a person dying or surviving over a given year. The event of interest (claim, death) is generally coded as 1, and $\pi$ is the probability of the event occurring.

Elementary calculations show that the mean and variance of a Bernoulli random variable are $\pi$ and $\pi(1 - \pi)$ respectively. The variance is a maximum when $\pi = 0.5$. The probability function is

$$f(y) = \pi^y (1 - \pi)^{1-y}\;, \qquad y = 0, 1\;. \tag{2.1}$$

**Vehicle insurance.** This data set consists of 67 856 policies enacted in a given year, of which 4624 had a claim. If the probability $\pi$ of the occurrence of a claim for each policy is assumed constant, then a rough estimate of $\pi$ is $4624/67\ 856 = 0.068$.

In practice each policy is not exposed for the full year. Some policies come into force partly into the year while others are canceled before the year's end. Define $0 < t \leq 1$ as the amount of exposure during the year, with $t = 1$ indicating full exposure. For these data the average amount of exposure is $0.469$. This suggests a modified model for the claim probability

$$f(y) = (t\pi)^y (1 - t\pi)^{1-y} , \qquad y = 0, 1 . \tag{2.2}$$

A reasonable estimate of $\pi$ is the average number of claims weighted by exposure. This leads to an estimate of $\pi$ of $0.145$, considerably higher than the previous estimate. Exposure adjustments are often appropriate in insurance studies and a more detailed treatment is given in Section 7.4.

## 2.3 Binomial

The binomial distribution generalizes the Bernoulli distribution and is used to model counts such as the total number of policies making a claim. If there are $n$ independent Bernoulli random variables, each with success probability $\pi$, then the total number of successes has the binomial distribution denoted $y \sim B(n, \pi)$. The probability function is given by

$$f(y) = \binom{n}{y} \pi^y (1 - \pi)^{n-y} , \qquad y = 0, 1, \ldots, n . \tag{2.3}$$

The distribution depends on one unknown parameter $\pi$ since $n$ is known. Some typical shapes are displayed in Figure 2.1. Elementary calculations show the mean and variance are $E(y) = n\pi$ and $Var(y) = n\pi(1 - \pi)$, respectively. A Bernoulli random variable is a special case of the binomial random variable with $n = 1$, and hence $y \sim B(1, \pi)$. The binomial is practically and historically important and leads directly to the Poisson distribution as discussed below.

A binomial random variable is often transformed into a proportion by dividing by $n$. The resulting random variable $y/n$ is called the binomial proportion and has the probability function (2.3) shifted onto $0, 1/n, 2/n, \ldots, 1$.

**Grouped binary data.** Binary data is often grouped, in which case the number of occurrences of the event in each subgroup is analyzed. For example, policies may be grouped according to geographical area and the number of policies in each area on which there is a claim, recorded. If the Bernoulli trials within each area are independent with constant probability $\pi$, then the

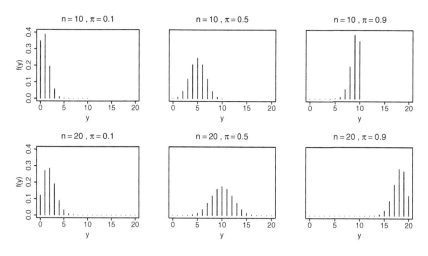

Fig. 2.1. Binomial distribution

number of claims arising from each area is binomial of the form (2.3), with varying numbers of policies $n$ and varying probabilities $\pi$. Of interest might be the relationship between $\pi$ and area characteristics such as socioeconomic indicators.

## 2.4 Poisson

Suppose with the binomial distribution $n$ becomes large while $\pi$ becomes small but in such a way that the mean $\mu = n\pi$ stays constant. In the limit this yields the probability function

$$f(y) = \frac{e^{-\mu}\mu^y}{y!}, \qquad y = 0, 1, 2, \ldots, \tag{2.4}$$

which is the Poisson distribution, denoted $y \sim P(\mu)$. The probability function depends on the single parameter $\mu$ and has $E(y) = \mu$ and $Var(y) = \mu$. Thus the variance equals the mean. Examples of (2.4) for different values of $\mu$ are shown in Figure 2.2.

**Number of children.** The frequency distribution of the number of children of 141 pregnant women, described on page 15, is given in the "Observed" column in Table 2.1. The mean number of children in the sample is 0.603, which is taken as the estimate of $\mu$. The observed frequencies are compared with expected frequencies from the $P(0.603)$ distribution:

$$141 \times f(y) = 141 \times \frac{e^{-0.603}0.603^y}{y!}, \qquad y = 0, 1, 2, \ldots.$$

Table 2.1. *Observed and expected number of children per mother*

| Children | Observed | P(0.603) | Expected |
|---|---|---|---|
| 0 | 89 | 0.547 | 77.2 |
| 1 | 30 | 0.330 | 46.5 |
| 2 | 15 | 0.099 | 14.0 |
| 3 | 6 | 0.020 | 2.8 |
| 4 | 0 | 0.003 | 0.4 |
| 5 | 0 | 0.000 | 0.1 |
| 6 | 0 | 0.000 | 0.0 |
| 7 | 1 | 0.000 | 0.0 |
| ≥ 8 | 0 | 0.000 | 0.0 |
| Total | 141 | 1 | 141.0 |

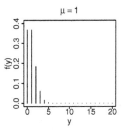 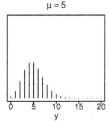 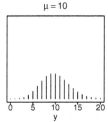

Fig. 2.2. Poisson distribution

The fitted Poisson probabilities and expected frequencies are given in Table 2.1, and the observed and expected frequencies graphed in Figure 2.3. There is good agreement of the data with the Poisson model. In the sample there are more women with no children, and fewer with one child, compared to the Poisson model predictions.

## 2.5 Negative binomial

The classic derivation of the negative binomial distribution is as the number of failures in Bernoulli trials until $r$ successes. Having $y$ failures implies that trial $r + y$ is a success, and in the previous $r + y - 1$ trials there were exactly $r - 1$ successes and $y$ failures. If $\pi$ is the probability of success on each Bernoulli trial, then the number of failures $y$ has the probability function

$$
\begin{aligned}
f(y) &= \pi \times \binom{r + y - 1}{r - 1} \pi^{r-1}(1 - \pi)^y \\
&= \binom{r + y - 1}{r - 1} \pi^r (1 - \pi)^y, \qquad y = 0, 1, 2, \ldots,
\end{aligned}
$$

which depends on $\pi$ and $r$.

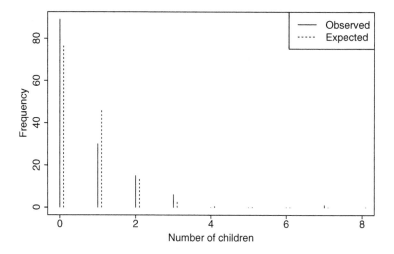

Fig. 2.3. Number of children: Poisson fit

The above formulation supposes $r$ is a positive integer. However, the negative binomial distribution can be defined for any positive values of $r$, by using the gamma function in place of factorials:

$$f(y) = \frac{\Gamma(y + r)}{y!\,\Gamma(r)}\,\pi^r(1 - \pi)^y\,, \qquad y = 0, 1, 2, \dots .$$

In generalized linear modeling the following parametrization is convenient:

$$\mu = \frac{r(1 - \pi)}{\pi}\,, \qquad \kappa = \frac{1}{r}.$$

Using this notation, the probability function of $y$ is

$$f(y) = \frac{\Gamma(y + \frac{1}{\kappa})}{y!\,\Gamma(\frac{1}{\kappa})}\left(\frac{1}{1 + \kappa\mu}\right)^{\frac{1}{\kappa}}\left(\frac{\kappa\mu}{1 + \kappa\mu}\right)^y\,, \qquad y = 0, 1, 2, \dots , \quad (2.5)$$

with

$$\mathrm{E}(y) = \mu\,, \qquad \mathrm{Var}(y) = \mu(1 + \kappa\mu)\,.$$

The parameter $\kappa$ is called the "overdispersion" or "shape" parameter. A random variable $y$ having the above distribution is denoted $y \sim \mathrm{NB}(\mu, \kappa)$. The $(\mu, \kappa)$ parametrization is used, for example, by SAS (where $\kappa$ is denoted as $k$). As $\kappa \to 0$, $\mathrm{NB}(\mu, \kappa)$ approaches $\mathrm{P}(\mu)$ and $\kappa = 0$ implies $\mathrm{E}(y) = \mathrm{Var}(y)$. When $\kappa$ is large, the distribution has a mode at zero and a long tail to the right. Plots of the distribution for different $(\mu, \kappa)$ combinations are displayed in Figure 2.4.

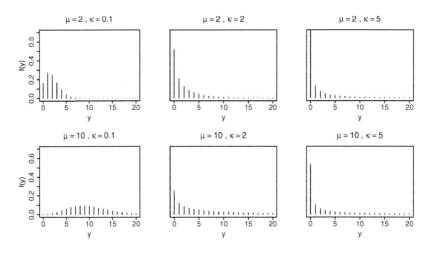

Fig. 2.4. Negative binomial distribution

## 2.6 Normal

The best known continuous distribution is the normal. Many variables occurring in nature appear to be approximately normally distributed. However in insurance and finance, quantities of interest such as claim size, personal income or time to a claim, are non-negative and generally have distributions that are markedly skewed to the right. The normal distribution is nevertheless important in the analysis of insurance data, since it is often possible to apply a transformation, such as the log-transform, in order to achieve normality. The normal distribution is also important in the distributional properties of estimators. Such normality often applies even if data are not normally distributed.

The normal probability function is

$$f(y) = \frac{1}{\sigma\sqrt{2\pi}} \exp\left\{-\frac{1}{2}\left(\frac{y-\mu}{\sigma}\right)^2\right\}, \qquad -\infty < y < \infty,$$

where $\mu$ is the mean and $\sigma$ the standard deviation. The normal probability function is a symmetric bell-shaped curve centred on $\mu$. The notation $y \sim N(\mu, \sigma^2)$ indicates $y$ has the normal distribution given above. The $N(0, 1)$ distribution is the so-called standard normal distribution.

**Claim size.** Histograms of the log-transformed personal injury and vehicle damage claim sizes, with normal curves superimposed, are shown in Figure 2.5. The log-transformed personal injury claim sizes appear approximately normally distributed. Vehicle log claim sizes do not.

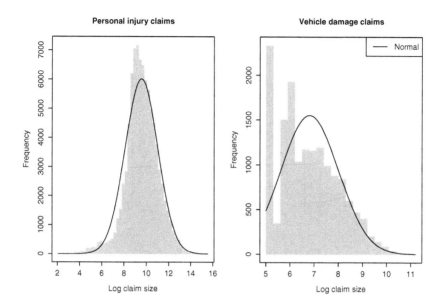

Fig. 2.5. Distribution of log of claim size

**Multivariate normal.** The $p$-dimensional multivariate normal distribution is defined for a random vector $y = (y_1, \ldots, y_p)'$. The joint density is

$$f(y) = (2\pi)^{-p/2} |\Sigma|^{-\frac{1}{2}} e^{-\frac{1}{2}(y-\mu)'\Sigma^{-1}(y-\mu)} ,$$

where $\mathrm{E}(y) = \mu \equiv (\mu_1, \ldots, \mu_p)'$, $\Sigma$ is the covariance matrix of $y$ and $|\Sigma|$ is the determinant of $\Sigma$. This is denoted as $y \sim \mathrm{N}(\mu, \Sigma)$. The multivariate normal has the following properties:

- The marginal distributions of the components $y_i$ are univariate normal, $y_i \sim \mathrm{N}(\mu_i, \sigma_i^2)$, $i = 1, \ldots, p$, where $\sigma_i^2$ is diagonal element $i$ of $\Sigma$.
- The covariance matrix $\Sigma$ is any positive definite $p \times p$ matrix.

## 2.7 Chi-square and gamma

The chi-square distribution is the distribution of the sum of squares of $\nu$ independent $\mathrm{N}(0, 1)$ random variables, denoted as $y \sim \chi_\nu^2$. The parameter $\nu$ is called the degrees of freedom. Chi-squared random variables are non-negative, and their distribution is skewed to the right. The mean and variance are $\nu$ and $2\nu$, respectively. For large $\nu$, $y$ is approximately normal. The chi-square distribution is also defined for non-integral $\nu > 0$ degrees of freedom;

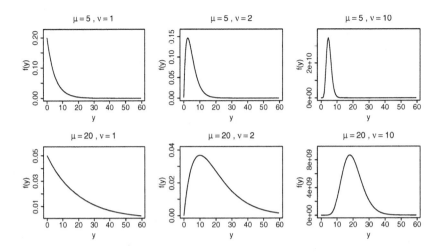

Fig. 2.6. Gamma probability functions

this distribution is conveniently thought of as intermediate between the two chi-square distributions with integer degrees of freedom which bracket $\nu$.

Multiplying a $\chi^2_{2\nu}$ random variable by $\mu/(2\nu)$ yields a gamma random variable with parameters $\mu$ and $\nu$, denoted $G(\mu, \nu)$. The gamma is often a reasonable fit for variables such as claim size and annual income. Gamma random variables are continuous, non-negative and skewed to the right, with the possibility of large values in the upper tail.

The $G(\mu, \nu)$ probability function is

$$ f(y) = \frac{y^{-1}}{\Gamma(\nu)} \left( \frac{y\nu}{\mu} \right)^{\nu} e^{-y\nu/\mu} , \qquad y > 0 , \tag{2.6} $$

with

$$ E(y) = \mu , \qquad \text{Var}(y) = \frac{\mu^2}{\nu} . $$

Small values of $\nu$ result in a distribution with a long tail to the right, i.e. a more right-skewed distribution. Gamma probability functions for various $(\mu, \nu)$ are displayed in Figure 2.6.

The "$(\alpha, \beta)$" parametrization of the gamma is also popular. Here the mean and variance are $\alpha/\beta$ and $\alpha/\beta^2$ respectively. Hence $\mu = \alpha/\beta$, $\nu = \alpha$ and $\beta = \nu/\mu$. In generalized linear modeling it is advantageous to use the parametrization (2.6) where one of the parameters is $E(y) = \mu$.

**Personal injury claims.** The distribution of personal injury claim sizes is displayed in the left panel of Figure 2.7. The fitted gamma distribution is shown as

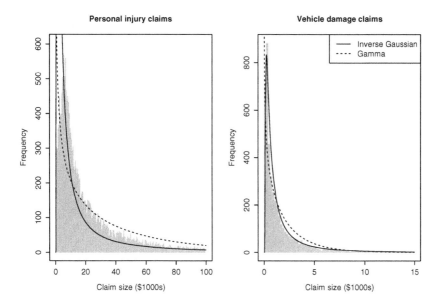

Fig. 2.7.  Distribution of claim size

the dashed line. While the observed distribution appears to have a gamma-like shape, the gamma fit does not cope with the extreme skewness.

**Vehicle damage claims.** The distribution of claim size for vehicle insurance claims and the fitted gamma distribution is shown in the right panel of Figure 2.7. The fitted gamma distribution does not reproduce the shape of the observed claim size distribution.

## 2.8  Inverse Gaussian

The inverse Gaussian is a continuous distribution with density similar to that of the gamma, but with greater skewness and a sharper peak. The inverse Gaussian has two parameters. Several alternative parameterizations appear in the literature. This text uses

$$f\left(y\right) = \frac{1}{\sqrt{2\pi y^3}\sigma} \exp\left\{-\frac{1}{2y}\left(\frac{y-\mu}{\mu\sigma}\right)^2\right\}, \qquad y > 0, \qquad (2.7)$$

denoted as $y \sim \mathrm{IG}(\mu, \sigma^2)$. Example inverse Gaussian densities are shown in Figure 2.8. The mean and variance are

$$\mathrm{E}(y) = \mu, \qquad \mathrm{Var}(y) = \sigma^2 \mu^3,$$

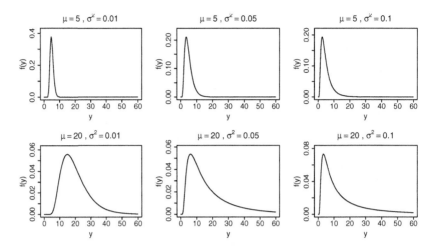

Fig. 2.8.  Inverse Gaussian distribution

and $\sigma^2$ is the dispersion parameter. The inverse Gaussian is used in situations of extreme skewness.

The name *inverse Gaussian* derives from the cumulant function, which bears an inverse relationship with the cumulant function of the normal (Gaussian) distribution.

**Claim size distributions.** The fitted inverse Gaussian distributions for the personal injury and vehicle insurance data sets are shown (solid lines) in Figure 2.7. In both cases, the inverse Gaussian fit is more successful than the gamma. For the personal injury claims data the inverse Gaussian appears inadequate.

**Note on claim size.** The terms *claim size*, *claim cost*, *claim severity*, *claim amount* and *loss* are all used more or less synonymously in the insurance literature. Many continuous, right-skewed distributions with positive support have been used to model these: for example, Hogg and Klugman (1984) describe the gamma, log-gamma, Weibull, Burr, Pareto, generalized Pareto, Makeham and Gompertz, all as candidates for loss distributions.

## 2.9  Overdispersion

The Poisson distribution is often suggested for count data but found to be inadequate because the data displays far greater variance than that predicted by the Poisson. This is termed *overdispersion* or *extra-Poisson variation*. Overdispersion may be modeled using compound Poisson distributions. With this model

Table 2.2. *Distribution of claims across 176 areas*

| Number of claims | Number of areas | Number of claims | Number of areas |
|---|---|---|---|
| 0–99 | 76 | 900–999 | 3 |
| 100–199 | 23 | 1000–1499 | 9 |
| 200–299 | 7 | 1500–1999 | 7 |
| 300–399 | 8 | 2000–2999 | 5 |
| 400–499 | 11 | 3000–3999 | 5 |
| 500–599 | 8 | 4000–4999 | 3 |
| 600–699 | 3 | 5000–5999 | 0 |
| 700–799 | 3 | 6000–6999 | 1 |
| 800–899 | 4 | | |

the count $y$ is Poisson distributed with mean $\lambda$, but $\lambda$ is itself a random variable which causes the variation to exceed that expected if the Poisson mean were fixed.

Thus suppose $\lambda$ is regarded as a positive continuous random variable with probability function $g(\lambda)$. Given $\lambda$, the count is distributed as $P(\lambda)$. Then the probability function of $y$ is

$$f(y) = \int_0^\infty \frac{e^{-\lambda}\lambda^y}{y!} g(\lambda)\, d\lambda \,. \tag{2.8}$$

A convenient choice for $g(\lambda)$ is the gamma probability function $G(\mu, \nu)$, implying (2.8) is $NB(\mu, \kappa)$ where $\kappa = 1/\nu$. In other words the negative binomial arises when there are different groups of risks, each group characterized by a separate Poisson mean, and with the means distributed according to the gamma distribution. Note this derivation of the negative binomial is unconnected with the classical derivation discussed in Section 2.5. Detailed calculations are given below.

As an illustration, consider the number $y$ of accidents involving a randomly chosen driver from a population. If the mean accident rate $\lambda$ over the population is homogeneous, then perhaps $y \sim P(\lambda)$. However, individuals may have different levels of accident-proneness, which implies that $\lambda$ is heterogeneous across individuals. If $\lambda \sim G(\mu, \nu)$ and hence accident-proneness is gamma distributed over the population, then $y \sim NB(\mu, \kappa)$.

**Third party claims.** The number of third party claims per area, described on page 17, has frequencies summarized in Table 2.2. The sample mean and variance are $586.7$ and $1.03 \times 10^6$ respectively, so clearly a Poisson model is not appropriate. The observed and expected frequencies for the Poisson and negative binomial distributions are shown in Figure 2.9, which demonstrates

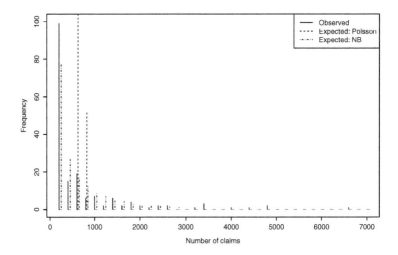

Fig. 2.9. Third party claims: Poisson and negative binomial fits

reasonably good agreement between the data and the negative binomial model, and a very poor fit of the Poisson model.

**Mathematical derivation.** To avoid notational confusion here the mean of the conditional distribution of $y$ is denoted as $\lambda$ (rather than $\mu$). Given $\lambda$, assume the distribution of $y$ is Poisson with mean $\lambda$:

$$y \mid \lambda \sim \mathrm{P}(\lambda) \qquad \Rightarrow \qquad f(y \mid \lambda) = \frac{\mathrm{e}^{-\lambda} \lambda^y}{y!} \; .$$

Suppose $\lambda$ is regarded as a continuous random variable with probability function $g(\lambda)$ where $g(\lambda) = 0$ for $\lambda < 0$. Then the unconditional probability function of $y$ is

$$f(y) = \int_0^\infty f(y \mid \lambda)\, g(\lambda)\, d\lambda \; . \tag{2.9}$$

Choosing $g(\lambda)$ as the gamma probability function, i.e. with $\lambda \sim \mathrm{G}(\mu, \nu)$ as given in (2.6):

$$
\begin{aligned}
f(y) &= \int_0^\infty \frac{\mathrm{e}^{-\lambda} \lambda^y}{y!} \, \frac{\lambda^{-1}}{\Gamma(\nu)} \left(\frac{\lambda \nu}{\mu}\right)^\nu \mathrm{e}^{-\lambda \nu / \mu}\, d\lambda \\
&= \frac{1}{y!\,\Gamma(\nu)} \left(\frac{\nu}{\mu}\right)^\nu \int_0^\infty \lambda^{y+\nu-1} \mathrm{e}^{-\lambda(1+\nu/\mu)}\, d\lambda \\
&= \frac{\Gamma(\nu+y)}{y!\,\Gamma(\nu)} \left(\frac{\nu}{\nu+\mu}\right)^\nu \left(\frac{\mu}{\nu+\mu}\right)^y \qquad y = 0, 1, 2, \ldots \; .
\end{aligned}
$$

Making the substitution $\kappa = 1/\nu$ results in the NB$(\mu, \kappa)$ probability function (2.5).

**Other compound Poisson distributions.** Any distribution of the form (2.8) is called a compound Poisson distribution, or Poisson mixture, and $g(\lambda)$ is called the mixing distribution. The weakness of the Poisson distribution in accommodating heavy tails was recognized in the early twentieth century, when Greenwood and Yule (1920) postulated a heterogeneity model for the overdispersion, in the context of disease and accident frequencies. This is the first appearance of the negative binomial as a compound Poisson distribution, as opposed to its derivation as the distribution of the number of failures till the $r$th success. Newbold (1927) and Arbous and Kerrich (1951) illustrated compound Poisson distributions in the context of modeling industrial accidents. In the actuarial literature, Lundberg (1940) further considered the negative binomial as a compound Poisson distribution, as a result of heterogeneity of risk over either time or individuals, as a model for claim frequencies; see also Seal (1982).

There are alternative choices to the gamma for the mixing distribution $g(\lambda)$. Two which have appeared in the actuarial literature are the generalized inverse Gaussian and inverse Gaussian distributions. The generalized inverse Gaussian is a three-parameter distribution which is highly flexible, but has the drawback that its computation is complex. Its two-parameter version, the inverse Gaussian, is computationally somewhat simpler. Substituting $g(\lambda)$ (as in (2.7)) as the mixing distribution in (2.8), results in the Poisson-inverse Gaussian distribution, which has greater skewness than the negative binomial, and so may be more suited to modeling heavy-tailed claim frequency distributions. Willmot (1987) compared their performance in fitting claim frequency distributions, and found that the Poisson-inverse Gaussian was more successful in accommodating the heavy tails than the negative binomial. However, this difference appears to be a marginal improvement only and the benefit of the Poisson-inverse Gaussian over the negative binomial was disputed by Lemaire (1991). In recent years the negative binomial has gained popularity as the distribution of choice when modeling overdispersed count data in many fields, possibly because of its simpler computational requirements and its availability in standard software.

## Exercises

2.1    Show that the mean and variance of a Bernoulli random variable are $\pi$ and $\pi(1 - \pi)$ respectively. More generally show that the mean and variance of binomial random variable are $n\pi$ and $n\pi(1 - \pi)$, respectively.

2.2    Show that the mean and variance of a $\chi^2_\nu$ random variable are $\nu$ and $2\nu$ respectively.

2.3    The distribution of the number of failures $y$ till the first success in independent Bernoulli trials, with probability of success $\pi$ at each trial, is the geometric:

$$f(y) = (1 - \pi)^y \pi \qquad y = 0, 1, \dots .$$

Show that the mean and variance of the geometric distribution are $E(y) = (1 - \pi)/\pi$ and $\mathrm{Var}(y) = (1 - \pi)/\pi^2$.

2.4    (a) Show that for the negative binomial $\pi = 1/(1 + \kappa\mu)$ and hence show (2.5).

(b) Show that the mean and variance of the negative binomial are $\mu$ and $\mu(1 + \kappa\mu)$, respectively.

# 3

# Exponential family responses and estimation

The exponential family of distributions is one of the key constructs in generalized linear modeling. This is the subject of the current chapter. Also discussed is maximum likelihood estimation, which is central to the fitting of generalized linear models.

## 3.1 Exponential family

All the probability functions discussed in the last chapter are of the general form

$$f(y) = c(y, \phi) \exp \left\{ \frac{y\theta - a(\theta)}{\phi} \right\} , \tag{3.1}$$

where $\theta$ and $\phi$ are parameters. The parameter $\theta$ is called the canonical parameter and $\phi$ the dispersion parameter. Probability functions which can be written as (3.1) are said to be members of the exponential family. The choice of the functions $a(\theta)$ and $c(y, \phi)$ determine the actual probability function such as the binomial, normal or gamma.

In terms of $a(\theta)$,

$$\mathrm{E}(y) = \dot{a}(\theta) , \qquad \mathrm{Var}(y) = \phi \, \ddot{a}(\theta) , \tag{3.2}$$

where $\dot{a}(\theta)$ and $\ddot{a}(\theta)$ are the first and second derivatives of $a(\theta)$ with respect to $\theta$, respectively. These results are proved in Section 3.3.

Table 3.1 displays different choices of $\theta$ and $a(\theta)$ leading to the distributions discussed in Chapter 2. Not shown in the table is the form of $c(y, \phi)$, which in most situations is not of interest. The proofs of the implicit relations in Table 3.1 are in Section 3.4.

Several authors define the dispersion parameter in (3.1) as $\phi/w$, where $w$ is a weight. It is appropriate to use this form in the case where grouped or frequency data are being analyzed, and $w$ is the frequency of raw observations in $y$. As the ungrouped data approach is preferred in this text (see Section 4.8), in all cases $w = 1$ and is ignored from consideration.

Table 3.1. *Exponential family distributions and their parameters*

| Distribution | $\theta$ | $a(\theta)$ | $\phi$ | $E(y)$ | $V(\mu) = \frac{\text{Var}(y)}{\phi}$ |
|---|---|---|---|---|---|
| $B(n, \pi)$ | $\ln \frac{\pi}{1-\pi}$ | $n \ln\left(1 + e^{\theta}\right)$ | $1$ | $n\pi$ | $n\pi(1 - \pi)$ |
| $P(\mu)$ | $\ln \mu$ | $e^{\theta}$ | $1$ | $\mu$ | $\mu$ |
| $N(\mu, \sigma^2)$ | $\mu$ | $\frac{1}{2}\theta^2$ | $\sigma^2$ | $\mu$ | $1$ |
| $G(\mu, \nu)$ | $-\frac{1}{\mu}$ | $-\ln(-\theta)$ | $\frac{1}{\nu}$ | $\mu$ | $\mu^2$ |
| $IG(\mu, \sigma^2)$ | $-\frac{1}{2\mu^2}$ | $-\sqrt{-2\theta}$ | $\sigma^2$ | $\mu$ | $\mu^3$ |
| $NB(\mu, \kappa)$ | $\ln \frac{\kappa\mu}{1+\kappa\mu}$ | $-\frac{1}{\kappa}\ln(1 - \kappa e^{\theta})$ | $1$ | $\mu$ | $\mu(1 + \kappa\mu)$ |

## 3.2 The variance function

For exponential family response distributions

$$\ddot{a}(\theta) = \frac{\partial \dot{a}(\theta)}{\partial \theta} = \frac{\partial \mu}{\partial \theta} \equiv V(\mu) \,,$$

and hence one can always write $\text{Var}(y) = \phi V(\mu)$ where $V(\mu)$ is called the variance function, indicating the relationship between the mean and variance.

The variance function $V(\mu)$ is a critical construct. In generalized linear modeling the mean $\mu$ is related to explanatory variables. Thus the mean varies with the explanatory variables. As the mean varies, so does the variance, through $V(\mu)$. A model connecting the mean to explanatory variables is thus, at the same time, a model for the relationship between the variance and the explanatory variables.

For the normal $V(\mu) = 1$. Hence the variance does not change with the mean – the response is homoskedastic. For the Poisson $V(\mu) = \mu$ and the variance equals the mean and hence changes in the mean directly impact the variance. For the gamma $V(\mu) = \mu^2$ and hence the standard deviation varies directly with the mean.

It must be stressed there are many functions $V(\mu)$ that cannot arise from an exponential family distribution. Thus there are many mean–variance relationships that cannot be captured with an exponential family density. This issue is addressed with quasi-likelihood methods. This is discussed, in the context of responses which are counts, in Section 6.3.

### 3.3 Proof of the mean and variance expressions

To show the relations in (3.2), define $\dot{f}(y)$ and $\ddot{f}(y)$ as the first and second derivatives of $f(y)$ in (3.1) with respect to $\theta$. Then

$$\dot{f}(y) = f(y)\left\{\frac{y - \dot{a}(\theta)}{\phi}\right\} , \qquad \ddot{f}(y) = f(y)\left\{\frac{y - \dot{a}(\theta)}{\phi}\right\}^2 - f(y)\frac{\ddot{a}(\theta)}{\phi} .$$

Integrating both sides of each of these expressions with respect to $y$ yields

$$0 = \frac{E(y) - \dot{a}(\theta)}{\phi} , \qquad 0 = \frac{E[\{y - \dot{a}(\theta)\}^2]}{\phi^2} - \frac{\ddot{a}(\theta)}{\phi} . \tag{3.3}$$

The left hand sides are zero since

$$\int \dot{f}(y)dy = \frac{\partial}{\partial\theta}\int f(y)\,dy , \qquad \int \ddot{f}(y)dy = \frac{\partial^2}{\partial\theta^2}\int f(y)\,dy ,$$

where $\int f(y)dy = 1$ and assuming integration and differentiation can be interchanged. The stated relations in (3.2) follow from (3.3).

### 3.4 Standard distributions in the exponential family form

This section shows how the probability functions discussed in Chapter 2 fit into the exponential family framework. For this family

$$\ln\{f(y)\} = \ln\{c(y, \phi)\} + \frac{y\theta - a(\theta)}{\phi} . \tag{3.4}$$

**Binomial.** Suppose $y \sim B(n, \pi)$. Then $\ln\{f(y)\}$ is, apart from the term involving factorials (which depends only on the known $n$ and $y$),

$$\ln\left\{\pi^y(1 - \pi)^{n-y}\right\} = y\ln\left(\frac{\pi}{1 - \pi}\right) + n\ln(1 - \pi) = \frac{y\theta - a(\theta)}{\phi} ,$$

where $\theta = \ln\{\pi/(1 - \pi)\}$, $a(\theta) = n\ln(1 + e^\theta)$ and $\phi = 1$. Thus the binomial is in the exponential family. Straightforward calculations show

$$E(y) = \dot{a}(\theta) = \frac{ne^\theta}{1 + e^\theta} = n\pi , \qquad Var(y) = \phi\ddot{a}(\theta) = n\pi(1 - \pi) .$$

The binomial proportion $y/n$ has exponential family probability function with the same $\theta$ but $a(\theta) = \ln(1 + e^\theta)$ and $\phi = 1/n$.

**Poisson.** If $y \sim P(\mu)$ then

$$\ln\{f(y)\} = -\mu + y\ln\mu - \ln y! = -\ln y! + \frac{y\theta - a(\theta)}{\phi} ,$$

provided $\phi = 1$, $\theta = \ln(\mu)$ and $a(\theta) = e^\theta$. This shows the Poisson is in the exponential family and

$$\dot{a}(\theta) = e^\theta = \mu = E(y) = \ddot{a}(\theta) = Var(y) .$$

**Normal.** Suppose $y \sim N(\mu, \sigma^2)$. Then $\ln\{f(y)\}$ is, apart from a numerical constant

$$-\ln\sigma - \frac{(y-\mu)^2}{2\sigma^2} = -\ln\sigma - \frac{y^2/2}{\sigma^2} + \frac{y\mu - \mu^2/2}{\sigma^2}. \tag{3.5}$$

The first two terms on the right involve only $y$ and $\sigma$ and serve to define $\ln c(y, \phi)$ with $\phi = \sigma^2$. The final term on the right is equivalent to the second term in (3.4) if $\theta = \mu$ and $a(\theta) = \theta^2/2$. Note $\dot{a}(\theta) = \theta = \mu$, $\mathrm{Var}(y) = \phi\,\ddot{a}(\theta) = \sigma^2$.

**Gamma.** The log of the $G(\mu, \nu)$ density function is

$$(\nu - 1)\ln y - \ln\Gamma(\nu) + \frac{y(-\mu^{-1})}{\nu^{-1}} - \frac{\ln\mu}{\nu^{-1}} + \nu\ln\nu$$

$$= \left\{\frac{y\theta - a(\theta)}{\phi}\right\} + (\nu - 1)\ln y - \ln\Gamma(\nu) + \nu\ln\nu,$$

with $\theta = -1/\mu$, $a(\theta) = -\ln(-\theta)$ and $\phi = 1/\nu$. Thus gamma densities are in the exponential family with

$$E(y) = \dot{a}(\theta) = -\frac{1}{\theta} = \mu, \qquad \mathrm{Var}(y) = \phi\,\ddot{a}(\theta) = \nu^{-1}\frac{1}{\theta^2} = \frac{\mu^2}{\nu}.$$

The $\chi^2_\nu$ distribution is $G(\nu, \nu/2)$, and hence the chi-square is also in the exponential family.

**Inverse Gaussian.** The log of the $IG(\mu, \sigma^2)$ density function is

$$-\tfrac{1}{2}\ln(2\pi y^3) - \ln\sigma - \tfrac{1}{2y}\left(\tfrac{y-\mu}{\mu\sigma}\right)^2$$

$$= -\frac{y}{2\mu^2\sigma^2} + \frac{1}{\mu\sigma^2} - \frac{1}{2y\sigma^2} - \tfrac{1}{2}\ln(2\pi y^3) - \ln\sigma$$

$$= \frac{y\theta - a(\theta)}{\phi} + \text{terms involving only } y \text{ and } \sigma^2$$

where $\theta = -1/(2\mu^2)$, $a(\theta) = -\sqrt{-2\theta}$ and $\phi = \sigma^2$. The inverse Gaussian is therefore in the exponential family with

$$E(y) = \dot{a}(\theta) = \frac{1}{\sqrt{-2\theta}} = \mu, \qquad \mathrm{Var}(y) = \phi\,\ddot{a}(\theta) = \frac{\sigma^2}{(-2\theta)^{3/2}} = \sigma^2\mu^3.$$

**Negative binomial.** The log of $f(y)$, apart from a constant involving $y$ and $\kappa$, is

$$y\ln\frac{\mu}{1+\kappa\mu} - \frac{1}{\kappa}\ln(1+\kappa\mu) = \frac{y\theta - a(\theta)}{\phi},$$

where $\phi = 1$, $\theta = \ln\{\mu/(1 + \kappa\mu)\}$ and $a(\theta) = -(1/\kappa)\ln(1 - \kappa e^\theta)$. For known $\kappa$, the negative binomial is thus in the exponential family and

$$E(y) = \dot{a}(\theta) = \frac{e^\theta}{1 - \kappa e^\theta} = \mu\,, \quad \text{Var}(y) = \phi\ddot{a}(\theta) = \frac{e^\theta}{(1 - \kappa e^\theta)^2} = \mu(1+\kappa\mu)\,.$$

Note that $\kappa$, while sometimes called the "dispersion parameter" of the distribution, is not the same as the exponential family dispersion parameter $\phi$.

## 3.5 Fitting probability functions to data

The probability functions $f(y)$ discussed previously have either one or two parameters, whose values are, in general, unknown. The functions are typically fitted to a sample of available data $y_1, \ldots, y_n$, i.e. the parameters are estimated on the basis of the sample. In the discussion below it is important to understand that in this chapter it is assumed each observation $y_i$ comes from exactly the same distribution: i.e. a given member of the exponential family with fixed but unknown parameters.

**Method of moments.** An intuitive method of estimation is the "method of moments." Estimating $\theta$ and $\phi$ by this method means finding $\theta$ and $\phi$ such that the population mean and variance are equal to their sample equivalents: $\dot{a}(\theta) = \bar{y}$ and $\phi\,\ddot{a}(\theta) = \hat{\sigma}^2$, where $\bar{y}$ and $\hat{\sigma}^2$ and the sample mean and variance, respectively. For example for the normal, the method of moment estimators are $\hat{\mu} = \bar{y}$ and $\hat{\phi} = \hat{\sigma}^2$, since $\dot{a}(\theta) = \theta$ and $\ddot{a}(\theta) = 1$.

**Maximum likelihood estimation.** The method of moments can often be improved upon. The usual improvement is to use maximum likelihood. Maximum likelihood estimation is based upon choosing parameter estimates which maximize the likelihood of having observed the sample $y_1, \ldots, y_n$.

Each $y_i$ is a realization from $f(y)$, and so has probability function $f(y_i)$. The probability depends on $\theta$ and, if applicable, $\phi$. To make this dependence explicit write the probability function as $f(y_i; \theta, \phi)$. If the $y_i$ are independent then their joint probability function is

$$f(y; \theta, \phi) = \prod_{i=1}^{n} f(y_i; \theta, \phi)\,.$$

The likelihood of the sample $(y_1, \ldots, y_n)$ is the above expression regarded as a function of $\theta$ and $\phi$. The log-likelihood $\ell(\theta, \phi)$ is the logarithm of the likelihood:

$$\ell(\theta, \phi) \equiv \sum_{i=1}^{n} \ln f(y_i; \theta, \phi)\,.$$

The method of maximum likelihood chooses those values of $\theta$ and $\phi$ which maximize the likelihood or equivalently, the log-likelihood. Maximization of the log-likelihood (as opposed to the likelihood) is preferred since the former is easier to work with analytically. The maximum likelihood estimators (MLEs) of $\theta$ and $\phi$ are denoted as $\hat{\theta}$ and $\hat{\phi}$ respectively.

**Maximum likelihood estimation for exponential family distributions.** When the $f(y_i; \theta, \phi)$ are an exponential family probability function then $\ell(\phi, \theta)$ is

$$\sum_{i=1}^{n} \left\{ \ln c(y_i, \phi) + \frac{y_i \theta - a(\theta)}{\phi} \right\} = \frac{n\{\bar{y}\theta - a(\theta)\}}{\phi} + \sum_{i=1}^{n} \ln c(y_i, \phi) .$$

Differentiating $\ell(\theta, \phi)$ with respect to $\theta$ and equating to zero leads to the first order condition for likelihood maximization

$$\frac{n\{\bar{y} - \dot{a}(\theta)\}}{\phi} = 0 \qquad \Rightarrow \qquad \dot{a}(\theta) = \bar{y} .$$

Hence the MLE of $\theta$ is obtained by finding $\theta$ such that $\dot{a}(\theta) \equiv \mu$ equals the sample mean $\bar{y}$. Thus for any exponential family distribution, $\hat{\mu} = \bar{y}$.

**Properties of MLEs.** Any estimator $\hat{\theta}$ depends on the sample values $(y_1, \ldots, y_n)$, and will vary from sample to sample, drawn from the same population. An estimator is therefore itself a random variable, and two important properties of an estimator are its bias and variance. An estimator $\hat{\theta}$ is unbiased if $E(\hat{\theta}) = \theta$. The variance of an estimator indicates its precision, in that an unbiased estimator with small variance is likely to produce estimates reliably close to the true value (high precision), whereas an estimator with large variance produces more unreliable estimates, i.e. having low precision.

Suppose $\hat{\theta}$ is the MLE of parameter $\theta$. Desirable properties possessed by a MLE include:

- **Invariance:** If $h$ is a monotonic function and $\hat{\theta}$ is the MLE of $\theta$, then $h(\hat{\theta})$ is the MLE of $h(\theta)$.
- **Asymptotically unbiased:** The expected value $E(\hat{\theta})$ approaches $\theta$ as the sample size increases.
- **Consistent:** As the sample size increases the probability distribution $\hat{\theta}$ collapses on $\theta$.
- **Minimum variance:** In the class of all estimators, for large samples, $\hat{\theta}$ has the minimum variance and is therefore the most precise estimate possible.

Disadvantages of MLEs include:

- **Small-sample bias.** For small $n$, $\hat{\theta}$ is often biased. For example, the MLE of $\sigma^2$ in the normal distribution is $\hat{\sigma}^2 = n^{-1} \sum_i (y_i - \bar{y})^2$, which has $E(\hat{\sigma}^2) = \{(n-1)/n\}\sigma^2$. As $n$ becomes large, $E(\hat{\sigma}^2)$ converges to $\sigma^2$. In insurance data sets, $n$ is generally very large and small-sample bias is usually not an issue.
- **Computationally difficult.** MLEs are not always in closed form, in which case they need to be computed iteratively. With modern computing equipment this is unlikely to be a disadvantage.

## Exercises

3.1     Show that the geometric distribution, defined in Exercise 2.3, is in the exponential family.

3.2     (a) Write down the likelihood equations for the estimation of $\mu$ and $\nu$ of the gamma distribution.
        (b) Show that the MLE of $\mu$ is $\hat{\mu} = \bar{y}$. (This has been shown to be true in general, for the mean of exponential family distributions, in Section 3.5.)
        (c) For R users:

        - For claim size in the vehicle insurance data, write a program to estimate $\mu$ and $\nu$.
        - Plot the fitted $G(\hat{\mu}, \hat{\nu})$ density, superimposed on a histogram of claim size.

3.3     (a) Write down the likelihood equations for the estimation of $\mu$ and $\sigma^2$ of the inverse Gaussian distribution.
        (b) Show that the MLE of $\mu$ is $\hat{\mu} = \bar{y}$.
        (c) Show that the MLE of $\sigma^2$ is $\hat{\sigma}^2 = n^{-1} \sum_i (1/y_i - 1/\bar{y})$.
        (d) For R users:

        - For claim size in the vehicle insurance data, write a program to estimate $\mu$ and $\sigma^2$.
        - Plot the fitted $IG(\hat{\mu}, \hat{\sigma}^2)$ density, superimposed on a histogram of claim size.

# 4

# Linear modeling

Regression modeling deals with explaining the movements in one variable by movements in one or more other variables. The classical linear model, or normal linear model, forms the basis of generalized linear modeling, and a thorough understanding is critical to an understanding of GLMs. Many of the regression concepts found in GLMs have their genesis in the normal linear model, and so are covered in this chapter. Response distributions encountered in the insurance world are typically strongly non-normal, with the result that the methodology covered in this chapter, while important background to understanding GLMs, is usually not directly applicable to insurance data.

## 4.1 History and terminology of linear modeling

There is a smooth line of development from Gauss' original idea of simple least squares to present day generalized linear modeling. This line of thought and development is surveyed in the current chapter.

(i) **Simple linear modeling.** The aim is to explain an observed variable $y$ by a single other observed variable $x$. The variable $y$ is called the response variable and $x$ the explanatory variable. Alternative terminology used in the literature for $y$ are dependent, outcome, or (in econometrics) endogenous variable. Alternative names for $x$ are covariate, independent, predictor, driver, risk factor, exogenous variable, regressor or simply the "$x$" variable. When $x$ is categorical it is also called a factor.

(ii) **Multiple linear modeling.** Here simple least squares is extended by supposing that $x$ contains more than one explanatory variable, the combination of which serve to explain the response $y$.

(iii) **Transforming the response.** A small extension is to replace $y$, the variable to be explained, by a transformation $g(y)$. In this case the aim is to explain observed values of the transformed response $g(y)$

by the observed explanatory variables in $x$. Typical transformations are the logarithm or logit. For obvious reasons $g$ is constrained to be monotonic.

(iv) **Classical linear modeling.** A more subtle, conceptual, change is to replace the response $y$ by its expected value $E(y)$, or more specifically, $E(y|x)$. In this case the statistical average of $y$ is modeled in terms of $x$.

(v) **Generalized linear modeling.** Here $g\{E(y|x)\}$ is explained in terms of $x$. Similar to above, $g$ is a monotonic function and called the "link."

The variables $x$ and $y$ variables play distinct roles. The $y$ variable is generally thought of as being caused or explained by $x$, not vice versa. This may seem overly prescriptive; however, if the direction of causation is from $y$ to $x$ then it can be shown that some of the other assumptions that are usually invoked will definitely not hold.

## 4.2 What does "linear" in linear model mean?

The word "linear" in linear modeling requires careful scrutiny. In this context, linear means that the variables in $x$ are linearly combined to arrive at the prediction of $y$, $g(y)$, $E(y)$ or $g\{E(y)\}$. "Linearly combined" means the following:

(i) If $x_1, x_2, \ldots, x_p$ are the explanatory variables in $x$ then linear combinations considered are of the form $\beta_0 + \beta_1 x_1 + \cdots + \beta_p x_p$, where the $\beta_j$ are parameters to be decided upon. Note the presence of $\beta_0$, called the intercept. The linear combination $\beta_0 + \beta_1 x_1 + \cdots + \beta_p x_p$ is called the linear predictor. The linear predictor is written in vector form as $x'\beta$ where $x = (1, x_1, \ldots, x_p)'$ and $\beta = (\beta_0, \beta_1, \ldots, \beta_p)'$.

(ii) The variables in $x$ may be, and often are, related. For example $\beta_0 + \beta_1 x_1 + \beta_2 x_1^2$ and $\beta_0 + \beta_1 x_1 + \beta_2 x_2 + \beta_3 x_1 x_2$ are both "linear." Thus linearity refers to linearity in the $\beta_j$ coefficients, not the $x$ variables.

## 4.3 Simple linear modeling

Simple regression supposes

$$y \approx \beta_0 + \beta_1 x . \tag{4.1}$$

The $\beta_0$ and $\beta_1$ are parameters to be inferred or estimated. The approximation sign indicates the relationship is not exact but "statistical" in the sense that a body of data would only be expected to conform to the linear relationship "on average." This is made more precise shortly. The parameters $\beta_0$ and $\beta_1$ are usually referred to as the intercept and slope, respectively.

The meaning of the linear relationship above is as follows: for each unit increase in the explanatory variable $x$, the response variable $y$ is expected to increase by about $\beta_1$. Generally there is little significance to the value of $\beta_0$ and it is usually a mistake to say that it represents the prediction of $y$ when $x$ is zero. This emphasizes that the relationship (4.1) is usually assumed to pertain only over a relevant range of $x$, i.e. the range of $x$ observed in the data.

**Simple least squares.** This is a method for assigning values to $\beta_0$ and $\beta_1$ in (4.1), given a sample of $n$ pairs of measurements or observations on $y$ and $x$ denoted $(y_i, x_i)$, $i = 1, \ldots, n$. In particular, least squares determines $\beta_0$ and $\beta_1$ by minimizing the error sum of squares criterion:

$$\sum_{i=1}^{n} \{y_i - (\beta_0 + \beta_1 x_i)\}^2 . \tag{4.2}$$

Using calculus, the values of $\beta_0$ and $\beta_1$ that minimize (4.2) are

$$\hat{\beta}_1 = \frac{\sum_{i=1}^{n} x_i y_i - n\bar{x}\bar{y}}{\sum_{i=1}^{n} x_i^2 - n\bar{x}^2} , \qquad \hat{\beta}_0 = \bar{y} - \hat{\beta}_1 \bar{x} ,$$

where $\bar{y} = \sum_{i=1}^{n} y_i / n$ and $\bar{x} = \sum_{i=1}^{n} x_i / n$. Predicted values based on the fit are $\hat{y}_i = \hat{\beta}_0 + \hat{\beta} x_i$ and goodness of fit is typically measured using

$$R^2 \equiv 1 - \frac{\sum_{i=1}^{n} (y_i - \hat{y}_i)^2}{\sum_{i=1}^{n} (y_i - \bar{y})^2} . \tag{4.3}$$

It can be shown $0 \leq R^2 \leq 1$ with $R^2 = 1$ indicating a perfect linear fit. The $R^2$ statistic is much abused and misinterpreted.

## 4.4 Multiple linear modeling

With multiple regression it is supposed that

$$y \approx \beta_0 + \beta_1 x_1 + \cdots + \beta_p x_p . \tag{4.4}$$

Here $x_1, x_2, \ldots, x_p$ are the explanatory variables. The meaning associated with $\beta_j$ in (4.4) is as follows: For every unit increase in $x_j$, $y$ increases by about $\beta_j$, holding all other variables $x_k$ constant. The coefficients $\beta_j$ are often called partial regression coefficients, to distinguish them from the simple regression coefficient $\beta_1$ in (4.1). Partial regression coefficients partial out explanation to each one of the $x_j$ variables, whereas with simple regression all of the explanation is attributed to a single variable.

The art of linear modeling centers on the choice and form of the explanatory variables given the questions to be answered. For example in actuarial contexts, the $x$ variables may be pricing or rating variables impacting on the likely value of claims cost.

Although the $x_j$'s are called "independent" variables, they are often man-ufactured from other explanatory variables appearing in the linear predictor. Sections 4.9–4.13 explore alternatives.

**Multiple least squares.** The $\beta_j$ coefficients are determined by minimizing the sum of squares criterion:

$$S = \sum_{i=1}^{n}\{y_i - (\beta_0 + \beta_1 x_{i1} + \cdots + \beta_p x_{ip})\}^2 . \tag{4.5}$$

$y_i$ and $x_{ij}$ denote case $i$ of variables $y$ and $x_j$, respectively. Minimizing $S$ with respect to the $\beta_j$ requires the solution to the $p + 1$ equations:

$$\frac{\partial S}{\partial \beta_j} = 0 , \qquad j = 0, \ldots, p .$$

Matters are simplified using matrix notation. Define:

$$y = \begin{pmatrix} y_1 \\ y_2 \\ \vdots \\ y_n \end{pmatrix} , \qquad X = \begin{pmatrix} 1 & x_{11} & \cdots & x_{1p} \\ 1 & x_{21} & \cdots & x_{2p} \\ \vdots & \vdots & \cdots & \vdots \\ 1 & x_{n1} & \cdots & x_{np} \end{pmatrix} , \qquad \beta = \begin{pmatrix} \beta_0 \\ \beta_1 \\ \vdots \\ \beta_p \end{pmatrix} .$$

The first column of $X$ consists of 1's corresponding to the intercept in the model. In terms of this notation, (4.4) is, for all the cases $i = 1, \ldots, n$ together

$$y \approx X\beta . \tag{4.6}$$

The least squares criterion (4.5) is then

$$S = (y - X\beta)'(y - X\beta) . \tag{4.7}$$

Differentiating $S$ with respect to each component in $\beta$ yields

$$\frac{\partial S}{\partial \beta} = -2X'(y - X\beta) . \tag{4.8}$$

Equating (4.8) to zero yields the least squares solution

$$\hat{\beta} = (X'X)^{-1}X'y , \tag{4.9}$$

which is a system of $p + 1$ equations called the "normal" equations. The $R^2$ of the fit is defined as in (4.3) with $\hat{y} = X\hat{\beta}$.

Note that the calculation in (4.9) can be applied to any data formed in $y$ and $X$. Use of these equations does not imply that what is being done is sensible.

### 4.5 The classical linear model

Classical linear modeling deals explicitly with the approximation involved in (4.4) by assuming

$$E(y|x) = \beta_0 + \beta_1 x_1 + \cdots + \beta_p x_p \ . \tag{4.10}$$

In other words, it is the expected value that is being explained by a linear combination of the explanatory variables. Any particular observation on $y$ will deviate from this average. The formulation (4.10) emphasizes $y$ is regarded as random whereas the $x$'s are considered given or "fixed."

The interpretation accorded to the $\beta_j$ is similar to before: each unit increase in $x_j$ increases the expected value of $y$ by $\beta_j$. As before, each $x_j$ need not be an "independent" variable in that, for example, one could define $x_3$ as $x_3 = x_1 x_2$.

Assumption or model (4.10) can be rewritten in a number of ways, facilitating interpretation, the imposition of further assumptions, and the analysis of consequences of different sets of further assumptions. For example (4.10) is often written as

$$y = \beta_0 + \beta_1 x_1 + \cdots + \beta_p x_p + \epsilon \ , \qquad E(\epsilon) = 0 \ . \tag{4.11}$$

Here $\epsilon$ is called the error term. The terminology "error" is misleading: there is no implication that deviation of $y$ from the theoretical model is in any way erroneous. The term arose in the context of agricultural statistics, where modern statistics has its genesis, and much of the deviation of responses from models was due to measurement error. In econometrics the term "disturbance" is used. Equation (4.11) emphasizes $y$ is viewed as determined by the $x$'s, with an error $\epsilon$ serving to mask or "disturb" the relationship.

Further assumptions usually imposed with the classical linear model are the following:

- **Homoskedastic.** The variance of $\epsilon$ is finite and does not vary with the $x$ variables, at least over the considered range: $\mathrm{Var}(\epsilon) = \sigma^2$.
- **Normal.** The distribution of $\epsilon$ is normal. Together with the previous assumptions, this is denoted $\epsilon \sim N(0, \sigma^2)$.
- **Uncorrelated.** Each observation on $y$ is uncorrelated with all the other observations. This is often implicit in the notation $\epsilon \sim N(0, \sigma^2)$, meaning different $\epsilon$ draws are independent, or at least uncorrelated.

The additional assumptions are summarized in matrix notation:

$$y = X\beta + \epsilon \ , \qquad \epsilon \sim N(0, \sigma^2 I) \ , \tag{4.12}$$

where $\epsilon = (\epsilon_1, \ldots, \epsilon_n)'$, $I$ is the $n \times n$ identity matrix, $\sigma^2 I$ is the covariance matrix of $\epsilon$, and the distribution of $\epsilon$ is multivariate normal (Section 2.6).

An equivalent way of stating (4.12) is in terms of the conditional distribution of $y$, given $X$:

$$y \mid X \sim \mathrm{N}(X\beta, \sigma^2 I) \,. \tag{4.13}$$

## 4.6 Least squares properties under the classical linear model

Under the assumptions of the classical linear model,

$$\hat{\beta} \sim \mathrm{N}\{\beta, \sigma^2 (X'X)^{-1}\} \,. \tag{4.14}$$

This statement summarizes the following properties:

- **Unbiased.** This means $\mathrm{E}(\hat{\beta}) = \beta$. Unbiasedness only requires the assumption $\mathrm{E}(\epsilon) = 0$ since

$$\mathrm{E}(\hat{\beta}) = \mathrm{E}\{(X'X)^{-1}X'y\} = (X'X)^{-1}X'\mathrm{E}(y) = (X'X)^{-1}X'X\beta = \beta \,.$$

Note $\mathrm{E}(\epsilon) = 0$ is equivalent to $\mathrm{E}(y) = X\beta$.
- **Maximum likelihood.** This states $\hat{\beta}$ is the MLE of $\beta$. This is seen by considering the log-likelihood of model (4.11):

$$\ell(\beta, \sigma^2) = -n \ln \sigma - \frac{n}{2} \ln 2\pi - \frac{1}{2} \sum_{i=1}^{n} \left( \frac{y_i - \hat{y}_i}{\sigma} \right)^2 \tag{4.15}$$

where $\hat{y}_i = \hat{\beta}_0 + \hat{\beta}_1 x_{i1} + \cdots + \hat{\beta}_p x_{ip}$ is the fitted value for case $i$. The first two terms of $\ell(\beta, \sigma^2)$ do not involve $\beta$. Hence maximizing $\ell(\beta, \sigma^2)$ with respect to $\beta$ is equivalent to minimizing $\sum_i (y_i - \hat{y}_i)^2$, which is the same as the least squares criterion (4.5). The MLE and least squares solutions for $\beta$ thus coincide.
- **Minimum variance, invariance, consistency.** Since $\hat{\beta}$ is the MLE of $\beta$, it possesses the minimum variance, invariance and consistency properties of MLEs (Section 3.5).

## 4.7 Weighted least squares

In a regression certain observations may be less precise than others, and in a fit it is reasonable to assign them less weight. Weighting cases according to their precision leads to weighted least squares.

The precision $w_i$ of case $i$ is signalled through $\mathrm{Var}(\epsilon_i) = \sigma^2/w_i$. Thus $w_i \to 0$ indicates no precision and $w_i \to \infty$ indicates complete precision. Multiplying case $i$ by $\sqrt{w_i}$ yields

$$y_i^* = \beta_0 \sqrt{w_i} + \beta_1 x_{i1}^* + \cdots + \beta_p x_{ip}^* + \epsilon_i^* \tag{4.16}$$

where

$$y_i^* \equiv \sqrt{w_i}\, y_i \,, \qquad x_{ij}^* \equiv \sqrt{w_i}\, x_{ij} \,, \qquad \epsilon_i^* \equiv \sqrt{w_i}\, \epsilon_i \,.$$

Thus the weighted observations are homoskedastic since $\mathrm{Var}(\epsilon_i^*) = \sigma^2$. Regressing $y_i^*$ on the $x_{ij}^*$ yields

$$\hat{\beta}^* = (X^{*'}X^*)^{-1}X^{*'}y^* = (X'WX)^{-1}X'Wy , \qquad (4.17)$$

where $W$ is the diagonal matrix with diagonal entries $w_i$. The estimator $\hat{\beta}^*$ is called the weighted least squares estimator. Since $\hat{\beta}^*$ is the least squares estimator computed relative to the model $y^* = X^*\beta + \epsilon^*$ it follows that

$$\hat{\beta}^* \sim \mathrm{N}\left\{\beta, \sigma^2(X'WX)^{-1}\right\} .$$

Weighted least squares estimators have all the desirable properties of least squares estimators, provided of course correct weights are used.

## 4.8 Grouped and ungrouped data

Insurance data are often represented in tabular or grouped format. As an example, consider an analysis of claim sizes in the vehicle insurance data, by age and sex of the driver. For policies which had a claim, mean claim sizes by age and sex are given in Table 4.1. For male drivers, mean claim size decreases with increasing age. For female drivers the pattern is not as clear. The question arises as to the appropriate analysis for data in this form. Although there are 12 cells of data, the table is based on the 4624 policies which had a claim.

A regression analysis with claim size as the response, and driver's age and sex as explanatory variables, is appropriate. This may be carried out in two ways:

  (i) the "grouped data" approach. This is based on the 12 observations in
      Table 4.1, with regression weights equal to the number of observations
      in each cell;
  (ii) the "ungrouped data" approach. This is based on the 4624 raw
      observations.

The two approaches yield the same parameter estimates. The grouped data approach has been, and still is, popular, as data representation and storage is dramatically simpler in cases such as the current example. Computation is also simplified. However, in realistic analyses many explanatory variables are typically considered, meaning that the summary table is highly multidimensional. In addition, with modern computing the saving in computation time is minimal. Thus while a summary table such as Table 4.1 is a useful preliminary data inspection tool, its use in analysis does not present any advantage over use of the raw observations. In any case, if there is at least one explanatory variable which is continuous, then the grouped data approach cannot be used.

The ungrouped data approach is used throughout this text, i.e. analyses are performed on the basis of raw observations such as individual policies. The

Table 4.1. *Vehicle insurance: mean claim size (dollars) by age and sex of driver, number of observations in brackets*

| Sex | Driver's age category | | | | | |
|---|---|---|---|---|---|---|
| | 1 | 2 | 3 | 4 | 5 | 6 |
| Male | 2 118 | 1 945 | 1 869 | 1 800 | 1 724 | 1 546 |
| | (276) | (537) | (688) | (643) | (322) | (182) |
| Female | 3 285 | 2 381 | 1 991 | 2 143 | 1 734 | 2 198 |
| | (220) | (395) | (425) | (461) | (292) | (183) |

grouped and ungrouped approaches are contrasted in the context of logistic regression, in Section 7.5.

## 4.9 Transformations to normality and linearity

Transformations of the response and explanatory variables are frequently carried out in order to view and analyze data on an appropriate scale. This has been discussed in Section 1.3. When performing a linear regression, data is transformed in order to satisfy the model assumptions of linearity between $y$ and the explanatory variables, homoskedasticity and normality of $\epsilon$. While normality of the explanatory variables is not necessary, when an $x$ variable is strongly skewed a linear relationship with $y$ is unlikely. Transformations which normalize, or at least symmetrize, the distribution of an explanatory variable frequently also linearize its relationship with $y$ or some transform of $y$.

**Third party claims.** Consider a model for the number of claims in an area as a function of the number of accidents. A scatterplot of claims against accidents is shown in the left panel of Figure 4.1. This is strongly heteroskedastic. Diagnostic checks on a linear model based on these data indicate clear violation of the homoskedasticity assumption. The concentration of points around the origin make it difficult to discern the relationship between $y$ and $x$. The top two panels of Figure 4.2 show the histograms of the number of accidents and the number of claims. Both are strongly skewed to the right. The bottom two panels are histograms of the log-transformed data, which appear more normal than those of the raw data. A scatterplot of the log-transformed data is shown in the right panel of Figure 4.1. This displays linearity and approximate homoskedasticity, and therefore a linear model based on log claims as the response and log accidents as the explanatory variable, is more amenable to analysis using the normal linear model than one based on the raw data. A GLM analysis is more appropriate for these data and is discussed in Section 6.2.

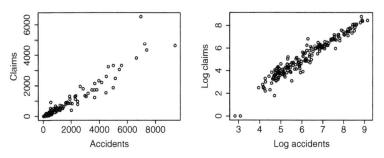

Fig. 4.1. Scatterplots of number of accidents and number of claims, raw and log scales

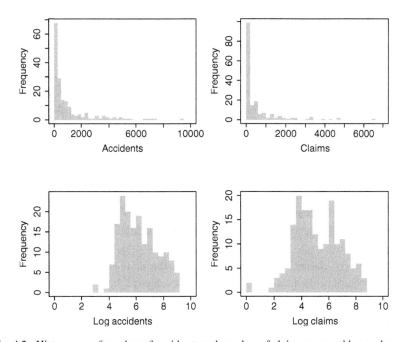

Fig. 4.2. Histograms of number of accidents and number of claims, raw and log scales

**Variance stabilizing transformations.** The above example demonstrates the use of the logarithmic transformation to both stabilize the variance of $y$ and linearize its relationship with $x$. If the variance of $y$ is of the form $\mathrm{Var}(y) = \phi\mu^p$, where $\phi > 0$ is a scale parameter, then the transformation $g(y)$, which makes the variance approximately independent of the mean, is such that the derivative of $g(y)$ with respect to $y$ is $y^{-p/2}$. This is established from

$$g(y) \approx g(\mu) + \dot{g}(\mu)(y - \mu) \qquad \Rightarrow \qquad \mathrm{Var}\{g(y)\} \approx \{\dot{g}(\mu)\}^2\mathrm{Var}(y)\,,$$

where $\dot{g}(y)$ is the derivative of $g$ evaluated at $y$. Integrating $\dot{g}(\mu) = \mu^{-p/2}$ with respect to $\mu$ yields

$$g(y) = \begin{cases} y^{1-p/2} & \text{for } p \neq 2 \\ \ln(y) & \text{for } p = 2 . \end{cases}$$

This is the Box–Cox transformation described in Section 1.3. As an example, when $y$ has variability proportional to the mean (such as in the case of Poisson data), $\text{Var}(y) = \phi\mu$, $p = 1$ and hence the variance stabilizing transform is $g(y) = \sqrt{y}$. If the standard deviation is proportional to the mean and hence $p = 2$, then the log transform stabilizes the variance.

Variance stabilizing transformations were important before the GLM methodology became available. When non-normal responses were modeled, the only option was to find a transformation which would render the data amenable to analysis using the normal linear model. For example, when analyzing count data which had the Poisson distribution, a normal linear model analysis was performed using the square root of $y$ as the response. With GLMs the data is modelled directly, using the appropriate response distribution.

## 4.10 Categorical explanatory variables

When a potential explanatory variable is categorical, then it is "dummied up" for inclusion into a multiple linear regression. For example, suppose the area of residence of a policyholder is considered to be a potential explanatory variable in a model for claim size $y$. If there are three areas A, B and C, then two indicator (dummy) variables $x_1$ and $x_2$ are defined:

| Area | $x_1$ | $x_2$ |
|------|-------|-------|
| A | 1 | 0 |
| B | 0 | 1 |
| C | 0 | 0 |

Suppose area is the only explanatory variable. Then the relationship is modeled as

$$y \approx \beta_0 + \beta_1 x_1 + \beta_2 x_2 .$$

This states that $y \approx \beta_0$ in area C, $y \approx \beta_0 + \beta_1$ in area A, and $y \approx \beta_0 + \beta_2$ in area B. Thus $\beta_1$ is the difference between areas C and A, while $\beta_2$ is the difference between areas C and B. Note the following:

(i) An indicator variable $x_3$ for C is not used. The "left out" category is called the base level. In the above example, area C is the base level, meaning that differences are measured between C and each of the other levels. The choice of base level is up to the analyst: this is discussed in more detail below.

(ii) In general, when the explanatory variable has $r$ levels, $r - 1$ indicator variables are introduced, modeling the difference between each category and the base level.

(iii) It is not sensible to define, for example, a variable $x = 1, 2$ or $3$ according to whether the level is A, B or C, since $y \approx \beta_0 + \beta_1 x$ implies equal spacing between A, B and C, i.e. a difference of $\beta_1$ between areas A and B; and $\beta_1$ between areas B and C.

**Choice of base level.** The base level should not be sparse. To explain this suppose one has a categorical explanatory variable with $r$ levels, and level $r$ has been chosen as the base level. In the extreme scenario, if there are no cases having level $r$ then for each case one of $x_1, \ldots, x_{r-1}$ is always equal to 1, and the others equal to zero. This in turn implies that $x_1 + \cdots + x_{r-1} = 1$ and hence the $X$ matrix is singular: the sum of the last $r - 1$ columns equals the intercept. More realistically, if the base level has very few cases, then for most cases $x_1 + \cdots + x_{r-1} = 1$, implying near linear dependency between the columns of $X$. Although $\hat{\beta}$ is computable, it would be numerically unstable, analogous to the result obtained when dividing by a number close to zero.

Any level which is not sparse is an appropriate base level. Since $\beta_j$ is the difference in the effect of the explanatory variable at level $j$ compared with the base level, it is convenient to choose the base level as the "normal" or "usual" level, against which other levels are to be compared. This is often the level having the most cases. For example, in the vehicle insurance data set, the most commonly occurring vehicle body type is "Sedan," which comprises almost a third of the cases. Comparing other body types with Sedan makes good sense, and makes the latter a good choice as the base level. Note, however, that one is not limited to making comparisons relative to the base level. Differences between non-base levels are of the form $\beta_j - \beta_k$.

**SAS notes.** The software chooses the base level as the highest level – numerically or alphabetically. When levels are coded numerically, the highest level is often the category "Other." This is not a good choice of base level as it is usually sparse, and comparisons relative to "Other" are generally not helpful. In this case a more suitable base level needs to be specified. The terminology for base level in the SAS manual is "reference level."

## 4.11 Polynomial regression

Given a single explanatory variable $x$ consider

$$y \approx \beta_0 + \beta_1 x + \beta_2 x^2 .$$

This is a linear regression since the right hand side is linear in the $\beta$ coefficients. The relationship between $y$ and $x$, however, is quadratic. In essence there is one explanatory variable, albeit used twice in different forms. A unit increase in $x$ has the effect of changing $y$ by about $\beta_1 + 2\beta_2 x$ and hence the slope of the relationship depends on the value of $x$.

This idea can be extended by defining further variables $x^3$, $x^4$, and so on. Incorporating more polynomial terms permits an increasingly complicated response structure. When a polynomial term of degree $m$, i.e. $x^m$, is included in a model, all lower order terms $x, x^2, \ldots, x^{m-1}$ are generally included. Note that fitting polynomials of an order which is unnecessarily high, results in models with fitted values close to the observations but low predictive ability. This is illustrated in Figure 4.3, in which a small data set ($n = 20$), simulated with a quadratic relationship between $x$ and $y$, has had polynomials of degree $m = 1, 2, 10$ and $19$ fitted. Clearly the linear relationship ($m = 1$) is

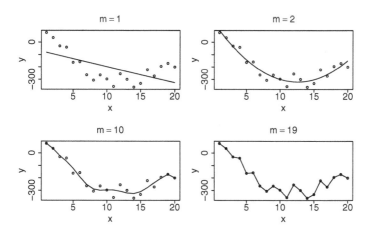

Fig. 4.3. Polynomial fits, simulated data set

inappropriate; $m = 2$ approximates the general shape of the relationship, without following local variation too closely; $m = 10$ produces fitted values much closer to the observations, but which tend to follow small local variations; and $m = 19$ (which fits 20 parameters to 20 observations) produces a perfect but useless fit, which "joins the dots." The $\hat{\beta}$s from the degree 10 fit will have lower precision, and the resulting fitted values will be less reliable, than those from the quadratic model. Judgement about what degree of polynomial to fit to a continuous explanatory variable is guided by significance testing of the coefficients (Section 4.15), and model selection criteria (Section 4.19). Typically one starts with a linear term, and adds in increasingly higher order terms. This is illustrated, in the context of logistic regression, in Section 7.3.

**Numerical difficulties.** These can arise when high order terms are included in a model, due to the finite length of computer storage. If $x$ is large (negative or positive), then overflow occurs in the computation of $x^m$ when $m$ is large. Frequently a further result of this is that underflow occurs in the corresponding $\hat{\beta}$. This problem is avoided if $x$ is suitably scaled before entering it into the regression. Specifically, denoting $x_{max}$ as the maximum value of $x$ in the data, and $x_{min}$ as the minimum, then $(x_{max} + x_{min})/2$ is the midrange of $x$, and $(x_{max} - x_{min})/2$ is half the range of $x$. The linear transformation

$$x^* = \frac{x - (x_{max} + x_{min})/2}{(x_{max} - x_{min})/2}$$

lies between $-1$ and $1$. Overflow and underflow problems are overcome by including $x^*$ rather than $x$ in the polynomial regression.

Further problems of collinearity (see Section 4.14) can arise when computing high order polynomial regressions. Successive powers of $x$ may be highly correlated, leading again to numerical instability and consequent unreliability of the estimates. This problem is avoided by the use of orthogonal polynomials. Interested readers are referred to Chambers and Hastie (1991). Orthogonal polynomials are used in a regression model for mortality in Section 6.2.

## 4.12  Banding continuous explanatory variables

When the relationship between explanatory variable and response is not linear an alternative, safer, approach to finding a parametric form of the relationship is to band or categorize the explanatory variable. Although banding results in loss of information, a model employing a banded version of a continuous variable is sometimes considered more practical than one which employs the (possibly misspecified) continuous variable. However, caution is required in the choice of cutoffs and there is no general rule as to the optimal choice of cutoffs.

- Excessively wide bands hide important features.
- Each band must have adequate numbers to ensure stable estimates.
- Ideally bands correspond to realistic groups. For example, external factors such as industry standards can guide appropriate levels of banding.

An example of banding a continuous explanatory variable in the context of logistic regression is given in Section 7.3.

## 4.13 Interaction

Consider the model with two explanatory variables $x_1$, $x_2$ and with

$$y \approx \beta_0 + \beta_1 x_1 + \beta_2 x_2 + \beta_3 x_1 x_2 \,.$$

This is a linear regression with $x_3 = x_1 x_2$, called an interaction term. A unit increase in $x_1$ increases $y$ by about $\beta_1 + \beta_3 x_2$, and hence the effect of $x_1$ depends on $x_2$. Similarly the effect of a unit increase in $x_2$ is about $\beta_2 + \beta_3 x_1$ which depends on $x_1$. Thus speaking of the effect of a unit increase in, for example, $x_1$, holding all other variables constant, does not make sense. The variables $x_1$ and $x_2$ are called the main effects and are distinguished from the interaction effect $x_3 = x_1 x_2$.

Interacting an ordinary quantitative variable with an indicator variable is a useful technique of linear modeling. Assume $x_1$ is continuous, and $x_2$ is an indicator taking on the values 0 and 1 (indicating one of two groups). Then

$$y \approx \begin{cases} \beta_0 + \beta_1 x_1 & \text{if } x_2 = 0 \\ (\beta_0 + \beta_2) + (\beta_1 + \beta_3)x_1 & \text{if } x_2 = 1 \,. \end{cases}$$

Thus the effect of $x_1$ – that is the intercept and slope – depends on the group indicated by $x_2$. For the base group $x_2 = 0$, the intercept and slope of the relation of $y$ to $x_1$ are $\beta_0$ and $\beta_1$, respectively. The intercept and slope when $x_2 = 1$ are $\beta_0 + \beta_2$ and $\beta_1 + \beta_3$. Hence these are an increase of $\beta_2$ and $\beta_3$ relative to the intercept and slope when $x_2 = 0$. This modeling idea is easily extended to more than two groups and a number of quantitative variables, so that the intercept and slopes with respect to quantitative variables may differ across many groups.

As an illustration of interaction, the age of a driver may have an effect on the probability of a claim, but this effect may differ according to whether the car is a sports car or otherwise. More generally the effect of the age of a driver may vary with the type of car.

## 4.14 Collinearity

Consider the effect of smoking on mortality. The following explanatory variables are available: $x_1$ the age at which smoking commenced, $x_2$ the number of years since smoking initiation and $x_3$ the current age. Obviously $x_3 = x_1 + x_2$ and

$$\beta_0 + \beta_1 x_1 + \beta_2 x_2 + \beta_3 x_3 = \beta_0 + (\beta_1 + \beta_3)x_1 + (\beta_2 + \beta_3)x_2 \,.$$

Hence the three variables $x_1, x_2$ and $x_3$ explain the same as any two of the variables. Thus the individual effects of each of the three variables cannot be assessed. The variables are perfectly "collinear." In terms of the multiple least squares model (4.6), the matrix $X$ has an exact linear dependence between its columns and hence $X'X$ is singular.

**Using perfectly collinear variables.** Many programs, when encountering perfect linear dependence in variables, exclude one or more variables to ensure the perfect collinearity disappears. Alternatively the software may just "crash" or even worse, report nonsensical results.

**Near collinearity.** The smoking example above is a case of exact collinearity. It is more usual to encounter situations of "near" and less obvious collinearity. For example, in a data set where the cases are policyholders, area of residence, income level and education level will be correlated. The result of the inclusion of highly correlated explanatory variables is the near singularity of $X'X$ and difficulties in the computing the inverse $(X'X)^{-1}$. If the inverse is computable, then it will typically have large diagonal entries, implying large estimation variances on one or more of the components of $\hat{\beta}$. The existence of collinearity may also mislead the analyst in the choice of explanatory variables. If $x_j$ and $x_k$ are highly correlated and both predictive of the response, then each one, in the presence of the other, will not contribute much additional explanation. Hypothesis tests for each variable, assuming that the other one is in the model, will show non-significance. The solution is to include only one of them in the model.

## 4.15  Hypothesis testing

Is a given coefficient $\beta_j$ equal to zero? This is equivalent to asking whether $x_j$ is relevant to the prediction of the response. More generally it may be asked if a group of coefficients are all zero i.e. if, for a given "hypothesis" matrix $C$ it is the case that $C\beta = 0$. For example, if $C$ picks out the trailing coefficients in $\beta$:

$$
C = \begin{pmatrix}
0 & \cdots & 0 & 1 & 0 & \cdots & 0 \\
0 & \cdots & 0 & 0 & 1 & \cdots & 0 \\
\vdots & & & & & & \\
0 & \cdots & 0 & 0 & 0 & \cdots & 1
\end{pmatrix},
$$

then the hypothesis $C\beta = 0$ is the hypothesis that the final coefficients in $\beta$ are all zero. More generally it may be asked whether a given coefficient is equal to some number different to zero, or whether for example the sum of coefficients equal a given number. All these hypotheses can be written as $C\beta = r$, where $C$ and $r$ are given. Throughout the following discussion it is assumed that $C$ has full row rank and hence there is no redundancy in the hypotheses contained in $C$.

Assume the hypothesis is that a subset of the $\beta$ coefficients are equal to zero, and that the number of rows of $C$ (i.e. the number of parameters being restricted to zero) is $q$. Further, let the number of parameters in the unrestricted model be $p$. Then the number of unknown parameters in the restricted model is $p - q$. To facilitate the discussion, write $\hat{\beta}$ as the unrestricted MLE of $\beta$, and let $\tilde{\beta}$ denote the MLE of $\beta$ when $\ell$ is maximized subject to the restrictions $C\beta = 0$. For the restricted model the $X$ matrix has the columns corresponding to the restricted parameters deleted, and is denoted as $X^*$.

The residual sums of squares for the unrestricted and restricted models are $(y - X\hat{\beta})'(y - X\hat{\beta})$ and $(y - X^*\tilde{\beta})'(y - X^*\tilde{\beta})$, respectively. The difference

$$(y - X^*\tilde{\beta})'(y - X^*\tilde{\beta}) - (y - X\hat{\beta})'(y - X\hat{\beta}) = \hat{\beta}'X'y - \tilde{\beta}'X^{*\prime}y \quad (4.18)$$

is a measure of the decrease in model fit due to the imposition of the restrictions. It is positive (as the residual sum of squares for the unrestricted model must be less than that for the restricted model) and if it is large then one would conclude that the deterioration in model fit as a result of the restrictions is too great. In that case the unrestricted model is chosen, i.e. the conclusion is made that $C\beta \neq 0$. The commonly used F test uses as test statistic the difference (4.18), scaled by the estimate of the variance of the unrestricted model:

$$\frac{(\hat{\beta}'X'y - \tilde{\beta}'X^{*\prime}y)/q}{\hat{\sigma}^2} \quad (4.19)$$

where $\hat{\sigma}^2 = (y - X\hat{\beta})'(y - X\hat{\beta})/(n - p)$. This test statistic, under the assumptions summarized in (4.12), has the $F_{q,n-p}$ distribution, if the restricted model is correct. One rejects the restricted model if it is "too large," i.e. in the upper tail of the $F_{q,n-p}$ distribution.

**Testing a single coefficient.** When the hypothesis is that a single coefficient is zero, i.e. $\beta_j = 0$, then (4.19) reduces to

$$\frac{\hat{\beta}_j^2}{\hat{\sigma}^2\psi_j} \sim F_{1,n-p} , \quad (4.20)$$

where $\psi_j$ is diagonal element $j$ of $(X'X)^{-1}$. From (4.14), the denominator of (4.20) is the estimated variance of $\beta_j$. The signed square root of (4.20) is the well-known "t statistic", which is $\hat{\beta}_j$ divided by its estimated standard error:

$$\frac{\hat{\beta}_j}{\hat{\sigma}\sqrt{\psi_j}} \sim t_{n-p} . \quad (4.21)$$

**Testing the effect of a categorical variable.** A test for the significance of a categorical explanatory variable with $r$ levels involves the hypothesis that the coefficients of all $r - 1$ indicator variables are zero. For example, consider a model with a continuous explanatory variable $x_1$ and a categorical explanatory variable with three levels, and corresponding indicator variables $x_2$ and

$x_3$. In this case the hypothesis concerning the significance of the categorical variable is

$$C\beta = \begin{pmatrix} 0 & 0 & 1 & 0 \\ 0 & 0 & 0 & 1 \end{pmatrix} \begin{pmatrix} \beta_0 \\ \beta_1 \\ \beta_2 \\ \beta_3 \end{pmatrix} = \begin{pmatrix} \beta_2 \\ \beta_3 \end{pmatrix} = \begin{pmatrix} 0 \\ 0 \end{pmatrix},$$

i.e. $\beta_2 = \beta_3 = 0$.

Sometimes the F test for the significance of a categorical explanatory variable is rejected, but tests for the coefficients of the individual indicator variables are not all rejected. This may signal the need for judicious grouping of levels, particularly levels which are sparse. Care needs to be taken in this exercise, as wholesale grouping of, for example, all non-significant levels, may not make any sense. It is important not to combine category levels which are dissimilar in nature and do not form a sensible group.

**Statistical versus practical significance.** Classical hypothesis testing was developed in an era when data sets were small, typically of the order of tens or hundreds of observations. Insurance data sets are usually orders of magnitude larger than this. The effect of increasing sample size is to increase the precision of parameter estimates. Consider, for simplicity, a test of the hypothesis $\beta_j = 0$. An estimate $\hat{\beta}_j$ which is close to zero, based on a small data set, may lead to non-rejection of the hypothesis since its standard error is large, resulting in a small value for the t statistic (4.21). However, the identical $\hat{\beta}_j$ based on a very large data set will have a small standard error. This results in a large t statistic and rejection of the hypothesis. However, one has to think about the magnitude of the effect, and whether the statistical significance translates into a practically useful effect or relativity. When the effect of an explanatory variable is statistically significant but small relative to the effects of other explanatory variables, it is acceptable to exclude it from a final model. In cases such as these, model selection criteria (Section 4.19) lead to the exclusion of statistically significant explanatory variables that have little explanatory power.

## 4.16 Checks using the residuals

A fitted model must be checked. These checks are aimed at confirming whether the assumptions underlying the fitted model are applicable. The distributional assumptions of model (4.12) are:

(i) The mean of $y$ varies linearly with the $x$'s.
(ii) The error terms $\epsilon$ are normally distributed.

(iii) The variance of the $y$'s – equivalently the variance of the $\epsilon$'s does not vary with the $x$'s, i.e. is constant. (Equivalent terms are homoskedasticity, constant variance, homogeneity of variance.)

(iv) The $\epsilon$'s are independent.

These assumptions must be checked. Note there is no assumption of normality of the explanatory variables $x_j$.

The assumptions on $\epsilon$ are not directly verifiable, since $\epsilon$ is not observable. However the $\epsilon_i$ can be estimated:

$$\hat{\epsilon}_i \equiv y_i - (\hat{\beta}_0 + \hat{\beta}_1 x_{i1} + \cdots + \hat{\beta}_p x_{ip}) = y_i - \hat{y}_i \ .$$

These are called the residuals. Since $y = X\beta + \epsilon$,

$$\hat{\beta} = (X'X)^{-1} X'y = (X'X)^{-1} X'(X\beta + \epsilon) = \beta + (X'X)^{-1} X'\epsilon \ ,$$

it follows that

$$\hat{\epsilon} = y - X\hat{\beta} = X\beta + \epsilon - X\hat{\beta} = \{I - X(X'X)^{-1}X'\}\epsilon \ .$$

The matrix $H \equiv X(X'X)^{-1}X'$ is called the "hat" matrix because it puts a hat on $y$, $\hat{y} = Hy$. If $M \equiv I - H$ then $\hat{\epsilon} = M\epsilon$. It is easy to verify $MM = M$ and $M' = M$ and hence

$$\mathrm{Var}(\hat{\epsilon}) = \mathrm{Var}(M\epsilon) = \sigma^2 M = \sigma^2 (I - H) \ .$$

Thus $\mathrm{Var}(\hat{\epsilon}_i) = \sigma^2(1 - h_{ii})$ where $h_{ii}$ is diagonal element $i$ of $H$.

Much of model checking is based on the residuals, $\hat{\epsilon}_i$, or alternatively the studentized residuals, defined as

$$r_i = \frac{\hat{\epsilon}_i}{\hat{\sigma}\sqrt{1 - h_{ii}}} \ . \tag{4.22}$$

**Checking for normality.** Normality is checked by examining the distribution of either the residuals $\hat{\epsilon}_i$ or the studentized residuals $r_i$. The best way is via the pp-plot discussed in Section 1.6, where the percentile ranks of the $\hat{\epsilon}_i$ or $r_i$ are compared to those of the normal.

**Checking for constant variance.** If the variance of $\epsilon$, or $y$, does not vary with the explanatory variables, then a plot of $\hat{\epsilon}_i$ or $r_i$ against each $x_j$ is a random scatter. The residuals are also commonly plotted against the fitted values $\hat{y}_i$, again yielding a random scatter if the constant variance assumption is true. Non-random scatters thus suggest heteroskedasticity.

**Checking for independence.** If $\text{Var}(\epsilon) = \sigma^2 I$, then $\text{Var}(\hat{\epsilon}) = \sigma^2 M$. Off-diagonal elements of $M$ are often relatively small and hence the $\hat{\epsilon}_i$ are generally approximately independent. While there exist formal tests for correlation, typically one checks for serial correlation (i.e. correlation between successive observations) by plotting the $\hat{\epsilon}_i$'s in an order wherein one suspects lack of independence, for example the order of occurrence in the sample. If there is no serial correlation then one would expect to see no pattern in this plot.

## 4.17  Checking explanatory variable specifications

Model diagnostics also provide guidance for identifying the correct specification of explanatory variables in the model. Two plots are useful and extend to the GLM: added-variable plots and partial residual plots.

**Added-variable plots.** Added-variable plots are useful for detecting whether a continuous explanatory variable $x_j$ should be in the model, and for identifying the possible cause of unduly large residuals. In this plot the effect of $x_j$ on the regression equation is isolated, given that all the other explanatory variables are in the model.

An added-variable plot for $x_j$, is a plot of $y$ against $x_j$ when both variables are adjusted for all the other explanatory variables. Adjusting for all other variables means performing a regression of $y$ and $x_j$ on all the other variables, and computing the residuals. This is done for $y$ and $x_j$ as the responses in two regressions. The residuals from the two regressions are plotted against each other. The least squares slope associated with this plot is the regression coefficient on $x_j$ when regressing $y$ on all the $x$ variables including $x_j$.

- A random scatter, i.e. a point cloud with zero slope, indicates that $x_j$ should not be in the model.
- An linear plot means that $x_j$ should be included in the model, i.e. the relationship between $y$ and $x_j$ is linear, given the other explanatory variables.
- Curvature in the plot indicates that a transformation is needed for $x_j$.

**Partial residual plots.** A nonlinear relationship between $y$ and $x_j$ is more easily detected with a partial residual plot. The partial residuals for $x_j$ are defined as

$$(y_i - \hat{y}_i) + x_{ij}\hat{\beta}_j \, ,$$

where $\hat{y}_i$ and $\hat{\beta}_j$ are based on the model including all explanatory variables (including $x_j$). Thus it is the residual with the explanation afforded by $x_j$ added back in.

The partial residuals are plotted against $x_{ij}$: the plot will have slope $\hat{\beta}_j$, and a curvature indicates a departure from linearity in the relationship between $y$ and $x_j$, adjusted for the other explanatory variables. Because the horizontal axis of this plot is $x_j$, it provides a better indication of nonlinearity than the added-variable plot, where the horizontal axis is on another scale.

**SAS notes.** Added-variable plots are also called partial regression plots, and partial leverage plots in SAS Insight. Partial residuals are not directly produced by SAS.

## 4.18 Outliers

Cases which are unusual or extreme, in comparison with the rest of the data, are of concern.

(i) They may be wrong, usually as a result of data entry error.
(ii) They may influence the fit disproportionately.

When an analysis is performed on very large data sets, as is usually the case with insurance data, it is unlikely a single case influences the regression coefficients. In this situation, diagnostic testing for extreme observations is an aid to data cleaning, where suspicious cases are flagged for checking.

In insurance data sets, explanatory variables are commonly categorical. Even continuous variables such as age are usually banded for analysis. With categorical explanatory variables, it is impossible for the value of a single variable to be extreme, assuming that elementary validity checks have been carried out. Nevertheless, a case may have an unusual combination of values that could be indicative of an error: for example, in a personal injury insurance file, a case with a driver in age band 0–4 years is a recording error.

Unusual cases on the response scale will have fitted values very different from the observed. The corresponding residual will be either large positive or large negative; examination of residual plots will therefore reveal these cases.

**Leverage.** A case which is an unusual combination of the explanatory variables, will have high leverage. To explain leverage, recall $\hat{y} = Hy$ and hence each $\hat{y}_i$ is a linear combinations of the responses:

$$\hat{y}_i = h_{i1}y_1 + h_{i2}y_2 + \cdots + h_{in}y_n ,$$

where $(h_{i1}, h_{i2}, \ldots, h_{in})$ is row $i$ of $H$. It can be shown that the diagonal elements of $H$ are in the range 0 to 1, and $h_{ii}$ is the weight case $i$ contributes to its own fitted value. The sum of the diagonal elements of $H$ is the number of parameters in the model $p$, so each case is expected to contribute $p/n$ to its own fitted value. If a single $h_{ii}$ is much greater than $p/n$, then that case is "isolated or self-estimating" (Lindsey 1997). The $h_{ii}$ measure the distance of a case from the center of $x$-space, as is seen from the simple form of $h_{ii}$ for a model with a single explanatory variable $x$:

$$h_{ii} = \frac{1}{n} + \frac{(x_i - \bar{x})^2}{\sum_j (x_j - \bar{x})^2} \ .$$

The further $x_i$ is from the mean $\bar{x}$, the greater $h_{ii}$ is. This extends to models with multiple explanatory variables.

The $h_{ii}$ are called "leverages", or "hat matrix diagonals." A rule of thumb is that $h_{ii} > 2p/n$ indicates the case is unusual in the space of explanatory variables, or equivalently is contributing disproportionately to its own fitted value. Leverages provide a useful mechanism for diagnosing subtle data errors undetectable using simple checks on single explanatory variables.

## 4.19 Model selection

Every explanatory variable added to a model improves fit. However adding unwarranted variables decreases the precision of parameter estimates. While an explanatory variable may be statistically significant, adding it to the model may not be worthwhile, because the improvement in fit may be outweighed by loss of estimation precision. The central concept is the bias–variance tradeoff. Bias refers to the lack of fit. Variance in this context means the variance of the regression estimates.

Increasing the number of explanatory variables increases the number of parameters $p$ and decreases the errors $y_i - \hat{y}_i$ of the fit. A large $p$ leads to low bias. However, the more parameters in the model, the greater the variances of the $\hat{\beta}_j$. The aim is to find a model compromising between:

- a large number of parameters and consequently a close fit to the observations. In this case parameter estimates $\hat{\beta}_j$ have low precision (high standard deviation); and
- a small number of parameters with a less good fit. In this case parameter estimates $\hat{\beta}_j$ have relatively high precision (low standard deviation).

There are a number of criteria which balance the goodness of fit of a model with a penalty term for the number of parameters. The best known are Akaike's Information Criterion (AIC) and the Bayesian Information Criterion (BIC):

$$\text{AIC} \equiv -2\ell + 2p \ , \qquad \text{BIC} \equiv -2\ell + p \ln n. \tag{4.23}$$

Here $\ell$ is the log-likelihood of the model given in (4.15). A good fit means a high value for the likelihood, and therefore a low value for $-2\ell$.

The first two terms in the expression for $\ell$ in (4.15) are usually omitted, yielding

$$\text{AIC} = \frac{S}{\sigma^2} + 2p\,, \qquad \text{BIC} = \frac{S}{\sigma^2} + p\ln n\,, \qquad (4.24)$$

where $S$ is the sum of squared residuals. The $S/\sigma^2$ term is the bias term quantifying the fit of the model to the observations. A good fit yields a low value for $S$. The second term in each of the criteria is the variance term, penalizing for the number of parameters in the model. A model with a large number of parameters and a good fit has a low value for the bias term, but the criterion is pushed up by the variance term. Conversely a model with small $p$ has a higher bias term but lower variance term. Other things equal, the model with the lowest value of AIC or BIC is selected.

A decision has to be made whether to use AIC or BIC. The latter applies a greater penalty for the number of parameters, so tends to choose models with fewer explanatory variables compared to AIC. When $n$ is large, as is the case in most insurance data sets, the BIC tends to selects model which most analysts consider too simple. In this case the AIC is preferable.

Models compared using AIC or BIC must be based on the same set of observations. This impacts when deciding between models which include at least one explanatory variable with missing values. Standard software omits from analysis any cases which have missing values on any of the variables in a model. This means that if one or other model includes a variable with missing values, then the models being compared will be based on different sets of observations, rendering the comparison invalid. The solution is to perform model selection on the subset of cases which have no missing values for any of the potential explanatory variables.

**Stepwise regression.** Stepwise regression is an automated form of model selection. Stepwise algorithms are available in most statistical software. The methodology has fallen out of favor in recent years, as it is ad hoc, and yields different results when implemented in different ways. It is often used to avoid careful thought about the model. It encourages the notion that model selection can be performed automatically.

Model selection is as much art as science. Understanding of the subject matter, and the interplay between all of the variables, is critical. Judgements about the inclusion or exclusion of a variable is validly made using information other than statistical criteria. For example, the expense of measuring or recording a variable, or the political sensitivity of a variable, may override purely statistical considerations.

# 5

# Generalized linear models

Generalized linear modeling is used to assess and quantify the relationship between a response variable and explanatory variables. The modeling differs from ordinary regression modeling in two important respects:

(i) The distribution of the response is chosen from the exponential family. Thus the distribution of the response need not be normal or close to normal and may be explicitly nonnormal.

(ii) A transformation of the mean of the response is linearly related to the explanatory variables.

A consequence of allowing the response to be a member of the exponential family is that the response can be, and usually is, heteroskedastic. Thus the variance will vary with the mean which may in turn vary with explanatory variables. This contrasts with the homoskedastic assumption of normal regression.

Generalized linear models are important in the analysis of insurance data. With insurance data, the assumptions of the normal model are frequently not applicable. For example, claim sizes, claim frequencies and the occurrence of a claim on a single policy are all outcomes which are not normal. Also, the relationship between outcomes and drivers of risk is often multiplicative rather additive.

## 5.1 The generalized linear model

Given a response $y$, the generalized linear model (GLM) is

$$f(y) = c(y, \phi) \exp\left\{\frac{y\theta - a(\theta)}{\phi}\right\}, \qquad g(\mu) = x'\beta . \qquad (5.1)$$

The equation for $f(y)$ specifies that the distribution of the response is in the exponential family. The second equation specifies that a transformation of the mean, $g(\mu)$, is linearly related to explanatory variables contained in $x$.

64

- The choice of $a(\theta)$ determines the response distribution.
- The choice of $g(\mu)$, called the link, determines how the mean is related to the explanatory variables $x$. In the normal linear model, the relationship between the mean of $y$ and the explanatory variables is $\mu = x'\beta$. In the GLM, this is generalized to $g(\mu) = x'\beta$, where $g$ is a monotonic, differentiable function (such as log or square root).
- The setup in (5.1) states that, given $x$, $\mu$ is determined through $g(\mu)$. Given $\mu$, $\theta$ is determined through $\dot{a}(\theta) = \mu$. (See (3.2).) Finally given $\theta$, $y$ is determined as a draw from the exponential density specified in $a(\theta)$.
- Observations on $y$ are assumed to be independent.

$\dot{a}(\theta) = \mu$
↑
first derivative

## 5.2 Steps in generalized linear modeling

Given a response variable $y$, constructing a GLM consists of the following steps:

(i) Choose a response distribution $f(y)$ and hence choose $a(\theta)$ in (5.1). The response distribution is tailored to the given situation.

(ii) Choose a link $g(\mu)$. This choice is sometimes simplified by choosing the so called "canonical" link corresponding to each response distribution. This is discussed in more detail below.

(iii) Choose explanatory variables $x$ in terms of which $g(\mu)$ is to be modeled. Similar considerations apply as in ordinary regression modeling.

(iv) Collect observations $y_1, \ldots, y_n$ on the response $y$ and corresponding values $x_1, \ldots, x_n$ on the explanatory variables $x$. Successive observations are assumed to be independent, i.e. the sample will be regarded as a random sample from the background population.

(v) Fit the model by estimating $\beta$ and, if unknown, $\phi$. The fitting is usually done using software such as SAS, which implements maximum likelihood estimation or its variants. This is discussed in Section 5.5.

→ fit does not have to be MLE

(vi) Given the estimate of $\beta$, generate predictions (or fitted values) of $y$ for different settings of $x$ and examine how well the model fits by examining the departure of the fitted values from actual values, as well as other model diagnostics. Also the estimated value of $\beta$ will be used to see whether or not given explanatory variables are important in determining $\mu$.

The extra steps compared to ordinary regression modeling are choosing $a(\theta)$ (implying the response distribution) and the link $g(\mu)$. The choice $a(\theta)$ is guided by the nature of the response variable. The choice of link is suggested by the functional form of the relationship between the response and the explanatory variables.

The above steps rarely proceed sequentially. For example, especially with insurance data, the data is often collected prior to the specification of a model, and may simply be an existing database, for example all policies of a particular type. Initial exploration of the data is likely to suggest different models and different response distributions. Fits are often followed by further refinements of fits in that some of the explanatory variables may be discarded or transformed. The data may be judiciously massaged by the exclusion of various cases, or the incorporation of different effects.

### 5.3 Links and canonical links

Commonly used link functions $g(\mu)$ are given in Table 5.1. With the exception of the logit link, the links are of the form $g(\mu) = \mu^p$, with the logarithmic case being the limit of $(y^p - 1)/p$ as $p \to 0$.

If $g(\mu) = \theta$ then $g$ is called the canonical link corresponding to $a(\theta)$. In this case $\theta = x'\beta$. Choosing the canonical link $g$ corresponding to a response distribution $f$ simplifies estimation, although with modern computing this is no longer an overriding consideration. In Table 5.1, the response distributions for which the commonly used links are canonical, are shown. Constants in $\theta$ are generally omitted from the canonical link. For example, with the inverse Gaussian $\theta = -1/(2\mu^2)$ and the canonical link is $1/\mu^2$.

**Third party claims.** Consider the relationship between the number of accidents and the number of third party claims in an area. Scatterplots of the number of claims against accidents, and log of number of claims against log of number of accidents, are given in Figure 4.1.

It is clear that the number of claims, as well as the variation in claims, increase with the number of accidents in an area. In the right panel of Figure 4.1, log of number of claims are graphed against log of number of accidents. This suggests the model

$$\ln \mu = \beta_0 + \beta_1 \ln z \tag{5.2}$$

where $\mu$ is the average number of claims, and $z$ is the number of accidents, of an area. Equation (5.2) specifies a log link, with explanatory variable log accidents.

### 5.4 Offsets

Modeling counts such as the number of claims or deaths in a risk group requires correction for the number $n$ exposed to risk. If $\mu$ is the mean of the count $y$, then the occurrence rate $\mu/n$ of interest and

Table 5.1. *Commonly used links*

| Link function | $g(\mu)$ | Canonical link for |
|---|---|---|
| identity | $\mu$ | normal |
| log | $\ln \mu$ | Poisson |
| power | $\mu^p$ | gamma $(p = -1)$ <br> inverse Gaussian $(p = -2)$ |
| square root | $\sqrt{\mu}$ | |
| logit | $\ln \frac{\mu}{1-\mu}$ | binomial |

*[handwritten: $\rightarrow g(\mu) = \theta$]*

$$g\left(\frac{\mu}{n}\right) = x'\beta .$$

When $g$ is the log function, this becomes *[handwritten: likely how the offset is applied in h2o]*

$$\ln\left(\frac{\mu}{n}\right) = x'\beta \quad \Rightarrow \quad \ln \mu = \ln n + x'\beta .$$

The variable $n$ is called the exposure and $\ln n$ is called an "offset." An offset is effectively another $x$ variable in the regression, with a $\beta$ coefficient equal to one. With the offset, $y$ has expected value directly proportional to exposure:

$$\mu = ne^{x'\beta} .$$

Offsets are used to correct for group size or differing time periods of observation. *[handwritten: or fixed class plan variables]*

## 5.5 Maximum likelihood estimation

The MLE of $\beta$ and $\phi$ are derived by maximizing the log-likelihood, defined, similar to Section 3.5, as

$$\ell(\beta, \phi) = \sum_{i=1}^{n} \ln f(y_i; \beta, \phi) = \sum_{i=1}^{n} \left\{ \ln c(y_i, \phi) + \frac{y_i\theta_i - a(\theta_i)}{\phi} \right\}, \quad (5.3)$$

which assumes independent exponential family responses $y_i$.

Consider the MLE of $\beta_j$. To find the maximum, $\ell(\beta, \phi)$ is differentiated with respect to $\beta_j$:

$$\frac{\partial \ell}{\partial \beta_j} = \sum_{i=1}^{n} \frac{\partial \ell}{\partial \theta_i} \frac{\partial \theta_i}{\partial \beta_j} ,$$

*[handwritten in left margin: sum of all parts of the given data]*

where

$$\frac{\partial \ell}{\partial \theta_i} = \frac{y_i - \dot{a}(\theta_i)}{\phi} = \frac{y_i - \mu_i}{\phi} , \qquad \frac{\partial \theta_i}{\partial \beta_j} = \frac{\partial \theta_i}{\partial \eta_i} \frac{\partial \eta_i}{\partial \beta_j} = \frac{\partial \theta_i}{\partial \eta_i} x_{ij} .$$

Here $\eta_i = x_i'\beta$ and $x_{ij}$ is component $i$ of $x_j$. Setting $\partial \ell/\partial \beta_j = 0$ yields the first order conditions for likelihood maximization:

$$\sum_{i=1}^{n} \frac{\partial \theta_i}{\partial \eta_i} x_{ij}(y_i - \mu_i) = 0 \qquad \Leftrightarrow \qquad X'D(y - \mu) = 0 , \qquad (5.4)$$

where $D$ is the diagonal matrix with diagonal entries $\partial \theta_i/\partial \eta_i$,

$$\left(\frac{\partial \theta_i}{\partial \eta_i}\right)^{-1} = \frac{\partial \eta_i}{\partial \theta_i} = \frac{\partial \eta_i}{\partial \mu_i} \frac{\partial \mu_i}{\partial \theta_i} = \dot{g}(\mu_i)\ddot{a}(\theta_i) = \dot{g}(\mu_i)V(\mu_i) .$$

Thus $D$ is diagonal with entries $\{\dot{g}(\mu_i)V(\mu_i)\}^{-1}$. The equations in (5.4) are often called the estimation equations for $\beta$. Note $\beta$ is implicit in these equations, working implicitly through $\mu$ and $D$.

Defining the diagonal matrices $G$ and $W$ with diagonal entries $\dot{g}(\mu_i)$ and $[\{\dot{g}(\mu_i)\}^2 V(\mu_i)]^{-1}$, respectively, then $D = WG$ and (5.4) is equivalent to

$$\underbrace{X'WG}(y - \mu) = 0 . \qquad (5.5)$$
$$D$$

**Connection to weighted least squares.** Using a Taylor series approximation

$$g(y_i) \approx g(\mu_i) + \dot{g}(\mu_i)(y_i - \mu_i) \qquad \Rightarrow \qquad g(y) \approx g(\mu) + G(y - \mu) , \quad (5.6)$$

where $g(y)$ is a vector with entries $g(y_i)$ and similarly for $g(\mu)$. Rearrangement and substituting $g(\mu) = X\beta$ yields $G(y - \mu) \approx g(y) - X\beta$. Substituting this last relation into (5.5) yields the approximate estimation equation

$$X'Wg(y) - X'WX\beta \approx 0 \qquad \Rightarrow \qquad \hat{\beta} \approx (X'WX)^{-1}X'Wg(y). \quad (5.7)$$

From the left relation in (5.6), $\{\dot{g}(\mu_i)\}^2 V(\mu_i)$ is, apart from the factor $\phi$, the first order approximation to the variance of $g(y_i)$. Thus solving the estimation equation (5.5) corresponds to, approximately, weighted regression of the transformed responses $g(y_i)$ with weights proportional to the variances.

With an identity link $g(y_i) = y_i$, (5.6) is exact and hence

$$\hat{\beta} = (X'WX)^{-1}X'Wy ,$$

where $W$ has diagonal entries $1/V(\mu_i)$. Thus with an identity link and $V(\mu_i)$ independent of $\mu_i$, the MLE of $\beta$ is the weighted least squares estimator (4.17).

**Newton–Raphson iteration.** The first order conditions (5.4) for likelihood maximization are usually difficult to solve directly except for cases such as the normal with the identity link. A fruitful suggestion going back to Newton assumes the first and second derivatives of the function to be maximized can be easily evaluated at each point. Using these derivatives, a quadratic approximation is made to the function at the point and it is the quadratic that is maximized. The resulting maximizer is then used to derive a new quadratic which in turn is maximized. This sequence of approximate maximizers is often found to converge quickly to the actual maximum.

To simplify the discussion, suppose $\phi$ is known and so write $\ell(\beta)$ to denote the log-likelihood as a function of the unknown parameter vector $\beta$. If $\beta$ contains a single parameter then the quadratic Taylor series approximation at any point $\beta$ is

$$\ell(\beta + \delta) \approx \ell(\beta) + \dot{\ell}(\beta)\delta + \frac{\delta^2}{2}\ddot{\ell}(\beta) \ .$$

Differentiating the right hand side as a function of $\delta$ and equating to zero yields

$$\dot{\ell}(\beta) + \delta\ddot{\ell}(\beta) = 0 \qquad \Rightarrow \qquad \delta = -\{\ddot{\ell}(\beta)\}^{-1}\dot{\ell}(\beta) \ .$$

With $\beta$ given and $\delta$ as specified, a higher point thus appears to be $\beta - \dot{\ell}(\beta)/\ddot{\ell}(\beta)$. Denoting $\beta^{(m)}$ as the value for $\beta$ at iteration $m$, the update equation is

$$\beta^{(m+1)} = \beta^{(m)} - \{\ddot{\ell}(\beta^{(m)})\}^{-1}\dot{\ell}(\beta^{(m)}) \ . \tag{5.8}$$

For a maximum $\ddot{\ell}(\beta) < 0$. Iteration of this equation, each time revising $\beta$, leads to a sequence which, as stated above, often rapidly converges.

The approach can be adapted when $\beta$ is vector. In this case a quadratic approximation is made to the surface $\ell(\beta)$, and it is this quadratic surface that is maximized. The update equation is as in (5.8) with the inverse interpreted as matrix inversion and where $\dot{\ell}(\beta)$ is the vector of partial derivatives $\partial\ell/\partial\beta_j$. The vector $\dot{\ell}(\beta)$ is called the "score" vector, and $\ddot{\ell}(\beta)$, the matrix of cross partial derivatives $\partial^2\ell/(\partial\beta_j\partial\beta_k)$, the "Hessian" matrix. The condition for a maximum is that the Hessian is non-positive definite, i.e. $-\ddot{\ell}(\beta)$ is non-negative definite. The procedure of repeatedly evaluating the score and Hessian to update the estimate as in (5.8) is called Newton–Raphson iteration.

**Fisher scoring.** Fisher suggested replacing $\ddot{\ell}(\beta)$ in (5.8) by its expectation $\mathrm{E}\{\ddot{\ell}(\beta)\}$. He also showed that given $\beta$, $\mathrm{E}\{\ddot{\ell}(\beta)\} = -\mathrm{E}\{\dot{\ell}(\beta)\dot{\ell}'(\beta)\}$. (See Exercise 5.2.) These results are true for all log-likelihoods, not just for those in the exponential family. The matrix $-\mathrm{E}\{\ddot{\ell}(\beta)\}$ is called the "Fisher information" matrix or simply the "information" matrix. For GLMs the information matrix is

$$\mathrm{E}\{\dot{\ell}(\beta)\dot{\ell}'(\beta)\} = \phi^{-2}X'D\mathrm{E}\{(y - \mu)(y - \mu)'\}DX = \phi^{-1}X'WX \ . \tag{5.9}$$

Hence, substituting $\ddot{\ell}(\beta)$ by its expectation in (5.8), and using the left hand side of (5.5) for $\dot{\ell}(\beta)$ yields

$$\beta^{(m+1)} = \beta^{(m)} + (X'WX)^{-1}X'WG(y - \mu) \,.$$

This equation is often rewritten as

$$\beta^{(m+1)} = (X'WX)^{-1}X'W\{X\beta^{(m)} + G(y - \mu)\} \,, \qquad (5.10)$$

where the expression in the curly brackets on the right is called the "local dependent variable." Equation (5.10) is similar to weighted least squares regression. The local dependent variable is computed by replacing $\mu$ by the estimate $\mu^{(m)}$ where $g(\mu^{(m)}) = X\beta^{(m)}$. Computing $\beta^{(m+1)}$, requires $V(\mu)$, the variance function of the distribution and $\dot{g}(\mu)$, the derivative of the link. The dispersion parameter $\phi$ is not required.

The inverse of the Fisher information matrix is approximately, for large $n$, the covariance matrix of $\hat{\beta}$. Also MLEs are asymptotically unbiased and, again for large samples, approximately normal. Hence

$$\hat{\beta} \sim \mathrm{N}\{\beta, \phi\,(X'WX)^{-1}\} \,.$$

This large sample result is the basis for significance testing using the Wald test, discussed in Section 5.8. In practice $W$ is evaluated at $\hat{\beta}$.

**Estimation of dispersion.** The dispersion parameter $\phi$ may be estimated by maximum likelihood or method of moments. Maximum likelihood estimation involves iterative solution of the equation $\partial\ell/\partial\phi = 0$, which is different for each response distribution. As estimation of $\phi$ is generally considered to be peripheral to generalized linear modeling, we do not focus on this issue.

**SAS notes.** The default estimate of $\phi$ in SAS is the MLE.

## 5.6 Confidence intervals and prediction

Given values of the explanatory variables $x$, the estimated value of the mean of $y$ is $\hat{\mu}$ where $g(\hat{\mu}) = x'\hat{\beta}$. For example, with a log link:

$$\ln\hat{\mu} = x'\hat{\beta} \qquad \Rightarrow \qquad \hat{\mu} = \mathrm{e}^{x'\hat{\beta}} \,.$$

A confidence interval around the estimate is used to indicate precision. The computation of the confidence interval requires the sampling distribution of $\hat{\mu}$. The variance of the linear predictor $x'\hat{\beta}$ is

$$\mathrm{Var}(x'\hat{\beta}) = \phi\,x'(X'WX)^{-1}x \,.$$

Thus an approximate confidence interval for the mean is $(\mu_\ell, \mu_u)$ where

$$g(\mu_\ell) = x'\hat{\beta} - z\sqrt{\phi\,x'(X'WX)^{-1}x} \,,$$

and $\mu_u$ similarly defined with a plus sign. Here $z$ is the appropriate point on the $N(0,1)$ distribution. The confidence interval is exact in the case of an identity link and normal response. In other cases it is an approximation, the accuracy of which improves with increasing sample size. The dispersion $\phi$ is replaced by an estimate, causing further approximation errors.

The estimate $\hat{\mu}$ is unbiased when using an identity link. For other links it is biased. To illustrate, with a log link and assuming $\hat{\beta}$ is approximately normal, then

$$E(e^{x'\hat{\beta}}) = \exp\left\{x'\beta + \frac{1}{2}\mathrm{Var}(x'\hat{\beta})\right\} \neq e^{x'\beta} = \mu \ .$$

The bias increases with $\mathrm{Var}(x'\hat{\beta})$. For large sample sizes, $\mathrm{Var}(\hat{\beta})$ is small and the bias is expected to be negligible.

The interval $(\mu_\ell, \mu_u)$ is a confidence interval for the mean of $y$ given $x$. Any particular case is a random outcome from the response distribution with mean at $\mu$ where $g(\mu) = x'\beta$. An actual outcome of $y$ will deviate from $\mu$. An interval constructed for an actual case or outcome is called a prediction interval. The width of a prediction interval factors in the uncertainty associated with both $\hat{\mu}$ and the outcome from the response distribution.

Consider predicting an actual value of $y$ given the value $x$ of the explanatory variables. This prediction is taken as $\hat{\mu}$ and hence the same as the estimate of $\mu$. If the response distribution is, for example, $G(\mu, \nu)$ at the given value of $x$, then a 95% prediction interval for a single realization of $y$ is the central 95% portion of the $G(\mu, \nu)$ distribution. However, $\mu$ and $\nu$ are estimated. Taking the prediction interval as the central portion of the $G(\hat{\mu}, \hat{\nu})$ distribution ignores the variability associated with the parameter estimates, and is thus optimistic. A more conservative approach is to take the lower point of the prediction interval as the lower 2.5% point of $G(\mu_\ell, \hat{\nu})$, and the upper point as the upper 97.5% point of $G(\mu_u, \hat{\nu})$. This ad hoc approach ignores any biases which arise similarly as for the mean.

## 5.7 Assessing fits and the deviance

The goodness of fit of a model to data is a natural question arising with all statistical modeling. The principles of significance testing, model selection and diagnostic testing, as discussed in Chapter 4, are the same for GLMs as for normal regression; however, the technical details of the methods differ somewhat.

One way of assessing the fit of a given model is to compare it to the model with the best possible fit. The best fit will be obtained when there are as many parameters as observations: this is called a saturated model. A saturated model will ensure there is complete flexibility in fitting $\theta_i$. Since

$$\frac{\partial \ell}{\partial \theta_i} = \frac{y_i - \mu_i}{\phi} = \frac{y_i - \dot{a}(\theta_i)}{\phi} ,$$

the MLE of $\theta_i$ under the saturated model is $\check{\theta}_i$, where $\dot{a}(\check{\theta}_i) = y_i$. Thus each fitted value is equal to the observation and the saturated model fits perfectly.

The value of the saturated log-likelihood is

$$\check{\ell} \equiv \sum_{i=1}^{n} \left\{ \ln c(y_i, \phi) + \frac{y_i \check{\theta}_i - a(\check{\theta}_i)}{\phi} \right\} ,$$

which is the maximum possible log-likelihood for $y$ given the response distribution specified by $a(\theta)$. This value is compared to $\hat{\ell}$, the value of the maximum of the log-likelihood based on $y$ and the given explanatory variables. The "deviance," denoted as $\Delta$, is defined as a measure of distance between the saturated and fitted models:

$$\Delta \equiv 2(\check{\ell} - \hat{\ell}) .$$

- When the model provides a good fit, then $\hat{\ell}$ is expected to be close to (but not greater than) $\check{\ell}$. A large value of the deviance indicates a badly fitting model.
- The size of $\Delta$ is assessed relative to the $\chi^2_{n-p}$ distribution (Dobson 2002). This is the approximate sampling distribution of the deviance, assuming the fitted model is correct and $n$ is large. The expected value of the deviance is $n - p$, and typically the deviance divided by its degrees of freedom $n - p$ is examined: a value much greater than one indicates a poorly fitting model.
- A direct calculation shows that for the exponential family

$$\Delta = 2 \sum_{i=1}^{n} \left\{ \frac{y_i(\check{\theta}_i - \hat{\theta}_i) - a(\check{\theta}_i) + a(\hat{\theta}_i)}{\phi} \right\} , \qquad (5.11)$$

since terms involving $c(y_i, \phi)$ cancel out, and where $\check{\theta}_i$ and $\hat{\theta}_i$ are such that $\dot{a}(\check{\theta}_i) = y_i$ and $g\{\dot{a}(\hat{\theta}_i)\} = x_i'\hat{\beta}$, respectively.

- When $\phi$ is unknown and estimated, then the $\chi^2_{n-p}$ distribution for the deviance is compromised. In the case of the Poisson distribution, $\phi = 1$ and the $\chi^2$ approximation is useful. In the case of the normal distribution, when $\sigma^2$ is known then the $\chi^2$ distribution of the deviance is exact; however, when $\sigma^2$ is estimated then we cannot rely on the deviance being $\chi^2$ distributed. Several authors, for example (McCullagh and Nelder 1989, pp. 119, 122) caution against using the deviance as an overall goodness of fit measure in general, as its approximate $\chi^2_{n-p}$ distribution depends on assumptions which are frequently not tenable. However, the deviance is useful for testing the significance of explanatory variables in nested models: see Section 5.8.

Table 5.2. *Deviance for exponential family response distributions*

| Distribution | Deviance $\Delta$ |
|---|---|
| Normal | $\frac{1}{\sigma^2} \sum_{i=1}^{n} (y_i - \hat{\mu}_i)^2$ |
| Poisson | $2 \sum_{i=1}^{n} \left\{ y_i \ln \left( \frac{y_i}{\hat{\mu}_i} \right) - (y_i - \hat{\mu}_i) \right\}$ |
| Binomial | $2 \sum_{i=1}^{n} n_i \left\{ y_i \ln \left( \frac{y_i}{\hat{\mu}_i} \right) + (n_i - y_i) \ln \left( \frac{n_i - y_i}{1 - \hat{\mu}_i} \right) \right\}$ |
| Gamma | $2\nu \sum_{i=1}^{n} \left\{ - \ln \left( \frac{y_i}{\hat{\mu}_i} \right) + \frac{y_i - \hat{\mu}_i}{\hat{\mu}_i} \right\}$ |
| Inverse Gaussian | $\frac{1}{\sigma^2} \sum_{i=1}^{n} \frac{(y_i - \hat{\mu}_i)^2}{\hat{\mu}_i^2 y_i}$ |
| Negative binomial | $2 \sum_{i=1}^{n} \left\{ y_i \ln \left( \frac{y_i}{\hat{\mu}_i} \right) - \left( y_i + \frac{1}{\kappa} \right) \ln \left( \frac{y_i + 1/\kappa}{\hat{\mu}_i + 1/\kappa} \right) \right\}$ |

**SAS notes.** In SAS the deviance is called the scaled deviance, and also the residual deviance by the SAS manual, while $\phi \Delta$ is called the deviance. This means that it is the *scaled deviance* that is relevant. (Both scaled and unscaled deviances are given in SAS output.)

**Deviance for well-known distributions.** Table 5.2 gives the expressions for the deviance for the exponential family distributions discussed previously. The derivation of the deviance expressions for the normal and Poisson distributions are illustrated and the others are left as exercises.

**Normal.** In this case

$$a(\theta) = \frac{1}{2}\theta^2 , \qquad \dot{a}(\theta) = \theta , \qquad \check{\theta}_i = y_i , \qquad \hat{\theta}_i = \hat{\mu}_i .$$

Hence each term in the sum (5.11) is, apart from the divisor $\phi = \sigma^2$

$$y_i(y_i - \hat{\mu}_i) - \frac{1}{2} \left( y_i^2 - \hat{\mu}_i^2 \right) = \frac{1}{2}(y_i - \hat{\mu}_i)^2 .$$

Thus the deviance is as given in Table 5.2 and is proportional to the residual sum of squares.

**Poisson.** In this case $\phi = 1$ and

$$a(\theta) = e^\theta , \qquad \dot{a}(\theta) = e^\theta , \qquad \check{\theta}_i = \ln y_i , \qquad \hat{\theta}_i = \ln \hat{\mu}_i .$$

Hence each term in sum (5.11) is

$$y_i \left( \ln y_i - \ln \hat{\mu}_i \right) - (y_i - \hat{\mu}_i) = y_i \ln \left( \frac{y_i}{\hat{\mu}_i} \right) - (y_i - \hat{\mu}_i)$$

and the deviance is as given in Table 5.2.

## 5.8 Testing the significance of explanatory variables

Testing the significance of explanatory variables in linear models was discussed in Section 4.15. A similar development applies in the case of GLMs. As before, hypotheses are written as $C\beta = r$ where $C$ is known matrix – sometimes called the hypothesis matrix – and $r$ is a set of given values.

There are three main approaches to testing hypotheses of the form $C\beta = r$. Each of these approaches considers the likelihood or log-likelihood as in (5.3). Write $\hat{\beta}$ as the unrestricted MLE of $\beta$, and let $\tilde{\beta}$ denote the MLE of $\beta$ when $\ell$ is maximized subject to the restrictions $C\beta = r$ (as in Section 4.15). Further, write $\hat{\ell}$ as the value of $\ell$ at $\hat{\beta}$, and $\tilde{\ell}$ the value of $\ell$ at $\tilde{\beta}$. Obviously $\hat{\ell} \geq \tilde{\ell}$.

**Likelihood ratio test.** Here $\hat{\ell}$ is compared to $\tilde{\ell}$. A value of $\hat{\ell}$ much larger than $\tilde{\ell}$ is evidence against the restrictions. Both $\hat{\beta}$ and $\tilde{\beta}$ are required. The likelihood ratio is defined as $\lambda = \hat{L}/\tilde{L}$ where $\hat{L}$ and $\tilde{L}$ are the likelihoods of the unrestricted and restricted models, respectively. The likelihood ratio test statistic is

$$2 \ln \lambda = 2(\hat{\ell} - \tilde{\ell}) . \tag{5.12}$$

This is always non-negative, and has the $\chi_q^2$ distribution if $C\beta = r$, where $q$ is the number of rows of $C$, i.e. the number of restrictions on $\beta$. If $2 \ln \lambda$ is small (close to zero) then the restricted model is almost as good as the unrestricted model, which would provide evidence that $C\beta = r$. The rejection region for the test is the upper tail of the $\chi_q^2$ distribution.

The $\chi_q^2$ distribution of the likelihood ratio statistic involves the dispersion parameter $\phi$, which is often unknown. In the case of the Poisson and binomial distributions, $\phi$ is given; in the case of other distributions, $\phi$ must generally be estimated. The $\chi^2$ distribution is still appropriate in this case, as long as a consistent estimator for $\phi$ is used (Fahrmeir and Tutz 2001). Note that MLEs are consistent estimators (see Section 3.5). The likelihood ratio statistic may be expressed as the difference in the deviances of the unrestricted and restricted models, as long as the same estimate for $\phi$ is used in both log-likelihoods.

Note that the approximate $\chi^2$ distribution of the deviance differences (i.e. the likelihood ratio test statistics) is not controversial; the approximate $\chi^2$ distribution of the deviance is far more questionable, except for the Poisson case where $\phi$ is known.

**Wald test.** This measures how far $C\hat{\beta}$ is from $r$, with a large difference $C\hat{\beta} - r$ providing evidence against the restrictions. The estimate $\hat{\beta}$ is required, but not $\tilde{\beta}$. If $C\beta = r$ then since $\hat{\beta} \sim N\{\beta, \phi(X'WX)^{-1}\}$ it follows that

$$C\hat{\beta} - r \sim N\left\{0, \phi\, C(X'WX)^{-1}C'\right\} .$$

This leads to the Wald statistic for testing $C\beta = r$:

$$(C\hat{\beta} - r)'\{\phi\, C(X'WX)^{-1}C'\}^{-1}(C\hat{\beta} - r) \sim \chi_q^2 . \qquad (5.13)$$

Thus the Wald statistic is the squared statistical distance of $C\hat{\beta}$ from $r$ using the covariance matrix of $C\hat{\beta}$. In practice $W$ is replaced by an estimate and hence the $\chi_q^2$ distribution is approximate.

**Testing single coefficients.** When testing $\beta_j = r$, the matrix $C$ is a row vector of zeros except in position $j$ where it is 1. Note that this assumes that all other explanatory variables in $X$ are in the model. The term in curly brackets in (5.13) reduces to a single diagonal entry of $\phi(X'WX)^{-1}$, the variance of $\hat{\beta}_j$, which is denoted as $\phi\,\psi_j$. The Wald statistic then becomes

$$\frac{(\hat{\beta}_j - r)^2}{\phi\,\psi_j} \sim \chi_1^2 .$$

Where $\phi$ is not known, it is replaced by its estimate $\hat{\phi}$. The signed square root of the Wald statistic is reported by some statistical software, with $p$-value calculated on either the standard normal or t distribution. Note the equivalence of this statistic with that for the normal linear model (4.20) or (4.21).

**Testing all coefficients.** For the global test that all coefficients except the intercept are zero, $C$ is the $(p-1) \times p$ matrix:

$$C = \begin{pmatrix} 0 & 1 & 0 & \cdots & 0 \\ 0 & 0 & 1 & \cdots & 0 \\ \vdots & & & & \\ 0 & 0 & 0 & \cdots & 1 \end{pmatrix} .$$

**Score test.** This test is based on the derivative or slope of $\ell$ at $\tilde{\beta}$, called the score. Large scores (slopes) suggest there is much to be gained from dropping the restrictions and hence constitutes evidence against the hypothesis $C\beta = r$. The estimate $\tilde{\beta}$ is required, but not $\hat{\beta}$. For GLMs, the score is $\dot{\ell}(\beta) = \phi^{-1}X'WG(y - \mu)$ – see Section 5.5. Further,

$$\mathrm{E}\{\dot{\ell}(\beta)\} = 0 , \qquad \mathrm{Var}\{\dot{\ell}(\beta)\} = \mathrm{E}\{\dot{\ell}(\beta)\dot{\ell}'(\beta)\} = \phi^{-1}X'WX .$$

If $C\beta = r$, $\dot{\ell}(\tilde{\beta})$ should not be too far away from 0. This motivates the score statistic

$$\dot{\ell}'(\tilde{\beta})[\mathrm{Var}\{\dot{\ell}(\beta)\}]^{-1}\dot{\ell}(\tilde{\beta}) \tag{5.14}$$

where $\dot{\ell}(\tilde{\beta}) = \phi^{-1}X'WG(y - \tilde{\mu})$, $\mathrm{Var}\{\dot{\ell}(\beta)\} = \phi^{-1}(X'WX)$ and $\tilde{\mu}$ is $\mathrm{E}(y)$ evaluated at $\tilde{\beta}$.

The score statistic is approximately $\chi^2_q$ distributed. In practice $W$ and $\phi$ are replaced with estimates, which makes the chi-square approximation to the distribution less accurate. Note that $X$ is defined as the full matrix, including any explanatory variables whose coefficients are assumed zero in the hypothesis $C\beta = r$.

As an example consider the test that a group of coefficients in $\beta$ are zero. Then the model is fitted without the corresponding explanatory variables, yielding $y - \tilde{\mu}$ containing the residuals of the fitted model. These residuals are then combined as in (5.14), using the matrix $X$ containing all the explanatory variables. A large score statistic is evidence against the hypothesis: the rejection region for the test is in the upper tail of the $\chi^2_q$ distribution.

**Identity link.** In this case $\tilde{\mu} = X\tilde{\beta}$ and $G = I$. Then the score statistic (5.14) reduces to

$$\phi^{-1}(\hat{\beta} - \tilde{\beta})'(X'WX)(\hat{\beta} - \tilde{\beta}) .$$

Note that $\mathrm{Var}(\hat{\beta}) = \phi(X'WX)^{-1}$ and hence the score statistic with an identity link measures the statistical distance between $\hat{\beta}$ and $\tilde{\beta}$ using the covariance matrix of $\hat{\beta}$. If the test is $\beta = 0$ then the score statistic reduces to $\phi^{-1}\hat{\beta}'(X'WX)^{-1}\hat{\beta}$.

**SAS notes.** The following items indicate the implementation of the above ideas in SAS.

- For all distributions except the gamma, the "scale parameter" is defined as $\sqrt{\phi}$, where $\phi$ is the dispersion parameter. For the gamma, the scale is defined as $1/\phi$.
- The Wald statistics for individual coefficients, and their $p$-values, are given in the table of parameter estimates. The Wald statistic column is headed "Chi-square".

- "Type I" tests are incremental or sequential tests. Explanatory variables are added in the sequence as specified in the model equation, and each ones significance is tested under the assumption that variables previously added, are present in the model. If an explanatory variable is categorical with $r$ levels, then all $r - 1$ indicator variables corresponding to that variable are tested together. Care needs to be taken in the interpretation of these statistics, as different results will be obtained when variables are specified in the model equation in a different order.

- "Type III" tests test for the significance of each explanatory variable, under the assumption that all other variables entered in the model equation, are present. This procedure is invariant to the order of specification of explanatory variables in the model equation.

- Type I and Type III tests based on likelihood ratios are produced optionally. In all cases, the hypothesis $C\beta = 0$ is tested. It sometimes happens that the $p$-values from the Wald and likelihood ratio tests are contradictory. In this case, conclusions based on likelihood ratio tests must be regarded as more reliable, as their statistical properties are superior.

- Wald tests are by their nature Type III tests, in that they assume that all other explanatory variables are in the model.

- Wald confidence intervals for individual parameters $\beta_j$ are given in the parameter estimates table, as $\hat{\beta}_j \pm z(\hat{\phi}\,\hat{\psi}_j)^{1/2}$, where $z$ is the appropriate point on the $N(0, 1)$ distribution. Likelihood ratio confidence intervals may be requested: these are obtained by finding the region of $\beta_j$, i.e. all values $\beta_j^*$, which would result in acceptance of the hypothesis $\beta_j = \beta_j^*$, using the likelihood ratio test at significance level $\alpha$. This confidence interval is found iteratively and is computationally intensive.

## 5.9 Residuals

Diagnostics relating to the normal linear model are discussed in Sections 4.16–4.18. These diagnostics focus on checking for evidence of non-normality, and/or heteroskedasticity of residuals; for evidence against appropriateness of the specification of continuous explanatory variables in the model; and for extreme observations.

The assumptions of the GLM are different from those of the normal linear model, leading to different diagnostic tests. The aims, however, are the same, i.e. to detect evidence against model assumptions.

Residuals are used to check the appropriateness of a chosen response distribution, and for outlying values. The residuals $\hat{\epsilon}_i = y_i - \hat{y}_i$, and their studentized version (4.22) are central to model checking for the normal linear model. For the GLM, these residuals are neither normally distributed, nor do they have constant variance, for any response distribution other than the normal. The definition of residual is broadened from the notion of the difference between observed and fitted values, to a more general quantification of the conformity of a case to the model specification. Two forms of residual are useful.

**Deviance residuals.** Suppose $\delta_i^2$ denotes a term in the deviance $\Delta$ given in (5.11)

$$\delta_i^2 \equiv \frac{2\{y_i(\breve{\theta}_i - \hat{\theta}_i) - a(\breve{\theta}_i) + a(\hat{\theta}_i)\}}{\phi} .$$

The $\delta_i^2$ for specific members of the exponential family are as given in Table 5.2. Then $\delta_i$ is called the deviance residual. The sign of $\delta_i$ is taken to be the sign of $y_i - \hat{\mu}_i$, and $\delta_i$ measures the square root of the contribution of case $i$ to the deviance (5.11).

If a particular contribution $\delta_i$ is large, then case $i$ is contributing "too much" to the deviance, indicating a departure from the model assumptions for that case. The question arises as to how large is "too large?" If the model is correct and $n$ is large, then the deviance is approximately $\chi^2_{n-p}$. The expected value of the deviance is thus $n - p$, and one expects each case to contribute approximately $(n - p)/n \approx 1$ to the deviance. Therefore $|\delta_i|$ much greater than one is an indication that case $i$ is contributing to a lack of fit. This suggests model misspecification or a data error. Typically deviance residuals are examined by plotting them against fitted values or explanatory variables.

**Anscombe residuals.** These are based on the difference $h(y_i) - h(\hat{y}_i)$, where $h$ is chosen so that $h(y)$ is approximately normal. The function $h$ is such that $\dot{h}(y) = \{V(y)\}^{-1/3}$ where $V(\mu)$ is the variance function of the response distribution. The residual is standardized, by dividing by the standard deviation of $h(y)$, whose first-order approximation is, apart from $\phi$, $\dot{h}(y)\sqrt{V(y)}$. Thus the Anscombe residual is

$$\frac{h(y_i) - h(\hat{y}_i)}{\dot{h}(\hat{y}_i)\sqrt{V(\hat{y}_i)}} ,$$

which is approximately normal if the response distribution is correctly specified. Approximate normality is checked using the tools described in Section 1.6.

As an example, consider the inverse Gaussian distribution where $V(\mu) = \mu^3$. Here $\dot{h}(y) = (y^3)^{-1/3} = y^{-1}$, implying $h(y) = \ln y$ and $\dot{h}(y)\sqrt{V(y)} = y^{-1}y^{3/2} = \sqrt{y}$. The appropriate scale for comparison of observed and fitted values is thus the log scale and the Anscombe residual is

$$\frac{\ln y_i - \ln \hat{y}_i}{\sqrt{\hat{y}_i}} .$$

McCullagh and Nelder (1989) show that Anscombe and deviance residuals are numerically similar, even though they are mathematically quite different. This means that deviance residuals are also approximately normally distributed, if the response distribution has been correctly specified. This is a useful feature when using software that does not produce Anscombe residuals. An adjustment to deviance residuals results in a distribution more closely approximating the normal:

$$\delta_i + \frac{1}{6} \mathrm{E} \left[ \left\{ \frac{y_i - \hat{\mu}_i}{\sqrt{\mathrm{Var}(y_i)}} \right\}^3 \right] .$$

These quantities are called adjusted residuals. The forms of the adjustment term for the binomial, Poisson and gamma response distributions are given by Fahrmeir and Tutz (2001).

**SAS notes.** Anscombe residuals may be requested as a model output in SAS Insight, but not in the command language. Deviance residuals are provided by SAS Insight and in the command language.

## 5.10 Further diagnostic tools

**Checking the link.** The first order Taylor series expansion of $g(y_i)$, as in (5.6) yields

$$g(y_i) \approx g(\mu_i) + \dot{g}(\mu_i)(y_i - \mu_i) \approx x_i'\beta . \tag{5.15}$$

Plotting $g(\hat{\mu}_i) + \dot{g}(\hat{\mu}_i)(y_i - \hat{\mu}_i)$ against $x_i'\hat{\beta}$ should produce points lying approximately on a straight line, and strong curvature would suggest that the link function $g$ is incorrect.

**Checking the specification of the explanatory variables.** In Section 4.17 the added-variable plot and partial residual plots are described for the normal linear model. These plots extend to the GLM, with the appropriate technical adjustments.

**Added-variable plot.** Here the fitted values for the $y$ regression are computed on the basis of the GLM which excludes $x_j$. The partial residual plot is then constructed as for the normal model.

**Partial residual plot.** For the normal linear model the partial residual is $(y_i - \hat{y}_i) + x_{ij}\hat{\beta}_j$. For the GLM, they are defined as $(y_i - \hat{y}_i)\dot{g}(\hat{y}_i) + x_{ij}\hat{\beta}_j$. The first term is the first order approximation to $g(y_i) - g(\hat{y}_i)$.

**Identification of outliers.** Leverage for GLMs is measured using the hat matrix:

$$H = W^{\frac{1}{2}} X \left(X'WX\right)^{-1} X'W^{\frac{1}{2}},$$

which is the same as the hat matrix for normal linear regression (defined in Section 4.16), with $X$ replaced by $W^{\frac{1}{2}}X$.

## 5.11 Model selection

The principle of balancing bias and variance applies to GLMs in the same way as to the normal linear model, discussed in Section 4.19. For GLMs, the model selection criteria AIC and BIC are defined in the same way, i.e. as equations (4.23).

## Exercises

5.1     Show that $\mathrm{E}\{\dot{\ell}(\beta)\} = 0$.

5.2     Show that the information matrix $-\mathrm{E}\{\ddot{\ell}(\beta)\}$ is equal to $\mathrm{E}\{\dot{\ell}(\beta)\dot{\ell}'(\beta)\}$.

5.3     Show that the deviances of the binomial, gamma, inverse Gaussian and negative binomial distributions are as given in Table 5.2.

5.4     Show that the Anscombe residual for the Poisson distribution is

$$\frac{3\left(y_i^{2/3} - \hat{y}_i^{2/3}\right)}{2\,\hat{y}_i^{1/6}}.$$

# 6

## Models for count data

This chapter deals with GLMs where the response is a count. Examples of count data models in insurance are:

- In mortality studies the aim is to explain the number of deaths in terms of variables such as age, gender and lifestyle.
- In health insurance, we may wish to explain the number of claims made by different individuals or groups of individuals in terms of explanatory variables such as age, gender and occupation.
- In general or casualty insurance, the count of interest may be the number of claims made on vehicle insurance policies. This could be a function of the color of the car, engine capacity, previous claims experience, and so on.

### 6.1 Poisson regression

When the response variable is a count, the Poisson is often used as the response distribution. With Poisson regression, the mean $\mu$ is explained in terms of explanatory variables $x$ via an appropriate link. The Poisson regression model is:

$$y \sim \mathrm{P}(\mu) , \qquad g(\mu) = x'\beta . \tag{6.1}$$

Popular choices for $g(\mu)$ are the identity link $\mu = x'\beta$ and log link $\ln \mu = x'\beta$. With the log link $\hat{\mu} = \exp(x'\hat{\beta})$ is positive. With the identity link, positivity is not guaranteed.

Consider the model with a single continuous explanatory variable $x_1$. Then

$$x = (1, x_1)' , \qquad \beta = (\beta_0, \beta_1)' , \qquad g(\mu) = \beta_0 + \beta_1 x_1 .$$

With the identity link, the effect of a change in the value of $x_1$ is additive: a unit increase in $x_1$ increases the expected value of $y$ by

$$\{\beta_0 + \beta_1(x_1 + 1)\} - (\beta_0 + \beta_1 x_1) = \beta_1 .$$

With the log link, the expected value of $y$ is $\mu = e^{\beta_0 + \beta_1 x_1}$ and the effect on $\mu$ of a unit increase in $x_1$ is:

$$e^{\beta_0 + \beta_1 (x_1 + 1)} = e^{\beta_0 + \beta_1 x_1} e^{\beta_1} \ ,$$

and hence there is a multiplicative effect on the mean of $e^{\beta_1}$, independent of $x_1$.

Next, consider the model with a single categorical explanatory variable with $r$ levels. Assuming level $r$ is the base level, then the variable is replaced by the $r - 1$ indicator variables $x_1, \ldots, x_{r-1}$, and

$$g(\mu) = \beta_0 + \beta_1 x_1 + \ldots + \beta_{r-1} x_{r-1} \ .$$

For the identity link, $\beta_j$ is the change in mean response due to the variable being in category level $j$ compared with the base level. For the log link,

$$\mu = e^{\beta_0 + \beta_1 x_1 + \ldots + \beta_{r-1} x_{r-1}} \ .$$

When the variable is at the base level, $\mu = e^{\beta_0}$ and when it is at level $j$, $\mu = e^{\beta_0 + \beta_j} = e^{\beta_0} e^{\beta_j}$, and there is a multiplicative effect on the mean of $e^{\beta_j}$ compared with the base level. If $\beta_j = 0$ the mean response for category $j$ is the same as that of the base level. If $\beta_j > 0$ the effect is an increase, since $e^{\beta_j} > 1$. Conversely, $\beta_j < 0$ means that the effect on the mean response of being in category $j$ is a decrease.

**Number of children.** Consider the number of children of a sample of 141 pregnant women, as described on page 15. In this example $y$, $\mu$ and $x$ are the number of children, the expected number of children, and the woman's age, respectively. The results for the Poisson model with log and identity link are summarized in Table 6.1 – see code and output on page 150. The model with log link yields the fit

$$\ln \hat{\mu} = -4.090 + 0.113x \qquad \Rightarrow \qquad \hat{\mu} = e^{-4.090 + 0.113x} \ .$$

The fit with the identity link is

$$\hat{\mu} = -0.965 + 0.057x \ .$$

The fitted curves for these two models are shown in Figure 6.1. For the log link model, the expected number of children changes by a factor of $e^{0.113} = 1.12$, i.e. a 12% increase, for every increasing year of mother's age. For the identity link model, the expected number of children increases by $\hat{\beta}_1 = 0.057$ with every increasing year of mother's age. These relationships only have validity during the childbearing years.

Table 6.1. *Poisson models for number of children*

| Response variable | Number of children |
|---|---|
| Response distribution | Poisson |
| Link | log |
| Deviance | 165.0 |
| Degrees of freedom | 139 |

| Parameter | df | $\hat{\beta}$ | se | $\chi^2$ | $p$-value |
|---|---|---|---|---|---|
| Intercept | 1 | −4.090 | 0.714 | 32.84 | <0.0001 |
| Age | 1 | 0.113 | 0.021 | 28.36 | <0.0001 |

| Response variable | Number of children |
|---|---|
| Response distribution | Poisson |
| Link | identity |
| Deviance | 171.4 |
| Degrees of freedom | 139 |

| Parameter | df | $\hat{\beta}$ | se | $\chi^2$ | $p$-value |
|---|---|---|---|---|---|
| Intercept | 1 | −0.965 | 0.460 | 4.40 | 0.0359 |
| Age | 1 | 0.057 | 0.016 | 13.39 | 0.0003 |

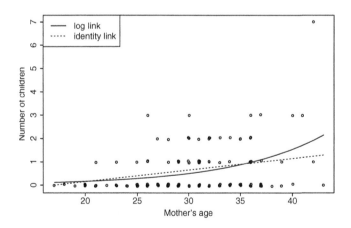

Fig. 6.1. Number of children versus mother's age

The deviances for both models indicate adequate fits: 165.0 on 139 degrees of freedom for the log link model, and 171.4 on 139 degrees of freedom for the identity link model. Significance of mother's age is assessed using deviance differences, as described in Section 5.8. As there is only one explanatory variable, Type I and Type III tests are identical. They are given in Table 6.2. The

Table 6.2. *Number of children, Poisson model, analysis of deviance*

|                     | Source    | $\Delta$ | df | $\chi^2$ | $p$-value |
|---------------------|-----------|----------|----|----------|-----------|
| Log link model      | Intercept | 194.4    |    |          |           |
|                     | Age       | 165.0    | 1  | 29.4     | <0.0001   |
| Identity link model | Intercept | 194.4    |    |          |           |
|                     | Age       | 171.4    | 1  | 23.0     | <0.0001   |

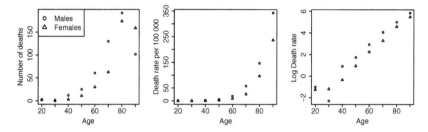

Fig. 6.2. Diabetes deaths: numbers and rates against age

"null deviance" of 194.4, for both models, is the deviance of the model with no explanatory variables, i.e. the model containing just an intercept. For the log link model, adding mother's age into the model reduces the deviance by 29.4 to 165.0. This deviance reduction is judged against the $\chi^2_1$ distribution. It is far in the right tail ($p$-value <0.0001), leading to the conclusion that mother's age is a significant explanatory variable. A similar conclusion holds for mother's age in the identity link model. Note that the $\chi^2$ statistic in the analysis of deviance table differs from that in the parameter estimates table. In the analysis of deviance table, deviance differences (or likelihood ratio test statistics) are given, whereas the parameter estimates table shows Wald test statistics. Occasionally these tests lead to different conclusions.

**Diabetes deaths.** This example deals with the number of deaths due to diabetes in New South Wales, Australia in 2002 (page 16). The data are graphed in Figure 6.2. The death rate increases exponentially into old age, for both genders, with the male death rate being consistently higher than that of females.

Let $y$ denote the number of deaths, $\mu$ the expected number of deaths, $x$ a vector of age and gender effects and $n$ the population size. The proposed model is

$$y \sim \mathrm{P}(\mu) , \qquad \ln \mu = \ln n + x'\beta$$

where $x = (1, x_1, x_2, \ldots, x_p)'$ with $x_1$ an indicator variable for gender and $x_2, \ldots, x_p$ age variables as discussed below. Population size $n$ enters the model as an offset term, as discussed in Section 5.4.

For simplicity in the discussion, models without age by gender interaction are considered first.

**Age effect.** This is modeled as either a continuous, or categorical variable, i.e. by means of indicator variables. For the former suppose midpoints of the age bands are used as the explanatory variable. To assess how best to enter this variable into the model, examine the relationship between log death rate and age midpoint, depicted in the rightmost panel of Figure 6.2. The nonlinearity in this plot suggests a polynomial in age, for example

$$\ln \mu = \ln n + \beta_0 + \beta_1 x_1 + \beta_2 x_2 + \beta_3 x_2^2 ,$$

where $x_1$ is a gender indicator variable and $x_2$ is the age midpoint. The appropriate degree of the age polynomial is to be determined. Generally when a polynomial of degree $m$ is considered, all the lower order terms are in the model.

Alternatively the age effect can be modeled using indicator variables based on, say, age group 45–54 years as the base level. This leads to the model

$$\ln \mu = \ln n + \beta_0 + \beta_1 x_1 + \beta_2 x_2 + \cdots + \beta_8 x_8 ,$$

where $x_1$ is again an indicator variable for gender and $x_2, \ldots, x_8$ are indicators of age groups $< 25$ through to $85+$, excluding the 45–54 base level.

Parameter estimates for the model which includes age as a categorical variable are given in Table 6.3 – see code and output on page 152. As expected, age and gender are both highly significant, $p$-value $<0.0001$. The deviance is 10.9 on 7 degrees of freedom, which indicates a good fit. On the $\chi_7^2$ distribution, a deviance value of 10.9 has $p$-value $= 0.143$. The "$e^{\hat{\beta}}$" column gives the multiplicative effect of the categorical variable levels on the mean death rate, compared with the base level. Further:

- The mean death rate for the base level, i.e. 45–54 year old males, is estimated as $e^{-9.892} = 0.00005$.
- Females have an expected death rate which is $e^{-0.523} = 0.593$ times that of males, that is 40.7% lower, at all ages.
- The effect of being in the 35–44 year age group, compared with 45–54 year olds, is to multiply the mean death rate by $e^{-0.997} = 0.369$, that is to decrease the mean death rate by an estimated 63.1%, for both genders.

Type I and Type III analysis of deviance tables are presented in Table 6.4. Differences between deviances reported here and those in the output on page 153 are due to rounding.

Table 6.3. *Diabetes deaths: age and gender as categorical variables*

| Response variable | Number of diabetes deaths |
|---|---|
| Response distribution | Poisson |
| Link | log |
| Offset | log population |
| Deviance | 10.9 |
| Degrees of freedom | 7 |

| Parameter | df | $\hat{\beta}$ | se | $e^{\hat{\beta}}$ | $\chi^2$ | $p$-value |
|---|---|---|---|---|---|---|
| Intercept | 1 | −9.892 | 0.168 | 0.00005 | 3 449.4 | <0.0001 |
| Gender | 1 | | | | | <0.0001 |
|   Female | 1 | −0.523 | 0.065 | 0.593 | 64.27 | <0.0001 |
|   Male | 0 | 0.000 | . | 1.000 | . | . |
| Age | 7 | | | | | <0.0001 |
|   <25 | 1 | −2.894 | 0.477 | 0.055 | 36.77 | <0.0001 |
|   25–34 | 1 | −3.67 | 1.014 | 0.025 | 13.11 | 0.0003 |
|   35–44 | 1 | −0.997 | 0.307 | 0.369 | 10.51 | 0.0012 |
|   45–54 | 0 | 0.000 | . | 1.000 | . | . |
|   55–64 | 1 | 1.236 | 0.197 | 3.442 | 39.39 | <0.0001 |
|   65–74 | 1 | 2.334 | 0.182 | 10.319 | 165.32 | <0.0001 |
|   75–84 | 1 | 3.418 | 0.175 | 30.508 | 382.67 | <0.0001 |
|   85+ | 1 | 4.306 | 0.178 | 74.143 | 583.27 | <0.0001 |

Table 6.4. *Gender and age (categorical) analysis of deviance*

| | | Type I | | | Type III | |
|---|---|---|---|---|---|---|
| Source | df | Δ | $\chi^2$ | $p$-value | $\chi^2$ | $p$-value |
| Intercept | | 3306.4 | | | | |
| Gender | 1 | 3298.3 | 8.1 | 0.0046 | 64.5 | <0.0001 |
| Age | 7 | 10.9 | 3287.4 | <0.0001 | 3287.4 | <0.0001 |

- The Type I analysis tests each explanatory variable sequentially, under the assumption that the previous explanatory variables are included in the model. With the entry of gender into the model, the deviance drops by 8.1, from 3306.4 to 3298.3. This is highly significant ($p$-value = 0.0046) as judged against the $\chi^2_1$ distribution. In the presence of gender in the model, the inclusion of age brings the deviance down to 10.9, a reduction of 3287.4. This indicates a much improved fit, achieved at a cost of seven degrees of freedom, since there are seven parameters associated with categorical age. This statistic has $p$-value <0.0001 on the $\chi^2_7$ distribution, indicating age is highly significant.

Table 6.5. *Gender and age (polynomial) analysis of deviance*

| Source | df | Δ | $\chi^2$ | $p$-value |
|---|---|---|---|---|
| Intercept | | 3306.4 | | |
| Gender | 1 | 3298.3 | 8.1 | 0.0046 |
| Age | 1 | 22.8 | 3275.5 | <0.0001 |
| Age$^2$ | 1 | 17.9 | 4.9 | 0.0260 |
| Age$^3$ | 1 | 15.3 | 2.6 | 0.1107 |

- The Type III analysis tests each explanatory variable under the assumption that all other variables are included in the model. Gender, in the presence of age, has a deviance reduction of $\chi_1^2 = 64.5$ with $p$-value <0.0001. Age, in the presence of gender, has $\chi_7^2 = 3287.4$, with $p$-value <0.0001 (as for the Type I analysis).

Type III tests are not useful for models with age as a polynomial. One does not test, for example, the significance of the linear term in the presence of the quadratic and cubic terms. The Type I analysis of deviance table for the model with gender and cubic ($m = 3$) age is presented in Table 6.5 – see code and output on page 154. As the degree $m$ of the polynomial increases the deviance falls, indicating an improved fit. Gender and the linear term are highly significant. The quadratic term is significant ($p$-value = 0.0260) in the presence of gender and the linear term. The cubic term is not significant ($p$-value = 0.1107) in the presence of gender and the linear and quadratic terms.

**Interaction.** In the light of the above, age by gender interaction is considered for models having gender and either quadratic age or categorical age. Model statistics are displayed in the bottom half of Table 6.6.

**Deciding between models.** Model selection is illustrated for this example using the AIC as criterion. For models without interaction, the cubic model (C) has the lowest AIC. However, the quadratic model B has a similar AIC value. The difference in AIC of less than one suggests the quadratic model is adequate. Note that the model with categorical age has the lowest deviance, but the highest AIC. For the interaction models, model F has the lowest AIC. Note that H, which has categorical age and age by gender interaction, has zero deviance and zero degrees of freedom. This occurs because it fits the data perfectly – it has 16 observations and 16 parameters. Fitted values for model F are depicted in Figure 6.3 and parameter estimates are given in Table 6.7.

The linear age by gender interaction term implies the slope of the age term is different for males and females. Thus the effects of age and gender cannot

Table 6.6. *Comparison of models explaining diabetes deaths*

| Model | | $\Delta$ | df | $p$ | AIC |
|---|---|---|---|---|---|
| **Without interaction** | | | | | |
| A | Gender + Age | 22.8 | 13 | 3 | −7187.3 |
| B | Gender + Age + Age$^2$ | 17.9 | 12 | 4 | −7190.2 |
| C | Gender + Age + Age$^2$ + Age$^3$ | 15.3 | 11 | 5 | −7190.8 |
| D | Gender + Age + Age$^2$ + Age$^3$ + Age$^4$ | 15.2 | 10 | 6 | −7188.9 |
| E | Gender + Age (categorical) | 10.9 | 7 | 9 | −7187.2 |
| **Including interaction** | | | | | |
| F | Gender + Age + Age$^2$ + Age × Gender | 13.4 | 11 | 5 | −7192.7 |
| G | Gender + Age + Age$^2$ + | | | | |
| | Age × Gender + Age$^2$ × Gender | 13.0 | 10 | 6 | −7191.1 |
| H | Gender + Age (categorical) + | | | | |
| | Age (categorical) × Gender | 0.0 | 0 | 16 | −7184.1 |

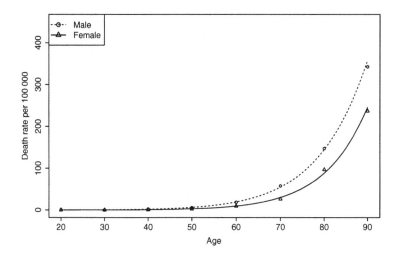

Fig. 6.3. Diabetes death rate: fitted values from preferred model

be quantified separately. The fitted numbers of deaths are given by

$$\hat{\mu} = \begin{cases} ne^{-16.297+0.150x_2+0.0004x_2^2} & \text{for males ,} \\ ne^{-17.715+0.162x_2+0.0004x_2^2} & \text{for females .} \end{cases}$$

Since the age effect $x_2$ is nonlinear, the effect of a change in age on the death rate depends on age. This is sometimes regarded as a disadvantage of specifying a polynomial model. On a logarithmic scale the rate of change in the age effect is $0.150 + 0.0008x_2$ for males, and $0.162 + 0.0008x_2$ for females.

Table 6.7. *Diabetes deaths: preferred model*

| Response variable | Number of diabetes deaths |
|---|---|
| Response distribution | Poisson |
| Link | log |
| Offset | log population |
| Deviance | 13.4 |
| Degrees of freedom | 11 |

| Parameter | df | $\hat{\beta}$ | se | $\chi^2$ | $p$-value |
|---|---|---|---|---|---|
| Intercept | 1 | $-16.297$ | 0.695 | 549.90 | $<0.0001$ |
| Gender: Female | 1 | $-1.418$ | 0.433 | 10.75 | 0.0010 |
| Gender: Male | 0 | 0.000 | · | · | · |
| Age | 1 | 0.150 | 0.020 | 55.68 | $<0.0001$ |
| Age$^2$ | 1 | 0.0004 | 0.000 | 5.80 | 0.0160 |
| Age×Gender: Female | 1 | 0.012 | 0.006 | 4.37 | 0.0365 |
| Age×Gender: Male | 0 | 0.000 | · | · | · |

Table 6.8. *Mean and variance of claims by number of accidents*

| | Number of accidents | | | | | |
|---|---|---|---|---|---|---|
| | 0–138 | 139–267 | 268–596 | 597–1 810 | $\geq 1\,811$ | Overall |
| Mean | 30 | 68 | 178 | 497 | 2176 | 587 |
| Variance | 397 | 1206 | 25 622 | 31 751 | $1.8\times10^6$ | $1.0\times10^6$ |
| Variance/Mean | 13 | 18 | 144 | 64 | 847 | 1 751 |
| Coefft of var | 0.66 | 0.51 | 0.90 | 0.36 | 0.62 | 1.73 |
| $n$ | 36 | 35 | 35 | 35 | 35 | 176 |

## 6.2 Poisson overdispersion and negative binomial regression

This section deals with regression models for count data with overdispersion. Overdispersion, or extra-Poisson variation, was discussed in Section 2.9.

**Third party claims.** Table 6.8 shows the observed mean and variance of the number of claims in 176 geographical areas, when the data is segmented into five groups corresponding to quintiles of the number of accidents. The variance is much larger than the mean. Thus a Poisson model for the number of claims is inappropriate.

One alternative to Poisson regression is negative binomial regression. In Section 2.9 it was shown that the negative binomial distribution may be viewed as a statistical model for counts, in the situation where overdispersion

Table 6.9. *Negative binomial regression results for third party claims*

| Response variable | Number of claims |
| --- | --- |
| Response distribution | negative binomial |
| Link | log |
| Offset | log population |
| Deviance | 192.3 |
| Degrees of freedom | 174 |

| Parameter | df | $\hat{\beta}$ | se | $\chi^2$ | $p$-value |
| --- | --- | --- | --- | --- | --- |
| Intercept | 1 | $-6.954$ | 0.162 | 1836.69 | $< 0.0001$ |
| log accidents | 1 | 0.254 | 0.025 | 100.04 | $< 0.0001$ |
| $\kappa$ | | 0.172 | 0.020 | | |

is explained by heterogeneity of the mean over the population. The negative binomial regression model, using the log link, is

$$y \sim \text{NB}(\mu, \kappa) , \qquad \ln \mu = \ln n + x'\beta . \tag{6.2}$$

**Third party claims.** In Section 5.3 a linear relationship between the log of the number of third party claims and log of the number of accidents, was demonstrated. A suitable negative binomial regression model is then

$$y \sim \text{NB}(\mu, \kappa) , \qquad \ln \mu = \ln n + \beta_1 + \beta_2 \ln z , \tag{6.3}$$

where $y$ is the number of third party claims, $z$ is the number of accidents and $n$ is the population size, of an area. Statistical division is also significant in the regression, and it is shown in Section 10.3 that the model selected according to the AIC has both log accidents and statistical division as explanatory variables. However, for simplicity of the discussion this section considers only log accidents.

The results of the fit are given in Table 6.9 – see code and output on page 156. The mean number of claims is related to log accidents, correcting for exposure:

$$\hat{\mu} = n e^{-6.954 + 0.254 \ln z} .$$

If $z$ increases by a factor of $a$ to $az$ then the rate $\mu/n$ is estimated to increase by a factor of $e^{0.254 \ln a} = a^{0.254}$. For example, with a 10% increase in the number of accidents, $a = 1.1$, the estimated effect on the expected claim rate is $1.1^{0.254} = 1.02$, a 2% increase.

The above fit can be compared to a fit with $\kappa = 0$, that is the Poisson model – see code and output on page 155. This fitted model has a deviance of 15 836.7 on 174 degrees of freedom, indicating a clear lack of fit, which cannot be remedied by the addition of more explanatory variables to the model.

In comparison, the negative binomial model has a deviance of 192.3 on 174 degrees of freedom.

**SAS notes.** The log link is the default link for negative binomial fits in SAS. The canonical link $g(\mu) = \ln\{\mu/(1 + \kappa\mu)\}$ is generally not useful.

**Testing for Poisson overdispersion.** With a negative binomial fit, an estimated $\kappa$ close to zero suggests a Poisson response. A formal test of $\kappa = 0$ is based on the likelihood ratio test. Since $\kappa = 0$ is at the boundary of the possible range $\kappa \geq 0$, the distribution of the test statistic is non-standard and requires care. The likelihood ratio test statistic is $2(\ell_{NB} - \ell_P)$ where $\ell_{NB}$ and $\ell_P$ are the values of the log-likelihood under the negative binomial and Poisson models, respectively. The distribution of the statistic has a mass of 0.5 at zero, and a half-$\chi_1^2$ distribution above zero. A test at the $100\alpha\%$ significance level, requires a rejection region corresponding to the upper $2\alpha$ point of the $\chi_1^2$ distribution (Cameron and Trivedi 1998).

**Third party claims.** The Poisson and negative binomial regressions yield $\ell_P = 644\ 365$, $\ell_{NB} = 651\ 879$. Hence the likelihood ratio statistic is $15\ 027$. The hypothesis $\kappa = 0$ is rejected, at all significance levels. The conclusion is that overdispersion is indeed present. For a significance level $\alpha = 0.05$, the hypothesis $\kappa = 0$ is rejected if the likelihood ratio statistic is greater than the upper 10% point of the $\chi_1^2$ distribution, which is 2.71.

**SAS notes.** The log-likelihoods for the Poisson and negative binomial reported by SAS are correct up to a constant – they omit the $\ln c(y, \phi)$ terms, which for both Poisson and negative binomial are $-\ln y!$. These terms cancel in the computation of the likelihood ratio.

**Swedish mortality.** These data, described on page 17, are displayed in the top panel of Figure 6.4. For male deaths, the Poisson GLM which treats both age and year as categorical variables is

$$y_{ij} \sim P(\mu_{ij}), \qquad \ln(\mu_{ij}) = \ln(n_{ij}) + x'_{ij}\beta. \tag{6.4}$$

Here $i = 0, \ldots, 109$ refers to age, and $j = 1, \ldots 55$ to calendar years 1951 through to 2005. Response $y_{ij}$ is the number of deaths while $n_{ij}$ is the number at risk. The vector $x_{ij}$ contains the values of the explanatory variables for each age $i$, year $j$ combination. The explanatory variables are the usual intercept 1, indicator variables corresponding to age, and indicators corresponding to calendar year. The model has $109 + 54 + 1 = 164$ parameters.

The deviance for the fitted Poisson regression is $21\ 589$ on 5704 degrees of freedom, suggesting overdispersion. Using a negative binomial response

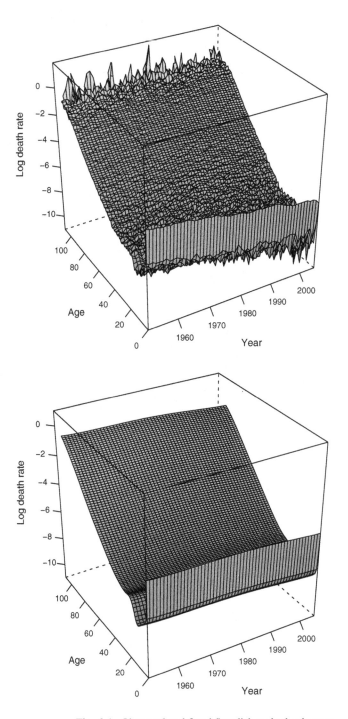

Fig. 6.4. Observed and fitted Swedish male death rates

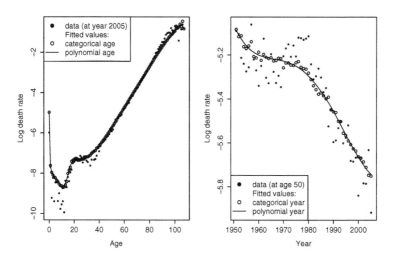

Fig. 6.5. Fitted Swedish male deaths rates using negative binomial model

yields a much better fit: a deviance of 2838 on 5704 degrees of freedom. The fitted regression coefficients are displayed in Figure 6.5 – see code and output on page 157.

The smooth progression of estimated beta coefficients over age and year suggests fewer parameters. Smoothness is exploited by specifying polynomials in the regression, for both age and year:

$$\ln(\mu_{ij}) = \ln(n_{ij}) + \beta_0 + \beta_1 i + \cdots + \beta_p i^p + \beta_{p+1} j + \cdots + \beta_{p+q} j^q \ .$$

Using the AIC as a selection criterion for $p$ and $q$ yields $p = 25$ and $q = 4$, and hence a model with 30 parameters. The AIC for this "optimal" model is 53 898, compared to a value of 54 023 corresponding to unconstrained coefficients. Figure 6.5 and the bottom panel of Figure 6.4 display the fitted values in two and three dimensions respectively – see code and output on page 157.

More weight can be given to recent data by using weights which increase with calendar year. Weighted fits are appropriate when future rates are predicted and the more recent data is seen as more relevant for prediction.

**SAS notes.** Numerical problems often occur when there are a large number of polynomial terms, as in the current Swedish mortality example. These problems manifest themselves in spuriously large standard errors of one or more coefficient estimates or the unavailability of coefficients for the high order polynomials. Standardization of the $x$ variable is suggested in Section 4.11; however, in this case this is not successful. Orthogonal polynomials are used to avoid these numerical problems. These are not implemented in SAS proc genmod, but are available in the statistical language R (Ihaka and Gentleman 1996). The above application was carried out using R.

## 6.3 Quasi-likelihood

For every exponential family response, $\text{Var}(y) = \phi V(\mu)$. For example, for a Poisson response $V(\mu) = \mu$ and $\phi = 1$. However many combinations of $\phi$ and $V(\mu)$ do not correspond to an exponential family response. An example is $\text{Var}(y) = \phi \mu$, with $\phi > 1$. Hence for such combinations of $\phi$ and $V(\mu)$ the expression (5.4)

$$\phi^{-1} X' D(y - \mu) = \sum_{i=1}^{n} \frac{\partial \mu_i}{\partial \beta} \frac{y_i - \mu_i}{\phi V(\mu_i)} , \qquad (6.5)$$

is not the derivative of an exponential family log-likelihood. This prohibition on certain choices of $\mu$ and $V(\mu)$ excludes interesting and practical mean–variance specifications.

A solution to this problem is to maximize the "quasi-likelihood." A quasi-likelihood $Q(\beta)$ is any function of $\beta$ which has derivatives $\dot{Q}(\beta)$ given in (6.5). With quasi-likelihood estimation, it is $Q(\beta)$ which is maximized with respect to $\beta$. Obviously, since $\dot{Q}(\beta)$ is as in (6.5), the quasi-likelihood estimate of $\beta$ coincides with $\hat{\beta}$ in those cases where (6.5) corresponds to the derivative of a likelihood. Similar to the proper maximum likelihood situation, the covariance matrix of $\hat{\beta}$ is determined from the second derivatives of $Q(\beta)$.

**Poisson variance function.** Suppose $V(\mu) = \mu$ and $\text{Var}(y) = \phi V(\mu)$. Then each term in the sum appearing in the right hand side of (6.5) equals the derivative of $y_i \ln \mu_i - \mu_i$ with respect to $\beta$. Hence

$$Q(\beta) = \sum_{i=1}^{n} (y_i \ln \mu_i - \mu_i) .$$

Maximizing $Q(\beta)$ yields $\hat{\beta}$ identical to that obtained from a Poisson regression. However standard errors are multiplied by the factor $\sqrt{\phi}$ reflecting the greater degree of uncertainty on account of overdispersion. The dispersion $\phi$ is estimated as the deviance divided by its degrees of freedom. If $\phi = 1$ then quasi-likelihood estimation is maximum likelihood.

**Other variance functions.** A similar development applies to other variance functions such as the "gamma variance function" $\text{Var}(y) = \phi \mu^2$. The quasi-likelihood estimates $\hat{\beta}$ are identical to that of a gamma fit, but standard errors are inflated.

Table 6.10. *Third party claims: comparison of estimates (standard errors)*

| Model | Variance | Dispersion parameter | $\hat{\beta}_1$ (se) | $\hat{\beta}_2$ (se) |
|---|---|---|---|---|
| Poisson | $\mu$ | $\phi = 1$ | −7.094 (0.027) | 0.259 (0.003) |
| Quasi-likelihood | $\phi\mu$ | $\hat{\phi} = 91.02$ | −7.094 (0.258) | 0.259 (0.032) |
| Negative binomial | $\mu(1 + \kappa\mu)$ | - | −6.954 (0.162) | 0.254 (0.025) |

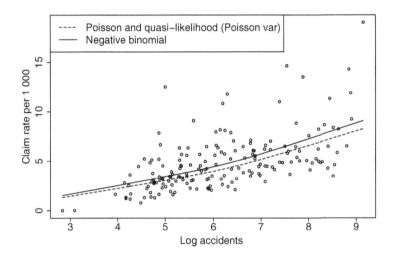

Fig. 6.6. Third party claim rates: fitted values

**Third party claims.** Using the Poisson variance function $V(\mu) = \mu$ results in parameter estimates given in the second line of Table 6.10 – see code and output on page 159. The quasi-likelihood estimates of $\beta$ are identical to those of the Poisson model, but with standard errors larger by a factor of $\hat{\phi}^{1/2} = 9.54$. Parameter estimates, and their standard errors, of the negative binomial model are shown for comparison: these are similar to the quasi-likelihood estimates. Fitted values are shown in Figure 6.6.

**SAS notes.** The quasi-likelihood model with Poisson variance function is estimated in SAS `proc genmod` by adding the option `dscale` in the model statement, and specifying a Poisson response distribution (`dist=poisson`). Other variance functions may be specified: for example the quasi-likelihood model with the gamma variance function $\text{Var}(y) = \phi\mu^2$ is implemented by specifying a gamma response distribution (`dist=gamma`) and `dscale`. SAS uses the term "scale parameter" for $\hat{\phi}^{1/2}$.

**Negative binomial or quasi-likelihood?** The negative binomial is intuitively more appealing than quasi-likelihood, because it explains the mechanism underlying the overdispersion. However, quasi-likelihood provides estimates which are comparable and the results of the two analyses are usually equivalent. The only difference between the Poisson and quasi-likelihood (Poisson variance) models is an inflation factor on the standard errors of the Poisson parameter estimates.

## 6.4 Counts and frequencies

Counts are often converted to frequencies by dividing the count by the number "exposed to risk." For example, suppose the response is the number of deaths as a function of age and other risk factors. The frequency of deaths is then the proportion of deaths given the total number in each group. In the mortality context the exposed to risk is the total number in the sample who are at risk of dying. In the health insurance area, models for disease frequency are of relevance, and here the number of people exposed to the risk of disease is important. For example, if we were modeling the incidence of childhood measles by postcode area, the number exposed to risk is the number of children resident in the postcode areas, and would usually be obtained from census data.

If counts are converted to frequencies, they cannot be modeled using a response distribution such as the Poisson or negative binomial. A preferable approach is to model raw counts, with offsets correcting for the number exposed to risk.

### Exercises

6.1   Develop a statistical model for the number of claims, in the vehicle insurance data set, described on page 15.
6.2   The SAS data file `nswdeaths2002` contains all-cause mortality data for New South Wales, Australia in 2002, by age band and gender. Develop a statistical model for the number of deaths, using the AIC as a model selection criterion.
6.3   Develop a model for female deaths, in the Swedish mortality data set.

# 7

# Categorical responses

Categorical variables take on one of a discrete number of categories. For example, a person is either male or female, or a car is one of a number of models. Other examples are colors, states of wellbeing, employment status and so on.

The simplest example of a categorical variable is where the outcome is binary, meaning it can take on only one of two values such as claim or no claim on a policy, dead or alive. These outcomes are usually coded as 0 or 1, with the occurrence of the event of interest (claim, death) coded as 1, and non-occurrence as 0. The terms "success" and "failure" are also often used for the occurrence and non-occurrence of the event.

Categorical variables fall into two distinct classes: those whose categories have a natural ordering or otherwise. For recording purposes, it is often convenient to code the categories numerically. For example 1 may denote Red, 2 Blue, and so on. In this case the numbers are purely "nominal" and for example 2 does not mean better than 1. In injury classification, however, 1 may denote minor injury, 2 more major up to 8 indicating catastrophic injury and 9 death. In this case the categories are ordered, although it is not necessarily the case that 4 is twice as bad as 2.

Categorical variables are often used as explanatory variables in regressions – see Section 4.10. In other situations a categorical variable is the response to be explained in terms of other explanatory variables. This is dealt with in the current chapter.

## 7.1 Binary responses

Consider a binary response variable $y$ with $y = 0$ or $y = 1$. For example $y$ indicates whether a person died, or whether there was a claim on a policy. The aim is to explain $y$ in terms of explanatory variables contained in $x$. If $\pi$ is the probability that $y = 1$ then $y \sim B(1, \pi)$ (Section 2.2) and

$$\mathrm{E}(y) \equiv \mu = \pi \,, \qquad \mathrm{Var}(y) = \pi \left(1 - \pi\right) \,.$$

The Bernoulli distribution is a special case of the Binomial with $n = 1$, which in turn is a member of the exponential family of distributions. The Bernoulli GLM is

$$y \sim B(1, \pi), \qquad g(\pi) = x'\beta \qquad (7.1)$$

where $g$ is a suitable link.

The ratio $\pi/(1 - \pi)$ is called the odds, and indicates proportionally how much more likely the occurrence of the event is, compared to non-occurrence.

## 7.2 Logistic regression

With logistic regression the log of the odds, called the logit, is modeled in terms of explanatory variables:

$$g(\mu) = \ln \frac{\pi}{1 - \pi} = x'\beta \qquad \Rightarrow \qquad \pi = \frac{e^{x'\beta}}{1 + e^{x'\beta}}. \qquad (7.2)$$

The logit link ensures predictions of $\pi$ using $x$ are in the interval (0,1) for all $\beta$ and $x$. Using a Bernoulli response distribution and logit link defines logistic regression. The logit link is the canonical link for the Bernoulli and binomial distributions.

To estimate $\beta$, measurements are collected on the (0,1) response $y$ and on the corresponding values of the explanatory variables $x$. Maximum likelihood estimation is performed using the generic method for GLM estimation, as described in Section 5.5.

Parameters in a logistic regression are interpreted as follows. Consider a single continuous explanatory variable $x$ and hence

$$\ln \frac{\pi}{1 - \pi} = \alpha + \beta x.$$

Exponentiating both sides shows that the odds are $e^{\alpha + \beta x}$. Suppose $x$ is increased by one unit, then the odds change from $e^{\alpha + \beta x}$ to $e^{\alpha + \beta(x+1)} = e^{\beta} e^{\alpha + \beta x}$. In other words, increasing the explanatory variable by one unit multiplies the odds by $e^{\beta}$. If $\beta$ is small then $(e^{\beta} - 1) \approx \beta$ and in this case $100\beta$ is the approximate percentage change in odds when the explanatory variable increases by one unit. If $\beta < 0$ the effect of an increase in $x$ is to decrease the odds of an occurrence. Conversely, if $\beta > 0$, then the effect of an increase in $x$ is to increase the odds. Finally if $\beta = 0$ then $e^{\beta} = 1$ and there is no effect on the odds.

Now consider a categorical explanatory variable $x$ with $r$ levels. Assuming the level $r$ to be the base level then the model is

$$\ln \frac{\pi}{1 - \pi} = \beta_0 + \beta_1 x_1 + \ldots + \beta_{r-1} x_{r-1},$$

where $x_j$ are indicator variables with $x_j = 1$ if $x$ is at level $j$ and 0 otherwise, $j = 1, \ldots, r-1$. When $x$ is at level $r$, the odds of occurrence are $\pi/(1-\pi) = e^{\beta_0}$. When $x$ is at level $j \neq 1$, the odds are $e^{\beta_0 + \beta_j}$. Thus the effect of $x$ being at level $j$, compared with level $r$, is to multiply the odds by a factor of $e^{\beta_j}$. If $\beta_j < 0$ then $x = j$ decreases the odds, compared with $x = r$, while $\beta_j > 0$ implies $x = j$ increases the odds.

**Probit and complementary log–log links.** While the logit link is the most popular link when dealing with Bernoulli responses, other links are also used. The probit and complementary log–log links are

$$\Phi^{-1}(\pi), \qquad \ln\{-\ln(1-\pi)\},$$

respectively, where $\Phi^{-1}$ is the inverse of the standard normal distribution function. Thus predicted values are

$$\Phi(x'\beta), \qquad 1 - \exp(-e^{x'\beta}).$$

Predicted means are guaranteed to fall in the interval (0,1). The complementary log–log link is important in the analysis of survival data and is not symmetric about $\pi = 1/2$.

## 7.3 Application of logistic regression to vehicle insurance

In this section, logistic regression is applied to the vehicle insurance data set, described on page 15. The occurrence of a claim is the response. Data displays for the relationship between the occurrence of a claim and vehicle value are discussed in Section 1.4. The right panels of Figure 1.7 suggest a nonlinear, possibly quadratic, relationship between vehicle value and the probability of a claim.

**Logistic fits.** Suppose the cubic model

$$\ln \frac{\pi}{1-\pi} = \beta_0 + \beta_1 x + \beta_2 x^2 + \beta_3 x^3, \tag{7.3}$$

where $x$ is the vehicle value and $\pi$ is the probability of a claim on the policy. The cases $\beta_3 = 0$ and $\beta_3 = \beta_2 = 0$ are the quadratic and linear models, respectively. The fits for these models are given in Table 7.1 – see code and output on page 160. The fits show $\hat{\beta}_3$ is not significant. If $\beta_3 = 0$ then $\beta_2$ is significant. Hence a quadratic model appears appropriate while a linear model appears inadequate. The difference between the AIC of the cubic and quadratic models is less than one, suggesting a quadratic model is preferred. Further, the AIC of the quadratic model is much less than that of the linear, suggesting the linear model is inadequate.

Table 7.1. *Logistic fits for vehicle insurance claims*

|  | Linear | Quadratic | Cubic |
|---|---|---|---|
| $\hat{\beta}_0$ (se) | −2.716 (0.026) | −2.893 (0.044) | −2.925 (0.048) |
| *p*-value | < 0.0001 | < 0.0001 | < 0.0001 |
| $\hat{\beta}_1$ (se) | 0.066 (0.012) | 0.220 (0.036) | 0.261 (0.042) |
| *p*-value | < 0.0001 | < 0.0001 | < 0.0001 |
| $\hat{\beta}_2$ (se) | . | −0.026 (0.006) | −0.038 (0.008) |
| *p*-value | . | < 0.0001 | 0.0018 |
| $\hat{\beta}_3$ (se) | . | . | 0.001 (0.000) |
| *p*-value | . | . | 0.1377 |
| $\Delta$ | 33745.1 | 33712.9 | 33710.7 |
| *p* | 2 | 3 | 4 |
| AIC | 33749.1 | 33718.9 | 33718.7 |

For the linear model the effect of an increase in vehicle value by $10 000 is estimated to be an increase in the odds of a claim by $e^{0.066} - 1 \approx 7\%$. For the quadratic model, the effect of an increase in vehicle value depends on the vehicle value. This dependence illustrates a disadvantage of using a nonlinear form of a continuous explanatory variable.

**Model fit.** While the AIC provides an objective measure deciding between given models, there is no guarantee that the model with the smallest AIC fits the data well. The fitted equations from the linear and quadratic models are $-2.716 + 0.066x$ and $-2.893 + 0.220x - 0.026x^2$, respectively. These are converted to estimates of $\pi$ using the inverse to the logit transform as in (7.2). Figure 7.1 displays the scatterplot smoother and the fitted values. The linear model fits badly. The quadratic fit captures claims behavior up to around value $100 000 while between $100 000 and $150 000, where the data is sparse, the fit is problematic.

This example highlights the danger of misspecifying the parametric form for a continuous explanatory variable. This is discussed further in Section 4.12.

**Banding vehicle value.** An alternative to finding a parametric form for vehicle value in the model, is to band it. The banding scheme used for vehicle value is shown in Table 7.2. Using band 1 as the base level, the linear predictor of the log odds of claiming is

$$\ln \frac{\pi}{1 - \pi} = \beta_0 + \beta_2 \, x_2 + \beta_3 \, x_3 + \beta_4 \, x_4 + \beta_5 \, x_5 + \beta_6 \, x_6 \qquad (7.4)$$

where $x_j$ is the indicator variable defined for band $j$. Table 7.3 displays the results of the fit – see code and output on page 161. The "$e^{\hat{\beta}}$" column contains

Table 7.2. *Banding scheme for vehicle value*

| Band | Vehicle value ($000's) | Number of policies |
|------|------------------------|--------------------|
| 1 | ≤25 | 54 971 |
| 2 | 25–50 | 11 439 |
| 3 | 50–75 | 1265 |
| 4 | 75–100 | 104 |
| 5 | 100–125 | 44 |
| 6 | >125 | 33 |

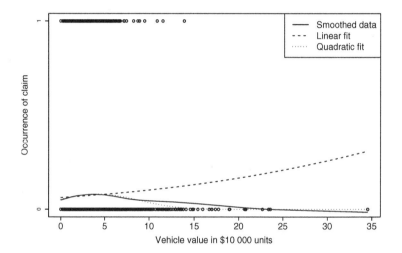

Fig. 7.1. Claim occurrence with scatterplot smoother, linear and quadratic fits

the estimated effect on the odds of a claim, of a policy being in a vehicle value band compared to band 1. For example, the odds of a claim increase by 19% for a vehicle in band 2 and decrease by 44% for a vehicle in band 4, both compared to band 1. The fitted probabilities for this model are shown in Figure 7.2. The fitted values follow the scatterplot smoother closely, excepting in the upper tail of vehicle value (band 6, vehicle value >$125 000), which spans a large range of sparse data values.

**SAS notes.** Logistic regression is implemented in SAS using either `proc genmod` with the binomial response distribution, or `proc logistic`. The latter gives output which is specific to logistic regression, whereas the former gives generic GLM output. Parameter estimates computed by the two procedures are identical.

Table 7.3. *Logistic regression for vehicle insurance claims*

| Response variable | Occurrence of a claim |
|---|---|
| Response distribution | Bernoulli |
| Link | logit |
| Deviance | 33 744.0 |
| Degrees of freedom | 67 850 |

| Parameter | df | $\hat{\beta}$ | se | $e^{\hat{\beta}}$ | $\chi^2$ | $p$-value |
|---|---|---|---|---|---|---|
| Intercept | 1 | −2.648 | 0.017 | 0.07 | 23799.7 | < 0.0001 |
| Vehicle value | 5 | | | | | 0.0004 |
| 1 | 0 | 0.000 | 0.000 | 1.00 | - | - |
| 2 | 1 | 0.174 | 0.039 | 1.19 | 19.93 | < 0.0001 |
| 3 | 1 | 0.102 | 0.110 | 1.11 | 0.87 | 0.3523 |
| 4 | 1 | −0.571 | 0.510 | 0.56 | 1.25 | 0.2627 |
| 5 | 1 | −0.397 | 0.724 | 0.67 | 0.30 | 0.5834 |
| 6 | 1 | −0.818 | 1.016 | 0.44 | 0.65 | 0.4205 |

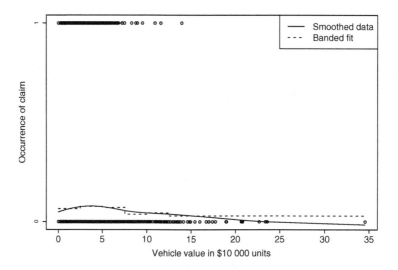

Fig. 7.2. Occurrence of a claim with scatterplot smoother and banded fit

## 7.4 Correcting for exposure

When policies have exposures to risk $t$, where $0 < t \leq 1$, the probability of a claim is proportionally reduced by the time at risk. As discussed in Section 2.2, the response distribution is $B(1, t\pi)$. However the appropriate logistic link is based on $\pi$, the probability of a claim over the entire period.

Table 7.4. *Model selection for car insurance claims*

| Model | Δ | p | AIC |
|---|---|---|---|
| age | 32 561.9 | 6 | 32 573.9 |
| area | 32 637.7 | 6 | 32 649.7 |
| vehicle body | 32 616.6 | 13 | 32 642.6 |
| vehicle value | 32 626.9 | 6 | 32 638.9 |
| age + area | 32 550.2 | 11 | 32 572.2 |
| age + vehicle body | 32 525.6 | 18 | 32 561.6 |
| age + value | 32 539.8 | 11 | 32 561.8 |
| area + vehicle body | 32 602.4 | 18 | 32 638.4 |
| area + vehicle value | 32 611.4 | 11 | 32 633.4 |
| vehicle body + vehicle value | 32 594.7 | 18 | 32 630.7 |
| age + vehicle body + vehicle value | 32 505.0 | 23 | 32 551.0 |
| age + area + vehicle body + vehicle value | 32 493.5 | 28 | 32 549.5 |

Defining $\pi^* = t\pi$:

$$\ln \frac{\pi^*/t}{1 - \pi^*/t} = x'\beta \qquad \Rightarrow \qquad \pi^* = t \, \frac{e^{x'\beta}}{1 + e^{x'\beta}} \, . \qquad (7.5)$$

The adjustment for exposure is therefore achieved by a simple modification to the logit link. This is different to the exposure adjustment in the case of count data, which is the offset term in the linear predictor (see Section 5.4). The appearance in the link of the observation-specific exposure $t$ is non-standard. This exposure adjustment has been used in the applications below.

**SAS notes.** The adjustment for exposure is implemented in proc genmod, with the user-defined link and inverse link (7.5). This is demonstrated on page 162.

**Vehicle insurance.** The risk factors driver's age, area, vehicle body type and vehicle value are all significant in separate regressions, and in the fit having all as explanatory variables. Results for different models and their associated AIC values are displayed in Table 7.4.

The model with all risk factors yields the lowest AIC. However, the model excluding area has an AIC only 1.5 greater. The statistical significance of area is marginal ($p$-value = 0.0435) and it would not be unreasonable to prefer the simpler model.

Table 7.5 displays the estimates for the model with driver's age, area, vehicle body and vehicle value (banded). The base levels are driver's age 3, area C, vehicle body Sedan and vehicle value less than \$25 000 – see code and output on page 162. The odds of a claim for a vehicle in this base level are therefore

Table 7.5. *Vehicle insurance claims logistic regression*

| Response variable | Occurrence of a claim |
| --- | --- |
| Response distribution | Bernoulli |
| Link | logit, adjusted for exposure |
| Deviance | 32 493.5 |
| Degrees of freedom | 67 848 |

| Parameter | df | $\hat{\beta}$ | se | $e^{\hat{\beta}}$ | $\chi^2$ | $p$-value |
| --- | --- | --- | --- | --- | --- | --- |
| Intercept | 1 | $-1.750$ | 0.049 | 0.174 | 1297.98 | $< 0.0001$ |
| | | | | | | |
| Driver's age | 5 | | | | | $< 0.0001$ |
| 1 | 1 | 0.288 | 0.062 | 1.333 | 21.35 | $< 0.0001$ |
| 2 | 1 | 0.064 | 0.050 | 1.066 | 1.66 | 0.1978 |
| 3 | 0 | 0.000 | 0.000 | 1.000 | - | - |
| 4 | 1 | $-0.036$ | 0.048 | 0.965 | 0.57 | 0.4492 |
| 5 | 1 | $-0.265$ | 0.056 | 0.767 | 22.77 | $< 0.0001$ |
| 6 | 1 | $-0.255$ | 0.067 | 0.775 | 14.56 | 0.0001 |
| | | | | | | |
| Area | 5 | | | | | 0.0435 |
| A | 1 | $-0.036$ | 0.045 | 0.965 | 0.63 | 0.4272 |
| B | 1 | 0.053 | 0.047 | 1.055 | 1.3 | 0.2543 |
| C | 0 | 0.000 | 0.000 | 1.000 | - | - |
| D | 1 | $-0.138$ | 0.058 | 0.871 | 5.62 | 0.0178 |
| E | 1 | $-0.066$ | 0.065 | 0.936 | 1.05 | 0.3052 |
| F | 1 | 0.021 | 0.076 | 1.021 | 0.08 | 0.7839 |
| | | | | | | |
| Vehicle body | 12 | | | | | 0.0010 |
| Bus | 1 | 1.136 | 0.456 | 3.115 | 6.22 | 0.0127 |
| Convertible | 1 | $-0.371$ | 0.640 | 0.690 | 0.34 | 0.5622 |
| Coupe | 1 | 0.433 | 0.147 | 1.542 | 8.64 | 0.0033 |
| Hatchback | 1 | $-0.012$ | 0.043 | 0.988 | 0.08 | 0.7729 |
| Hardtop | 1 | 0.099 | 0.105 | 1.104 | 0.9 | 0.3439 |
| Minicaravan | 1 | 0.596 | 0.324 | 1.815 | 3.39 | 0.0654 |
| Minibus | 1 | $-0.111$ | 0.172 | 0.895 | 0.42 | 0.5173 |
| Panel van | 1 | 0.019 | 0.144 | 1.020 | 0.02 | 0.893 |
| Roadster | 1 | 0.070 | 0.816 | 1.072 | 0.01 | 0.932 |
| Sedan | 0 | 0.000 | 0.000 | 1.000 | - | - |
| Station wagon | 1 | $-0.019$ | 0.050 | 0.981 | 0.15 | 0.7013 |
| Truck | 1 | $-0.097$ | 0.108 | 0.908 | 0.8 | 0.3709 |
| Utility | 1 | $-0.246$ | 0.076 | 0.782 | 10.48 | 0.0012 |
| | | | | | | |
| Vehicle value ($000's) | 5 | | | | | 0.0009 |
| <25 | 0 | 0.000 | 0.000 | 1.000 | - | - |
| 25–50 | 1 | 0.210 | 0.049 | 1.234 | 18.19 | $< 0.0001$ |
| 50–75 | 1 | 0.137 | 0.124 | 1.146 | 1.22 | 0.2697 |
| 75–100 | 1 | $-0.607$ | 0.541 | 0.545 | 1.26 | 0.2622 |
| 100–125 | 1 | $-0.290$ | 0.771 | 0.748 | 0.14 | 0.707 |
| >125 | 1 | $-0.797$ | 1.062 | 0.451 | 0.56 | 0.453 |

estimated as

$$e^{\hat{\beta}_0} = e^{-1.750} = 0.174.$$

This translates to an estimated probability of a claim of

$$\hat{\pi} = \frac{0.174}{1 + 0.174} = 0.148.$$

The multiplicative effect on the odds of a claim, for a policy being in a category other than the base level, for any of the risk factors, is given in the column "$e^{\hat{\beta}}$." For example, the effect of driver's age being in age band 1 on the odds of a claim is 1.333, or a 33.3% increase. The estimate of the odds of a claim for a vehicle with driver's age band 1 and all of the other risk factors at base levels, is therefore $0.174 \times 1.333 = 0.232$, giving an estimated probability of a claim of $0.232/(1 + 0.232) = 0.188$. The effect of any other combination of risk factors is calculated in this way. For example, the estimated odds of a claim on a policy with driver's age band 1, area A, vehicle body panel van and vehicle value $25 000 to $50 000, is

$$0.174 \times 1.333 \times 0.965 \times 1.020 \times 1.234 = 0.282$$

giving an estimated probability of a claim of $0.282/(1 + 0.282) = 0.220$.

## 7.5  Grouped binary data

If all explanatory variables are categorical, it is possible to express a data set in grouped form, as discussed in Section 4.8. A group consists of all cases with the same explanatory variable values and may correspond to a homogeneous risk set.

In the case of a binary response, once the data are grouped the observed response is number of events occurring in the group. This is different from the situation with a continuous response, where the response is the group mean – see the example in Section 4.8. Write

| | | |
|---|---|---|
| $m$ | = | number of groups |
| $n_i$ | = | number of cases (policies) in group $i$ |
| $y_i$ | = | number of events occurring in group $i$ |
| $\pi_i$ | = | probability of the event occurring for a case (policy) in group $i$ |
| $n$ | = | total sample size $= \sum_{i=1}^{m} n_i$. |

Then $y_i$ is the number of occurrences of the event, out of a possible $n_i$, where the probability of the event occurring in each case is $\pi_i$. The observed response is assumed to have a binomial distribution: $y_i \sim B(n_i, \pi_i)$, where the probability $\pi_i$ is modeled as a function of explanatory variables. With this

Table 7.6. *Subset of vehicle insurance claims grouped data*

| $i$ | Driver's age | Area | Vehicle body | Vehicle value ($000's) | Number of policies $n_i$ | Number of claims $y_i$ |
|---|---|---|---|---|---|---|
| 1 | 1 | A | Bus | <25 | 2 | 0 |
| 2 | 1 | A | Convertible | <25 | 1 | 0 |
| 3 | 1 | A | Convertible | 25–50 | 1 | 0 |
| 4 | 1 | A | Convertible | 75–100 | 2 | 0 |
| 5 | 1 | A | Coupe | <25 | 18 | 2 |
| 6 | 1 | A | Coupe | 25–50 | 2 | 0 |
| 7 | 1 | A | Coupe | 75–100 | 1 | 0 |
| 8 | 1 | A | Hatchback | <25 | 554 | 47 |
| 9 | 1 | A | Hatchback | 25–50 | 8 | 0 |
| 10 | 1 | A | Hardtop | <25 | 19 | 2 |
| 11 | 1 | A | Hardtop | 25–50 | 9 | 3 |
| 12 | 1 | A | Hardtop | 50–75 | 1 | 0 |
| 13 | 1 | A | Minicaravan | <25 | 3 | 2 |
| 14 | 1 | A | Minibus | <25 | 4 | 0 |
| 15 | 1 | A | Minibus | 25–50 | 1 | 0 |
| 16 | 1 | A | Panel van | <25 | 30 | 5 |
| 17 | 1 | A | Panel van | 25–50 | 4 | 0 |
| 18 | 1 | A | Sedan | <25 | 318 | 25 |
| 19 | 1 | A | Sedan | 25–50 | 26 | 3 |
| 20 | 1 | A | Sedan | 50–75 | 7 | 0 |
| 21 | 1 | A | Sedan | 100–125 | 2 | 1 |
| 22 | 1 | A | Sedan | >125 | 1 | 0 |
| 23 | 1 | A | Station wagon | <25 | 108 | 11 |
| 24 | 1 | A | Station wagon | 25–50 | 86 | 5 |
| 25 | 1 | A | Station wagon | 50–75 | 30 | 1 |
| 26 | 1 | A | Station wagon | 75–100 | 2 | 0 |
| 27 | 1 | A | Truck | <25 | 24 | 2 |
| 28 | 1 | A | Truck | 25–50 | 15 | 2 |
| 29 | 1 | A | Utility | <25 | 66 | 6 |
| 30 | 1 | A | Utility | 25–50 | 42 | 2 |

approach, differing exposure of individual policies cannot be adjusted for, nor can one include continuous explanatory variables in the model.

**Vehicle insurance.** Consider the explanatory variables driver's age, area, vehicle body type and vehicle value. There are $6 \times 6 \times 13 \times 6 = 2808$ combinations of the levels. Two–thirds of these are empty with just $m = 929$ non-empty combinations. A subset of the grouped data is shown in Table 7.6, those of age band 1 and area A. For example, group 8 consists of policies having driver's age 1, area A, hatchback body type and a value of less than $25 000. There are $n_8 = 554$ policies in this category, of which $y_8 = 47$ have a claim. The model estimates are identical to those computed from the individual policy data, without the exposure adjustment.

## 7.6  Goodness of fit for logistic regression

A variety of goodness of fit statistics or methods are available for logistic regression. This section considers some of them.

**Deviance.** The deviance $\Delta$ is not a useful measure of goodness of fit of the logistic regression model. To see this suppose $\hat{\pi}_i$ is the predicted probability of success:

$$\hat{\pi}_i = \frac{e^{x_i'\hat{\beta}}}{1 + e^{x_i'\hat{\beta}}} \, ,$$

where $\hat{\beta}$ is the maximum likelihood estimate. Algebraic manipulation shows that the deviance is (Collett 2003):

$$\Delta = -2 \sum_{i=1}^{n} \left\{ \hat{\pi}_i \ln \frac{\hat{\pi}_i}{1 - \hat{\pi}_i} + \ln\left(1 - \hat{\pi}_i\right) \right\} \, .$$

This depends on the counts $y_i$ only through the fitted values $\hat{\pi}_i$. Hence the deviance is not informative about the goodness of fit of the $\hat{\pi}_i$ to the $y_i$. In addition (Collett 2003), "... the deviance is not even approximately distributed as $\chi^2$."

A further problem with the deviance for logistic regression is that its value depends on whether the data are ungrouped or grouped. For the vehicle insurance data, the deviance for the ungrouped fit is 33 624 on 67 828 degrees of freedom. The same fit on the grouped data yields a deviance of 868 on 901 degrees of freedom. The deviance of the individual-level data compares individual responses (0 or 1) with the individual fitted probabilities $\hat{\pi}_i$, $i = 1, \ldots, n$. The deviance of the grouped data fit compares group means $y_i/n_i$ to fitted group probabilities $\hat{\pi}_i$, $i = i, \ldots, m$.

**Pearson chi-square statistic.** This is defined as

$$\sum_{i=1}^{n} \frac{(y_i - \hat{\pi}_i)^2}{\hat{\pi}_i (1 - \hat{\pi}_i)} \, .$$

This has the usual form of the square of the difference between observed and expected values, divided by the expected value. The statistic has, approximately, the $\chi^2_{n-p}$ distribution and is asymptotically equivalent to the deviance (Dobson 2002). Unlike the deviance, this statistic does depend on the actual counts $y_i$. However, the approximate chi-square distribution can be poor and the statistic is not considered a reliable measure of fit.

**SAS notes.** The deviance and Pearson chi-square statistic are produced by default by `proc genmod`.

Table 7.7. *Classification table with 0.08 threshold*

|            |       | Predicted claim | | |
|            |       | No | Yes | Total |
|------------|-------|---------|-------|--------|
| Actual     | No    | 54 196  | 9 036 | 63 232 |
| Claim      | Yes   | 3740    | 884   | 4624   |
|            | Total | 57 936  | 9 920 | 67 856 |

**Classification tables and ROC curves.** One way of examining the performance of a model for binary data is via a classification table. The fitted probabilities $\hat{\pi}_i$ are computed and each case $i$ is predicted (or classified) as an "event" or "non-event" depending on whether $\hat{\pi}_i$ is greater than or less than a given threshold. The resulting $2 \times 2$ classification table compares actual occurrences to predictions.

To illustrate, consider Table 7.7 constructed using a threshold of 0.08 with the exposure-adjusted logistic regression of vehicle insurance claims. Of the 4624 claims, 884 had $\hat{\pi}_i > 0.08$ and are correctly predicted to have a claim. Of the 63 232 policies with no claim, 54 196 are correctly predicted not to have a claim.

Given the classification table, the predictive usefulness of a model is often summarized using the following two measures:

- **Sensitivity.** This is the relative frequency of predicting an event when an event does take place.
- **Specificity.** This is the relative frequency of predicting a non-event when there is no event.

Ideally both sensitivity and specificity are near 1. If the threshold is set at 0 then the sensitivity and specificity are 1 and 0, respectively. As the threshold increases, fewer events are predicted, the sensitivity declines and the specificity increases. If the threshold is 1 then the sensitivity and specificity are 0 and 1, respectively.

In the above example a threshold of 0.08 leads to a sensitivity of 884/4624 = 0.19 and specificity of 54 196/63 232 = 0.85. Thus while the model has good ability to identify policies on which there is no claim, it does not accurately predict situations where there is a claim. The fact that the specificity is high is partly a consequence of the fact that most policies do not lead to a claim.

The ROC (Receiver Operating Characteristic) curve plots the sensitivity against specificity for each threshold. Traditionally one minus the specificity is plotted on the horizontal axis, and sensitivity on the vertical axis. With this orientation of the axes, a value near zero on the $x$ axis (high specificity) generally implies a low value on the $y$ axis (low sensitivity) and vice versa.

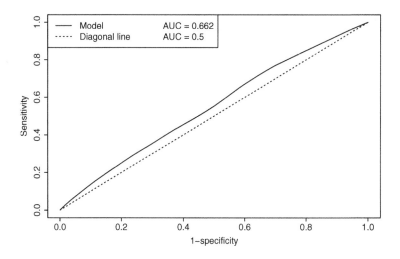

Fig. 7.3. ROC curve, exposure-adjusted model for vehicle claim

Figure 7.3 shows the ROC curve for the exposure-adjusted vehicle insurance claim model.

All ROC curves start at (0,0) and end at (1,1) as these points correspond to threshold probabilities 0 and 1, respectively. ROC curves increase monotonically. A model with perfect predictive ability has sensitivity and specificity both equal to one, giving a ROC curve consisting of the single point in the top left hand corner. A "good" ROC curve rises quickly to 1: the further a curve is to the top left hand corner, the better its predictive ability. This is quantified by computing the area under the ROC curve (AUC), as a measure of the model's predictive ability. The AUC has a maximum of 1. A model with ROC equal to the 45° line (AUC = 0.5) has a predictive ability no better than chance. For the exposure-adjusted model, AUC = 0.662. In comparison, the model unadjusted for exposure has AUC = 0.548, indicating weaker predictive ability.

The concepts of sensitivity and specificity are of particular interest in the area of medical diagnosis. Here an individual case is a patient, the event of interest is whether or not the patient has a particular disease, and the predictors are diagnostic tests. Accurate prediction of presence of a disease at the individual patient level, is critical. In insurance applications, however, prediction of a claim or no claim on an individual policy is rarely the point of statistical modeling. Rather, it is the average prediction which is of interest. For this reason, a model with low sensitivity is often adequate. The model is useful provided it explains the variability in claims behavior, as a function of risk factors. The ROC curve is a sensible means of comparing the performance of differing models.

**SAS notes.** The classification table and other output specific to logistic regression, are computed in `proc logistic`, but not in `proc genmod`. However, the exposure-adjusted model needs to be computed in `proc genmod` because `proc logistic` does not allow user-defined link functions. ROC curves and the AUC are demonstrated on page 169.

## 7.7 Categorical responses with more than two categories

Models for a categorical response with more than two outcomes fall into two broad classes:

- ordinal response models, in which response categories have a natural ordering; and
- nominal response models, in which response categories have no natural ordering.

Ordinal response variables measure responses to questions such as "How do you rate your health?" (excellent, good, moderate, poor) or assessments such as "Degree of crash" (fatal, injury, non-casualty). Examples of nominal responses are "Type of household insurance claim" (theft, fire, storm damage) and "Type of health insurance cover" (hospital and ancillary, hospital, ancillary, none) which is partially ordered.

**The multivariate GLM.** Consider a categorical response with $r$ categories labeled $1, 2, \ldots, r$. Similar to the way a categorical explanatory variable with $r$ levels is replaced by a set of $r - 1$ indicator variables, the response is formalized as a set of $r - 1$ indicator response variables $y_j, j = 1, \ldots, r - 1$, with $y_j = 1$ if the response is at level $j$ and 0 otherwise. In this way, the response $y \equiv (y_1, \ldots, y_{r-1})'$ is multivariate. Models for nominal and ordinal responses thus fall under the class of the multivariate GLM, based on the multivariate exponential family. The development of the multivariate GLM is not covered in this text. Interested readers are referred to Fahrmeir and Tutz (2001). The familiar GLM concepts of the link and variance functions carry over to the multivariate GLM.

Given $n$ independent observations on the response $y$, the number of times that category $j$ occurred, $n_j = \sum y_j$, is of interest. The joint distribution of $n_1, \ldots, n_r$ is multinomial:

$$f(n_1, \ldots, n_r) = \frac{n!}{n_1! \cdots n_r!} \pi_1^{n_1} \cdots \pi_r^{n_r}$$

where $\pi_j$ is the probability of response category $j$, $\sum_j \pi_j = 1$ and $n = \sum_j n_j$. If $r = 2$ then the multinomial is the binomial distribution. The multinomial distribution underpins the nominal regression model and

$$\mathrm{E}(n_j) = n\pi_j , \qquad \mathrm{Var}(n_j) = n\pi_j(1 - \pi_j) , \qquad \mathrm{Cov}(n_j, n_k) = -n\pi_j\pi_k ,$$

where Cov denotes covariance.

## 7.8 Ordinal responses

Consider an ordinal response $y$ with $r$ ordered categories. This can be thought of as arising from an underlying continuous variable $y^*$ and thresholds $\theta_0, \ldots, \theta_r$ such that

$$y = j \quad \text{if} \quad \theta_{j-1} \leq y^* < \theta_j , \qquad j = 1, \ldots, r .$$

Thus $y$ is a banded version of $y^*$. For example, the ordinal response to "How do you rate your health" can be thought of as a banded version of an underlying continuous variable, the state of one's health, which is intangible and difficult to measure on a single continuous scale. This threshold setup is a useful framework around which to base models with ordinal responses.

The model for the ordinal category $y$ is formulated in terms of cumulative probabilities:

$$\tau_j \equiv P(y \leq j) = P(y^* < \theta_j) , \qquad j = 1, \ldots, r .$$

The aim is to relate the cumulative probabilities $\tau_j$ to explanatory variables $x$. Assume $y^* = -x'\beta + \epsilon$ with $\mathrm{E}(\epsilon) = 0$, implying $y^*$ has mean $x'\beta$. It follows that

$$\tau_j = P(\epsilon \leq \theta_j + x'\beta) .$$

The distribution of $\epsilon$ determines the exact form of the model.

**Cumulative logistic or proportional odds model.** Suppose $\epsilon$ has the standard logistic distribution:

$$P(\epsilon \leq x) = \frac{1}{1 + e^{-x}} .$$

Then

$$\tau_j = P(\epsilon \leq \theta_j + x'\beta) = \frac{1}{1 + e^{-(\theta_j + x'\beta)}} ,$$

and hence

$$\ln \frac{\tau_j}{1 - \tau_j} = \theta_j + x'\beta , \qquad j = 1, \ldots, r - 1 , \tag{7.6}$$

where the $\theta_j$ are intercept terms that depend only on $j$, and $x$ does not contain a 1 corresponding to an intercept term. The coefficient $\beta$ does not depend on $j$, so that the $r - 1$ relationships in (7.6) all have the same slopes with respect to the explanatory variables $x$.

Model (7.6) is called the cumulative logistic or proportional odds model. The terminology arises as follows. The ratio of the odds of $y \leq j$ at two settings of $x$, say $x_1$ and $x_2$ is

$$\frac{e^{\theta_j + x_1'\beta}}{e^{\theta_j + x_2'\beta}} = e^{(x_1' - x_2')\beta} ,$$

which is independent of $j$. Thus the effect of a change in $x$ on the odds of $y \leq j$ is the same for all $j$. For example, if there is one explanatory variable $x$ indicating the presence ($x = 1$) or absence ($x = 0$) of a factor, then the ratio of odds is $e^{\beta}$. This factor effect is independent of the category $j$.

**Cumulative complementary log–log model.** Assuming the extreme minimal-value distribution for $\epsilon$ gives the model (Fahrmeir and Tutz 2001):

$$\ln\left\{-\ln(1 - \tau_j)\right\} = \theta_j + x'\beta , \qquad j = 1, \ldots, r - 1 .$$

This model is also called the discrete proportional hazards model or the grouped Cox model, as it is closely related to the Cox proportional hazards model in survival analysis (Hosmer and Lemeshow 1999).

**Cumulative probit model.** If $\epsilon$ is normally distributed, then the probit model results:

$$\Phi^{-1}(\tau_j) = \theta_j + x'\beta, \qquad j = 1, \ldots, r - 1 .$$

In other words the probability of being in group $j$ or lower is the standard normal probability integral evaluated at $\theta_j + x'\beta$. The response to changes in $x$ is, on a z-score scale, again the same for all categories and the category effect arises through the intercept $\theta_j$.

As in logistic regression, parameter estimates for the proportional odds, log–log and probit models are usually similar. However the parameters of the proportional odds model are more interpretable.

**Other models.** The above models are analogous to logistic regression with the logit, complementary log–log or probit links, respectively. Other models are based on other functions of the $\tau_j$ or $\pi_j = \tau_j - \tau_{j-1}$. In particular, the continuation ratio is defined as the conditional probability of being in category $j$ given one is in category $j$ or lower:

$$\delta_j = \frac{\pi_j}{\pi_1 + \pi_2 + \cdots + \pi_j} .$$

The continuation ratio model is

$$\ln \frac{\delta_j}{1 - \delta_j} = \theta_j + x'\beta , \qquad j = 2, \ldots, r .$$

**Application of the proportional odds model: the degree of a vehicle crash.**
Model (7.6) is the most well-known and commonly used ordinal regression
model. Its use is illustrated in this example.

In the degree of vehicle crash data set (page 18) there are $n = 76\,341$ drivers
involved in vehicle crashes. Suppose the response variable is the ordinal degree
of crash:

| $j$ | Degree of crash |
|---|---|
| 1 | Non-casualty |
| 2 | Injury |
| 3 | Fatal |

The cumulative probabilities $\tau_j$, $j = 1, 2, 3$ are modeled in terms of driver's
age, sex and road user class. The parameter estimates for the proportional odds
model are given in Table 7.8 – see code and output on page 169. Base levels
are car, 30 to 39 years and male.

The two fitted equations are

$$\ln \frac{\hat{\tau}_j}{1 - \hat{\tau}_j} = \hat{\theta}_j - 0.151 x_1 + \cdots + 0.148 x_{16} , \qquad j = 1, 2 ,$$

with $\hat{\theta}_1 = 0.470$ (non-casualty) and $\hat{\theta}_2 = 5.049$ (injury). Here $x_1, x_2, x_3$ are
the indicator variables for road user class, $x_4, \ldots, x_9$ for age, $x_{10}$ for sex, and
$x_{11}, \ldots, x_{16}$ for the age by sex interaction term.

**Parameter interpretation.** A "degree of crash" less than $j$, for $j = 1, 2$,
means either non-casualty, $j = 1$, or non-casualty or injury, $j \leq 2$.

- For light truck driver, $e^{\hat{\beta}} = 0.860$. This means that the odds of having
  degree of crash $j$ or better are 14% less for a light truck driver than a car
  driver (the base level). Therefore the odds of less serious crash are smaller
  for a light truck driver than a car driver. This means light truck drivers are
  more likely to have serious crashes than car drivers.
- The $e^{\hat{\beta}}$ for bus/heavy truck drivers, and motorcycle drivers, are 0.743 and
  0.086 respectively. The odds of having a crash of degree $j$ or better, compared with car drivers, are even less for the former group, and markedly less
  for the latter group.
- Because of the age by sex interaction, the effects of age and sex must be
  evaluated together. The base level is 30–39 year-old males. Hence, for

Table 7.8. *Degree of crash, ordinal regression*

| Response variable | Degree of crash | | | | |
| Response distribution | Multinomial | | | | |
| Link | cumulative logit | | | | |

| Parameter | df | $\hat{\beta}$ | se | $e^{\hat{\beta}}$ | $\chi^2$ | p-value |
|---|---|---|---|---|---|---|
| Intercept 1 (non-casualty) | | 0.470 | 0.021 | 1.600 | 494.09 | <0.0001 |
| Intercept 2 (injury) | | 5.049 | 0.045 | 155.867 | 12518.49 | <0.0001 |
| Road user class | 3 | | | | 1897.94 | <0.0001 |
|   Car | 0 | 0.000 | 0.000 | 1.000 | | |
|   Light truck | 1 | −0.151 | 0.027 | 0.860 | 31.23 | <0.0001 |
|   Bus/heavy truck | 1 | −0.297 | 0.037 | 0.743 | 66.1 | <0.0001 |
|   Motorcycle | 1 | −2.449 | 0.057 | 0.086 | 1858.78 | <0.0001 |
| Age | 6 | | | | 116.23 | <0.0001 |
|   17–20 | 1 | 0.179 | 0.032 | 1.196 | 30.73 | <0.0001 |
|   21–25 | 1 | 0.112 | 0.032 | 1.119 | 12.23 | 0.0005 |
|   26–29 | 1 | 0.058 | 0.036 | 1.060 | 2.55 | 0.1106 |
|   30–39 | 0 | 0.000 | 0.000 | 1.000 | | |
|   40–49 | 1 | −0.055 | 0.03 | 0.946 | 3.37 | 0.0664 |
|   50–59 | 1 | −0.070 | 0.033 | 0.932 | 4.47 | 0.0345 |
|   $\geq 60$ | 1 | −0.151 | 0.860 | 1.163 | 19.09 | <0.0001 |
| Sex | 1 | | | | 26.45 | <0.0001 |
|   F | 1 | −0.172 | 0.033 | 0.842 | 26.45 | <0.0001 |
|   M | 0 | 0.000 | 0.000 | 1.000 | | |
| Age × Sex | 6 | | | | 24.35 | <0.0001 |
|   17–20, F | 1 | −0.129 | 0.053 | 0.879 | 5.90 | 0.0152 |
|   21–25, F | 1 | −0.118 | 0.052 | 0.889 | 5.11 | 0.0238 |
|   26–29, F | 1 | −0.042 | 0.06 | 0.959 | 0.49 | 0.4855 |
|   30–39, F | 0 | −0.000 | 0.000 | 1.000 | | |
|   40–49, F | 1 | −0.028 | 0.049 | 0.972 | 0.34 | 0.5600 |
|   50–59, F | 1 | −0.018 | 0.056 | 0.982 | 0.11 | 0.7412 |
|   $\geq 60$, F | 1 | 0.148 | 0.06 | 1.160 | 6.22 | 0.0127 |

example, the effect on the odds of having degree of crash $j$ or better, for 17–20 year-old females, compared with the base level, is $1.196 \times 0.842 \times 0.879 = 0.885$, an 11.5% decrease in the odds of degree of crash $j$ or better.

**SAS notes.** Ordinal regression is performed in `proc genmod` or `proc logistic`.

- In `proc genmod`, one specifies `dist=multinomial` (or `dist= mult`), which has as default the proportional odds or cumulative logit model (`link = cumlogit`). Other available links are `link=cumprobit` (cumulative probit) and `link=cumcll` (cumulative complementary log–log). Note that `dist=multinomial` implies an ordinal response.

- In `proc logistic`, logit is the default link. When the link is unspecified and there are two distinct levels in the response variable, it performs logistic regression; when there are more than two distinct levels, it performs ordinal regression (cumulative logistic model).
- `Proc logistic` produces output specific to ordinal regression, such as the score test for the proportional odds assumption (see below), which `proc genmod` does not produce.

**Test for the proportional odds assumption.** A strong assumption in the cumulative logistic model is that the $r - 1$ regression equations (7.6) are parallel, i.e. the coefficients $\beta$ are common across all levels of the response. Relaxing this assumption yields

$$\ln \frac{\tau_j}{1 - \tau_j} = \theta_j + x'\beta_j, \qquad j = 1, \ldots, r - 1 ,$$

where the $\beta_j$ specify regression coefficient vectors particular to each group $j$. The hypothesis of parallel lines (or proportional odds) is $\beta_j = \beta$ for $j = 1, \ldots, r - 1$. The model is estimated, using the restrictions $\beta_j = \beta$, to obtain $\tilde{\beta}$ and score $\dot{\ell}(\tilde{\beta})$. The score statistic (5.14) is $\chi^2_{p(r-2)}$ if the restrictions are true. Here $p$ is the number of elements in $\beta$.

If the proportional odds assumption is rejected, options are:

- Fit the partial proportional odds model, described below, which allows the coefficients of some or all of the explanatory variables to differ across levels. This is awkward to implement.
- Fit a nominal regression model described in Section 7.9. This ignores the ordinality of the response categories but is straightforward to implement.

**Degree of crash.** The score statistic for the proportional odds hypothesis is 374.13. If the proportional odds hypothesis is true, this is $\chi^2_\nu$ distributed, where $\nu = p(r - 2) = 16(3 - 2) = 16$. Hence the proportional odds assumption is strongly rejected ($p$-value $<0.0001$).

**The partial proportional odds model.** If the proportional odds assumption is rejected, the partial proportional odds model (Peterson and Harrell 1990) may be appropriate:

$$\ln \frac{\tau_j}{1 - \tau_j} = \theta_j + x'\beta + w'\alpha_j , \qquad j = 1, \ldots, r - 1 , \qquad (7.7)$$

where $x$ is the full set of explanatory variables, and $w$ is a subset of $x$ for which the proportional odds assumption is believed not to hold. The $\alpha_j$ are increments to the $\beta$ coefficients at level $j$. The model permits proportional odds for some variables and non-proportional odds for others. If $\alpha_j = 0$ for

$j = 1, \ldots, r - 1$ then (7.7) reduces to the proportional odds model (7.6). If the component in $\alpha_j$ corresponding to $x_k$ is zero for each $j$, then the effect of $x_k$ on all odds $j$ is the same, i.e. the proportional odds assumption holds for $x_k$.

**Degree of crash.** The model with non-proportional odds for age, sex, road user class and age by sex interaction is fitted – see code and output on page 171. For each explanatory variable, the corresponding component in $\alpha_j$ is tested for significance, or equivalently for the proportional odds assumption. The proportional odds assumption is rejected for age ($p$-value = 0.0296), sex ($p$-value $<$0.001) and road user class ($p$-value $<$0.001), but is not rejected for age by sex interaction ($p$-value = 0.3210). The final model has proportional odds for age by sex interaction, and non-proportional odds for age, sex and road user class. The model equations are

$$
\ln \frac{\hat{\pi}_j}{1 - \hat{\pi}_j} = \begin{cases} 0.469 - 0.140x_1 + \cdots + 0.141x_{16} & \text{for } j = 1 \text{ (non-casualty)} \\ 5.092 - 0.681x_1 + \cdots + 0.141x_{16} & \text{for } j = 2 \text{ (injury)} \end{cases}
$$
(7.8)

where the explanatory variables are defined as for the proportional odds model.

The effects of age, sex and road user class are different at the two levels. For example, for a light truck driver and non-casualty, $e^{\hat{\beta}} = e^{-0.140} = 0.869$; for a light truck driver and injury, $e^{\hat{\beta}} = e^{-0.681} = 0.506$. This means that, for light truck drivers, the odds of having a non-casualty crash are approximately 13% less than for car drivers. The odds of having an injury or non-casualty crash are about half that of car drivers. For 17–20 year old females and non-casualty, $e^{\hat{\beta}} = e^{0.187-0.176-0.133} = 0.885$, while for injury, $e^{\hat{\beta}} = e^{-0.175+0.280-0.133} = 0.972$. Thus the odds of having a non-casualty crash are about 11% less than for 30–39 year old males. The odds of having an injury or non-casualty crash are about 3% less than for 30–39 year old males.

The estimates $e^{\hat{\beta}}$ for non-casualty are similar to the corresponding estimates for the proportional odds model; for injury they are quite different.

**SAS notes.** Estimation for the partial proportional odds model is complex, requiring restructuring of the data. In addition, the final parameter estimates given in (7.8) are computed by hand from the output, as demonstrated on page 174.

## 7.9 Nominal responses

Regression models for nominal responses are known by many names in the statistical literature: nominal regression, polytomous regression, polychotomous regression and multinomial logistic regression. These all refer to the same model, described as follows.

Consider a nominal response $y$ with $r$ unordered categories. The multinomial probabilities are $\pi_j = P(y = j)$ with $\sum_j \pi_j = 1$. As before the $\pi_j$ are related to explanatory variables. The odds of $y$ being in category $j$ relative to the base response level are modeled, giving the nominal regression model:

$$\ln \frac{\pi_j}{\pi_r} = \theta_j + x'\beta_j, \qquad j = 1, \ldots, r-1, \tag{7.9}$$

where $r$ is the base response level. Hence

$$\pi_r = \frac{1}{1 + \sum_{k=1}^{r-1} e^{\theta_k + x'\beta_k}}, \qquad \pi_j = \pi_r e^{\theta_j + x'\beta_j}, \qquad j = 1, \ldots r - 1.$$

Thus for each category $j$, there is a model (7.9) for the odds of the response being in category $j$ relative to the base response level.

**Application to private health insurance.** In the Australian National Health Survey data described on page 17, the type of private health insurance is regarded as the response. The aim of the analysis is to explain the uptake of private health insurance as a function of demographic factors.

There are 13 851 cases available for analysis, i.e. with valid values on all of the variables considered. ("Not applicable," "don't know," "insufficient information to calculate" and "not stated" are regarded as missing values.) The response variable, type of private health insurance, has $r = 4$ levels, and the level "none" ($j = 4$) is chosen as the base response level. As employment status is recorded as "not applicable" for all respondents 65 years and over, these cases have been omitted from analysis and age groups in the analysis are 20–34, 35–49 and 50–64 years.

Using BIC, the explanatory variables age group, sex, employment status, SEIFA quintile and income group are selected – see code and output on page 175. The equation for $j = 1$ ("Hospital and ancillary") is

$$
\begin{aligned}
\ln \tfrac{\pi_1}{\pi_4} = \quad &-1.736 \\
&+0.618x_1 + 1.128x_2 & \text{(age)} \\
&-0.491x_3 & \text{(sex)} \\
&-1.356x_4 - 0.716x_5 & \text{(employment status)} \\
&+0.502x_6 + \cdots + 1.245x_9 & \text{(SEIFA quintile)} \\
&+0.350x_{10} + \cdots + 1.301x_{12} & \text{(income group)}
\end{aligned}
\tag{7.10}
$$

There are similar equations for $j = 2$ ("Hospital only") and $j = 3$ ("Ancillary only"). The base levels for the explanatory variables are: 20–34 years, female, employed, SEIFA quintile 1 and income less than $20 000.

The interpretation of the parameters in the fitted equation is as follows. The effect on the odds of a 35–49 year old taking out hospital and ancillary insurance, compared with no private health insurance, compared to a 20–34 year

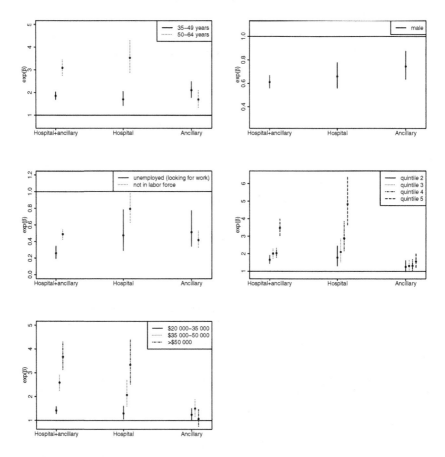

Fig. 7.4. Uptake of private health insurance: effects of age, sex, employment status, SEIFA quintile and income. Comparisons are with respect to base levels 20–34 years, female, employed, SEIFA quintile 1, income <$20 000

old, is $e^{0.618} = 1.856$. In other words, 35–49 year olds are 85.6% more likely than 20–34 year olds to take out hospital and ancillary.

The other parameters are explained similarly. It is easier to grasp the effect of the explanatory variables on the odds of uptake of private health insurance graphically, as in Figure 7.4. From these it is clear that:

- Higher income and socioeconomic status, and older age, are strongly associated with a greater degree of uptake of hospital and ancillary, and hospital only, private health cover.
- The uptake of ancillary only cover is only weakly affected by income and socioeconomic status.

- Males are less likely than females to take any type of private health cover.
- Unemployed people (looking for work or not in labor force) are less likely than employed people to have private health cover.

**SAS notes.** Nominal regression is implemented in `proc logistic`, with `link=glogit` (generalized logit).

## Exercises

7.1    For the degree of crash data, regard the event of interest as the occurrence of injury (fatal or non-fatal) in a crash. Develop a statistical model.

7.2    For the personal injury data, develop a statistical model for the occurrence of legal representation.

7.3    The RTA (Roads and Traffic Authority 2004) also publish driver crash statistics by age, sex and blood alcohol concentration. This data set is provided on the companion website. Develop

(a)  an ordinal regression model; and

(b)  a nominal regression model

for degree of crash.

7.4    In the Enterprise Miner data set, develop a statistical model for the occurrence of a claim.

# 8

# Continuous responses

---

Continuous responses of interest to insurers include claim size and time between the reporting of a claim and settlement. Continuous insurance variables are usually non-negative and skewed to the right. Options for modeling these variables are:

- Use a transformation to normality, and then employ the normal linear model on the transformed response. Thus $g(y) \sim N(\mu, \sigma^2)$ where $g$ is the transformation and $\mu = x'\beta$. The normal model is dealt with in Chapter 4.
- Generalized linear modeling, using a response distribution that is concentrated on the non-negative axis. Examples are the gamma and inverse Gaussian distributions. This is the subject of the current chapter.

 *tweedie*

## 8.1 Gamma regression

A gamma GLM is of the form

$$y \sim G(\mu, \nu) , \qquad g(\mu) = x'\beta . \tag{8.1}$$

The canonical link for the gamma distribution is the inverse function. Since parameters from a model with inverse link are difficult to interpret, the log link is usually regarded as more useful.

**Vehicle insurance claims.** Consider the claim sizes for the $n = 4624$ policies with a claim. The claim size distribution is graphed in the right panel of Figure 2.7, together with the fitted gamma density. The figure suggests the gamma does not fit well. However the fit ignores the effects of explanatory variables.

Fitting a gamma response leads to a model with the significant predictors age band, area of residence and gender of driver, vehicle body type and age by gender interaction – see code and output on page 178. The deviance for the fitted model is 5517.3 on 4595 degrees of freedom, indicating a lack of fit. This lack of fit is confirmed by examining model diagnostics. An inverse Gaussian regression is examined in the next section.

120

Table 8.1. *Gamma fit for personal injury claims*

| Response variable | Claim size |
| Response distribution | Gamma |
| Link | log |
| Deviance | 25 436.2 |
| Degrees of freedom | 22 033 |

| Parameter | df | $\hat{\beta}$ | se | $e^{\hat{\beta}}$ | $\chi^2$ | p-value |
|---|---|---|---|---|---|---|
| Intercept | 1 | 8.212 | 0.022 | 3684.905 | 139276 | <0.0001 |
| Operational time | 1 | 0.038 | 0.000 | 1.039 | 7991.3 | <0.0001 |
| Legal representation | 1 | | | | | <0.0001 |
| No | 0 | 0.000 | 0.000 | 1.000 | - | - |
| Yes | 1 | 0.467 | 0.028 | 1.595 | 279.36 | <0.0001 |
| Operational time × legal representation | 1 | −0.005 | 0.001 | 0.995 | 88.24 | <0.0001 |
| Scale ($\hat{\nu}$) | | 1.001 | 0.008 | | | |

**Personal injury claims.** In Section 1.3, it is demonstrated that the relationship between log claim size and operational time is roughly linear. In Figure 1.3, the association of legal representation with claim size is shown. This suggests a model for claim size with a log link, and operational time and legal representation as explanatory variables. As claim size is continuous and right-skewed, the gamma is a reasonable candidate response distribution.

Figure 1.3 suggests that the slope of claim size with operational time depends on legal representation. The first model fitted therefore includes an operational time by legal representation interaction term:

$$y \sim G(\mu, \nu) , \qquad \ln \mu = \beta_0 + \beta_1 x_1 + \beta_2 x_2 + \beta_3 x_1 x_2 ,$$

where $x_1$ is operational time, $x_2$ is an indicator variable for legal representation, and $x_1 x_2$ is the interaction. Estimates are displayed in Table 8.1, and fitted values are graphed in Figure 8.1 – see code and output on page 178.

It is clear from Figure 8.1 that the claims with low operational times, i.e. those settling quickly, have average claim sizes lower than predicted by the model. This systematic departure from the model is detected by model diagnostics, as shown in the plot of deviance residuals versus operational time in Figure 8.2. For cases without legal representation, there is a systematic dropoff in the size of deviance residuals for operational time close to zero.

To explain the dropoff, a model which allows a different slope for fast-settling claims is fitted. This is achieved by introducing an indicator variable $x_3$

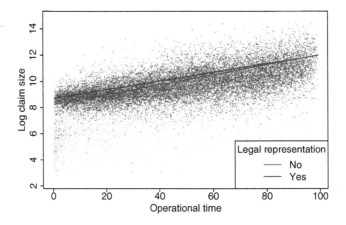

Fig. 8.1. Gamma fit for personal injury claim sizes

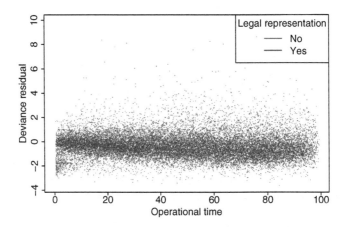

Fig. 8.2. Deviance residuals versus operational time with spline curve

for operational time under 5%, which interacts with the other variables operational time $x_1$ and legal representation $x_2$. The two- and three-way interaction terms permit different slopes for legal representation yes and no; and for operational time under and over 5%. The fitted values are graphed in Figure 8.3. These fit the data more closely at the lower end of operational time and for those claims without legal representation – see code on page 179.

**Runoff triangle.** The top triangle of Table 8.2 contains the totals of insurance payments classified with respect to accident years $i$ and development years $j$.

Table 8.2. *Actual and predicted claims payments*

| Accident year $i$ | Development year $j$ ← # of years until development | | | | | | | | | |
| | 0 | 1 | 2 | 3 | 4 | 5 | 6 | 7 | 8 | 9 |
| 1 | 5012 | 3257 | 2638 | 898 | 1734 | 2642 | 1828 | 599 | 54 | 172 |
| 2 | 106 | 4179 | 1111 | 5270 | 3116 | 1817 | -103 | 673 | 535 | 141 |
| 3 | 3410 | 5582 | 4881 | 2268 | 2594 | 3479 | 649 | 603 | 387 | 188 |
| 4 | 5655 | 5900 | 4211 | 5500 | 2159 | 2658 | 984 | 903 | 486 | 236 |
| 5 | 1092 | 8473 | 6271 | 6333 | 3786 | 225 | 914 | 766 | 412 | 200 |
| 6 | 1513 | 4932 | 5257 | 1233 | 2917 | 1711 | 660 | 553 | 298 | 145 |
| 7 | 557 | 3463 | 6926 | 1368 | 1885 | 1420 | 548 | 459 | 247 | 120 |
| 8 | 1351 | 5596 | 6165 | 3171 | 2691 | 2027 | 782 | 655 | 352 | 171 |
| 9 | 3133 | 2262 | 4480 | 2904 | 2464 | 1857 | 716 | 600 | 323 | 157 |
| 10 | 2063 | 4380 | 4402 | 2854 | 2422 | 1825 | 704 | 590 | 317 | 154 |

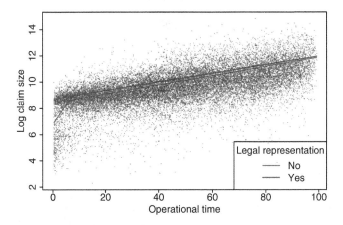

Fig. 8.3. Gamma fit for personal injury claim sizes, with adjustment for fast settlement

Lower shaded triangle entries in the are predictions discussed shortly. There are ten years of observations. England and Verrall (2002) use Poisson regression to analyze these payments. Gamma regression is considered here, since the totals $y_{ij}$ are not strictly counts but continuous quantities. Note the unusual negative amount in accident year two and development year six.

The proposed model is

$$y_{ij} \sim \mathrm{G}(\mu_{ij}, \nu) \,, \quad \ln \mu_{ij} = \alpha + \gamma_i + \delta_j \,, \quad i = 1, \ldots, n, \ j = 0, \ldots, n-1 \,.$$

The accident year $i = 1$, development year $j = 0$ combination serves as the base case. The negative value was replaced by a small positive value in the * replacing neg. values with pos. values. computation. Results are displayed in Table 8.3, and estimates and associated confidence intervals are displayed in Figure 8.4 – see code and output on page 180. The deviance of 59.7 on 36 degrees of freedom indicates lack of fit.

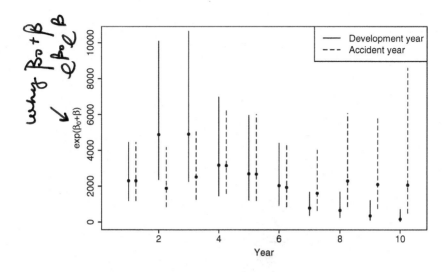

*(handwritten margin note: why $\beta_0 + \beta$ $e^{\beta_0 + \beta}$ ← $\exp(\beta_0+\beta)$)*

Fig. 8.4. Confidence intervals for accident and development year means

*(handwritten margin note: how is this p-value being generated ✱)*

The model fails to converge with an inverse Gaussian response distribution. Hence the gamma model, although not entirely satisfactory, is a more viable model.

Individual accident year effects are not significant and the hypothesis of no difference between all the accident year effects has a $p$-value of 0.95. Figure 8.4 indicates that confidence intervals widen with accident year. This reflects the decreasing number of cases for the more recent accident years: only one in the case of the final accident year.

Development year effects are generally significant. The overall hypothesis of no development year effect has a $p$-value of 0.0005. The width of the individual confidence intervals displayed in Figure 8.4 generally decrease with years. Hence there is apparent higher precision despite there being fewer observations. This is a result of the gamma variance function $V(\mu) = \mu^2$: a lower mean implies a lower response variability. Thus the lower response variability more than offsets the increased estimation error.

The lower triangle of Table 8.2 indicates the predicted means derived from the gamma fit. Totalling these numbers yields the total outstanding incurred claims liability. Standard errors and confidence intervals on this total outstanding liability are derived using the covariance matrix of the accident and development year effect estimates. As discussed in Section 5.6, the confidence interval factors in parameter estimation variability and is on the expected total outstanding liability rather than the actual outcome.

*(margin handwritten note: ~ ? continuous not better as a bit \* )*

Table 8.3. *Gamma fit for runoff triangle claims payments*

| Response variable | Claims payment |
|---|---|
| Response distribution | Gamma |
| Link | log |
| Deviance | 59.7 |
| Degrees of freedom | 36 |

| Parameter | df | $\hat{\beta}$ | se | $e^{\hat{\beta}}$ | $\chi^2$ | $p$-value |
|---|---|---|---|---|---|---|
| Intercept | 1 | 7.741 | 0.337 | 2299.852 | 526.72 | <0.0001 |
| Accident year | 9 | | | | | 0.9513 |
| 1 | 0 | 0.000 | 0.000 | 1.000 | - | - |
| 2 | 1 | −0.200 | 0.391 | 0.819 | 0.26 | 0.6096 |
| 3 | 1 | 0.089 | 0.362 | 1.094 | 0.06 | 0.8052 |
| 4 | 1 | 0.317 | 0.377 | 1.373 | 0.71 | 0.4001 |
| 5 | 1 | 0.153 | 0.423 | 1.165 | 0.13 | 0.718 |
| 6 | 1 | −0.173 | 0.440 | 0.841 | 0.15 | 0.6946 |
| 7 | 1 | −0.359 | 0.485 | 0.698 | 0.55 | 0.4585 |
| 8 | 1 | −0.004 | 0.524 | 0.997 | 0.00 | 0.9947 |
| 9 | 1 | −0.091 | 0.600 | 0.913 | 0.02 | 0.8791 |
| 10 | 1 | −0.109 | 0.803 | 0.897 | 0.02 | 0.8923 |
| Development year | 9 | | | | | 0.0005 |
| 0 | 0 | 0.000 | 0.000 | 1.000 | - | - |
| 1 | 1 | 0.753 | 0.361 | 2.123 | 4.35 | 0.0371 |
| 2 | 1 | 0.758 | 0.388 | 2.134 | 3.83 | 0.0505 |
| 3 | 1 | 0.325 | 0.401 | 1.383 | 0.66 | 0.4176 |
| 4 | 1 | 0.160 | 0.412 | 1.174 | 0.15 | 0.6968 |
| 5 | 1 | −0.123 | 0.427 | 0.884 | 0.08 | 0.7739 |
| 6 | 1 | −1.075 | 0.460 | 0.341 | 5.47 | 0.0193 |
| 7 | 1 | −1.252 | 0.517 | 0.286 | 5.86 | 0.0155 |
| 8 | 1 | −1.872 | 0.645 | 0.154 | 8.43 | 0.0037 |
| 9 | 1 | −2.593 | 0.803 | 0.075 | 10.43 | 0.0012 |
| Scale $(\hat{\nu})$ | 1 | 1.884 | 0.332 | | | |

## 8.2 Inverse Gaussian regression

The inverse Gaussian model states

$$y \sim \text{IG}\left(\mu, \sigma^2\right) , \qquad g(\mu) = x'\beta .$$

The canonical link is $g\left(\mu\right) = \mu^{-2}$. However the log link is usually preferred.

**Vehicle insurance claims.** Inverse Gaussian fit results are displayed in Table 8.4 – see code and output on page 181. The deviance of 4624 on 4612 degrees of freedom suggests a reasonable fit but further examination of model

Table 8.4. *Inverse Gaussian fit for vehicle claim sizes*

| Response variable | Claim size |
| --- | --- |
| Response distribution | Inverse Gaussian |
| Link | log |
| Deviance | 4624.0 |
| Degrees of freedom | 4612 |

| Parameter | df | $\hat{\beta}$ | se | $e^{\hat{\beta}}$ | $\chi^2$ | $p$-value |
| --- | --- | --- | --- | --- | --- | --- |
| Intercept | 1 | 7.683 | 0.073 | 2171.123 | 10946.8 | <0.0001 |
| Driver's age | 5 | | | | | 0.0041 |
| 1 | 1 | 0.251 | 0.098 | 1.285 | 6.62 | 0.0101 |
| 2 | 1 | 0.093 | 0.075 | 1.097 | 1.53 | 0.2154 |
| 3 | 0 | 0.000 | 0.000 | 1.000 | - | - |
| 4 | 1 | −0.005 | 0.070 | 0.995 | 0.01 | 0.9394 |
| 5 | 1 | −0.121 | 0.080 | 0.886 | 2.31 | 0.1285 |
| 6 | 1 | −0.068 | 0.098 | 0.935 | 0.48 | 0.4903 |
| Gender | 1 | | | | | 0.0022 |
| F | 1 | −0.153 | 0.051 | 0.858 | 9.14 | 0.0025 |
| M | 0 | 0.000 | 0.000 | 1.000 | - | - |
| Area | 5 | | | | | 0.0105 |
| A | 1 | −0.073 | 0.066 | 0.930 | 1.21 | 0.2718 |
| B | 1 | −0.103 | 0.069 | 0.902 | 2.24 | 0.1341 |
| C | 0 | 0.000 | 0.000 | 1.000 | - | - |
| D | 1 | −0.098 | 0.085 | 0.907 | 1.33 | 0.2488 |
| E | 1 | 0.070 | 0.099 | 1.072 | 0.49 | 0.4831 |
| F | 1 | 0.283 | 0.126 | 1.326 | 5.07 | 0.0244 |
| Scale ($\hat{\sigma}$) | 1 | 0.037 | 0.000 | | | |

diagnostics is warranted. Age, gender and area are significant but there are no significant interactions between these variables. The fitted model is

$$\hat{\mu} = e^{7.68+0.25x_1+\cdots-0.07x_5-0.15x_6-0.07x_7+\cdots+0.28x_{11}}, \qquad (8.2)$$

where $x_1, \ldots, x_5$ are the indicator variables for age band, $x_6$ indicates females and $x_7, \ldots, x_{11}$ are indicators for area.

The estimated area effects $e^{\hat{\beta}}$ and associated 95% confidence intervals are plotted in Figure 8.5. Area is significant ($p$-value 0.015), yet F is the only area significantly different from the base level C as confirmed with the Wald tests in Table 8.2. This suggests two area groups: F versus all other areas. However, the overlapping confidence intervals for the effects of E and F indicate that these are not significantly different. A Wald test of the hypothesis that the effects of areas E and F are equal, is couched in the form $C\beta = 0$ (Section 4.15

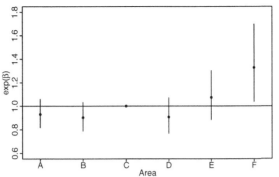

*95% Ci*
*= estimate*
*± 2 se*

Fig. 8.5. Area effects and 95% confidence intervals for vehicle claim sizes

*← what is the base class*
*for numeric variables?*

and Section 5.8). It yields a chi-square test statistic value of 2.11. The *p*-value is 0.1462, confirming that E and F are not significantly different. Hence the suggested grouping above, which is based purely on *p*-values, is inappropriate. Levels are grouped if there is an a priori basis for the grouping, such as geographical or demographic proximity in this example.

The estimated expected claim size for a male in the base age band 3, living in the base area C is $e^{7.68} = 2171$. The estimated effect associated with some other group is derived by multiplying this base estimate by $\exp(\hat{\beta}_j)$. For example, the estimated expected claim size of drivers in age band 1 multiplies the base by $e^{0.25} = 1.285$, indicating a 28.5% increase over a driver in age band 3. Similarly a policy with driver's age band 1, female and area A has expected claim size $2\,171 \times 1.285 \times 0.858 \times 0.930 = 2226$.

Both the gamma and inverse Gaussian models for claim size are conditional on the event that there is a claim. For example the estimated expected claim size of 2226 for policies with age band 1, female and area A applies to policies which make a claim. If claim size is set to zero for policies which did not have a claim, then the expected claim size for all policies in the above group is substantially lower than 2226. Sections 8.3, Section 10.4 and Section 10.5 deal with models for claim size which do not condition on there being a claim.

## 8.3 Tweedie regression

Many policies permit multiple claims. Write *c* as the number of claims on a policy and $z_1, \ldots, z_c$ as the individual claim sizes. Then the total claim size is $y = z_1 + \cdots + z_c$, with $y = 0$ if $c = 0$.

If $c$ is Poisson and the $z_j$ are independent gamma random variables then $y$ has the Tweedie distribution. This distribution has a non-zero probability at $y = 0$ equal to the Poisson probability of no claims. The rest of the distribution is similar to the gamma. The Tweedie distribution is a member of the exponential family and $\text{Var}(y) = \phi \mu^p$ where $1 < p < 2$. It is similar to the zero-adjusted inverse Gaussian distribution, discussed in Section 10.4. Jørgensen and de Souza (1994) and Smyth and Jørgensen (2002) have fitted Tweedie models to insurance claims data.

### Exercises

8.1    In the Enterprise Miner data set, develop a statistical model for claim size, amongst policies which had a claim.

8.2    In the personal injury data set, what is the impact of the level of injury on the dollar value of claims?

# 9

# Correlated data

The models of the previous chapters assume observed responses are independent. However many studies yield correlated observations. Correlation results from the sampling design or the way data are collected. Here are some practical situations leading to correlated responses.

- Claims experience is often studied on the same policy over successive time periods. For example claims on a given policy may be studied for each of five years. Claims for a given policyholder in successive years are correlated. A particularly bad driver will have higher than average claims in successive years, and conversely for a good driver. Here the average is calculated given the other rating variables. Responses on the same individual or policy at different points in time will tend to be more alike than responses on different individuals or policies with the same characteristics.

- When writing crop insurance policies in a given state, the state may be divided into geographical regions. Each region is likely to experience roughly the same weather conditions and hence different policies in the same region are likely to have a similar claims experience.

- Industries and companies are often classified into groups with a hierarchical structure. For example, a supermarket is a subdivision of "Supermarket and Grocery Stores" which in turn is a subdivision of "Food Retailing." Companies in the same industry group are more similar than a group of randomly selected companies.

- In a demographic study, a random sample of households is drawn and all the members of each household are surveyed. Members of the same household will tend to be more similar than randomly selected members of the population.

The above are examples of clustered or hierarchical data. Clusters are individuals or policies, geographical regions, divisions or subdivisions, and households. There is correlation between members of a cluster. Cases in different clusters are independent. Longitudinal data is a special case of correlated

Table 9.1. *Structure of vehicle insurance longitudinal data*

| Policy ID | Vehicle body type | Area | Driver's age | Vehicle value | Period | Number of claims |
|---|---|---|---|---|---|---|
| 1 | HBACK | C | 2 | 1 | 1 | 0 |
| 1 | HBACK | C | 2 | 1 | 2 | 0 |
| 1 | HBACK | C | 2 | 1 | 3 | 0 |
| 2 | SEDAN | A | 4 | 1 | 1 | 0 |
| 2 | SEDAN | A | 4 | 1 | 2 | 0 |
| 2 | SEDAN | A | 4 | 1 | 3 | 0 |
| 3 | UTE | E | 2 | 2 | 1 | 0 |
| 3 | UTE | E | 2 | 2 | 2 | 2 |
| 3 | UTE | E | 2 | 2 | 3 | 1 |
| ⋮ | ⋮ | ⋮ | ⋮ | ⋮ | ⋮ | ⋮ |
| 40 000 | SEDAN | A | 1 | 1 | 1 | 0 |
| 40 000 | SEDAN | A | 1 | 1 | 2 | 0 |
| 40 000 | SEDAN | A | 1 | 1 | 3 | 0 |

data, where a cluster is an individual (e.g. a policy or person) and the observations are taken over time. Ignoring the correlation can lead to erroneous conclusions (Goldstein 2003).

**Structure of clustered data.** With clustered data the following notation is useful. Suppose $m$ clusters labeled $c = 1, \ldots, m$, each consisting of $n_c$ correlated observations. The total sample size is $n = n_1 + \ldots + n_m$. The responses for cluster $c$ form a vector $y_c$ of length $n_c$. The response vector for the whole sample is the stack of these $y_c$ vectors. Further $X_c$ is the design matrix for cluster $c$ with $n_c$ rows. The $X$ matrix for the whole sample consists of the $m$ stacked $X_c$ matrices.

**Vehicle insurance.** Owing to the commercial sensitivity of much insurance data, a longitudinal data set is not available to illustrate methods. Accordingly methods are illustrated on a simulated longitudinal claims data set, which is based on the characteristics of the vehicle insurance data. The simulated data set contains counts of claims for 40 000 policies, for three periods (years). The risk factors are driver's age and vehicle value. Each policy is regarded as a cluster, and hence $m = 40\ 000$, $n_c = 3$ for $c = 1, \ldots, m$, and $n = 3 \times 40\ 000 = 120\ 000$. The structure of the longitudinal data set is shown in Table 9.1, which lists the first three and last policies. Each policy has three lines of data, one for each time period. The first six columns serve to define the $X$ matrix, and the rightmost column is the response vector $y$.

## 9.1 Random effects

An "effect" is a model coefficient. Random effects are coefficients which are random variables. Random effects are used to model the correlation between observed responses in a cluster. The same outcome of the random variable manifests itself in all observations in the same cluster. Random effect outcomes are different for different clusters. Under repeated sampling the outcomes of all the random effects change. However all responses in the same cluster receive the same outcome.

The $\beta$ coefficients of the previous chapters are fixed effects. They remain constant under hypothetical repeated sampling. For example, the effect of driver's age on car insurance claims is typically regarded as a fixed effect. The effect is assumed to be the same if, hypothetically, a new set of claims data is collected.

To illustrate random effects, consider a study of household insurance claims over a five-year period. Claims are observed on each policy in each of five years. Other demographics such as the geographical area or suburb are also recorded. The policies are clusters since claims on a given policy, in successive years, are correlated. Now consider a regression model with area and policy as explanatory variables. Area is regarded as a fixed effect in that under hypothetical repeated sampling, area effects are expected to be the same: interest centers on the effect of the given suburbs. The policy effect, however, is random in that under hypothetical repeated sampling, different policies are enacted and there is no interest in any particular policy *per se*. Both the fixed and random effects influence the outcome.

**Random intercept model.** The simplest random effects model is the "random intercept" model

$$g(\mu) = \alpha + x'\beta , \qquad \alpha \sim \mathrm{N}(0, \nu^2) . \qquad (9.1)$$

Here $\alpha$ is the random intercept term. The random variable $\alpha$ has the same outcome for all cases in a cluster, but different outcomes across clusters. The $\beta$ effect is constant both within and across clusters. As before, $g(\mu)$ models the mean of the exponential family response.

In (9.1) the explanatory variables $x$ contain the constant term 1, and $\beta$ contains the corresponding intercept parameter $\beta_0$. Hence the intercept for a cluster is $\alpha + \beta_0$. The effect of the cluster-specific draw $\alpha$ is to induce correlation between all responses within a cluster, while there is no correlation between clusters. Given $\alpha$, observations in a cluster are independent.

In terms of the cluster notation, model (9.1) is written as

$$g(\mu_{ic}) = \alpha_c + x'_{ic}\beta , \qquad \alpha_c \sim \mathrm{N}(0, \nu^2) , \qquad (9.2)$$

where $c$ denotes cluster and $i$ a case within the cluster. Thus case $i$ in cluster $c$ receives the random intercept applicable to cluster $c$. To this cluster-specific random effect is added the case-specific effect $x'_{ic}\beta$, where $\beta$ is common to all clusters.

**Credibility theory or experience rating.** Random intercept models are closely related to the credibility models of insurance. Suppose individual $c$ enacts an insurance policy over each of the years $i = 1, 2, \ldots$. In terms of (9.2), $\alpha_c$ is the individual or policy effect. In the first year $i = 1$ there is no claims experience for the individual $c$ and hence the price of insurance is based on rating variables contained in $x$ such as age, sex, suburb of residence and so on. In year $i = 2$ the claim for the first year is known – there is information on $\alpha_c$. As years pass, experience increases and information about $\alpha_c$ increases. Increasing weight is placed on the claims history of the policy as opposed to the general rating variables. The optimal relative weights are called the credibility weights and credibility formulas are sequential updating schemes for premiums as more information about a particular risk emerges.

In the GLM context, the experience is typically regarded as given and there is no special significance accorded to sequential updating. Of course fitting a random intercept model on say three years' data will lead to different estimates from the same analysis using four years' data. Estimated premiums $\hat{\mu}_{ic}$ derived from a fit of $g(\mu_{ic}) = \alpha_c + x'_{ic}\beta$ implicitly factor in the relative precisions of the estimates of $\alpha_c$ and $\beta$, that is the precision associated with the individual effect and the "group" effect.

**General random effects model.** Coefficients of explanatory variables may be regarded as random. If a coefficient is a random effect, then it varies from cluster to cluster, again inducing within-cluster homogeneity or correlation. To facilitate the discussion write $z$ as those explanatory variables with random coefficients and $\gamma$ as the corresponding parameter vector. The vectors $z$ and $\gamma$ have the same dimension. To ensure $\gamma$ has zero mean, write the model as

$$g(\mu) = x'\beta + z'\gamma , \qquad \gamma \sim N(0, G) , \qquad (9.3)$$

where $z$ is repeated in $x$ and $G$ is the covariance matrix of $\gamma$. To illustrate, suppose $x$ has a single explanatory variable: $x = (1, x_1)'$. If the coefficient of $x_1$ is a random effect with mean $\beta_1$, then

$$g(\mu) = \beta_0 + \beta_1 x_1 + \gamma x_1 , \qquad \gamma \sim N(0, \nu^2) ,$$

where $\beta_1 + \gamma$ is the random effect. In this case $x_1$ is retained in $x$ and $z$ can be thought of as a copy of the subset of $x$ which has random coefficients. The random intercept model is the special case where $z = 1$.

**Maximum likelihood estimation.** The treatment and estimation of the random coefficients model depends on the distribution of the response $y$, the link $g$ and the distribution of random effects. The simplest and classical situation is a normal response, identity link and normal random effects. This is an example of a fully specified model. Fully specified models – those that spell out both distributions – do lead to estimation intricacies.

For simplicity consider the random intercepts model (9.2). The extension to the more general random effects model (9.3) is straightforward. The conditional density for observation $i$ in cluster $c$, given $\alpha_c$, is $f(y_{ic}|\alpha_c)$. Given $\alpha_c$, observations in cluster $c$ are independent and the joint density of all observations in cluster $c$ is $\prod_i f(y_{ic}|\alpha_c)$. Integrating this density with respect to the density $f(\alpha_c)$ of $\alpha_c$ yields the joint distribution of cluster $c$ responses

$$\int f(\alpha_c) \prod_i f(y_{ic}|\alpha_c) \, d\alpha_c \, .$$

Usually $f(\alpha_c)$ is the $N(0, \nu^2)$ distribution. Clusters are independent and hence the overall joint density is the product over $c$ of the cluster densities displayed above.

The joint density depends on the unknown parameters, $\beta$, $\phi$ and $\nu^2$. The joint density, regarded as a function of the parameters and conditional on the given observations, is the likelihood. Generally this likelihood cannot be expressed in closed form and MLEs of the unknown parameters are computed iteratively, using numerical integration.

**Estimation of cluster-specific effects.** Estimates of $\beta$, $\phi$ and $\nu^2$ can be used to compute estimates of the $\alpha_c$ outcomes. Note that these are not model parameters, but random outcomes from the random effects distribution, so usual maximum likelihood estimation is not used. The distribution of $y$ given $\alpha_c$ is $f(y|\alpha_c)$. Using Bayes' theorem from elementary probability,

$$f(\alpha_c|y) = \frac{f(y|\alpha_c)f(\alpha_c)}{f(y)} \, . \tag{9.4}$$

The above is called the "post hoc" distribution of $\alpha_c$. Using the parameter estimates $\hat{\beta}$, $\hat{\phi}$ and $\hat{\nu}^2$ in the right hand side allows one to evaluate the expression. The estimate of $\alpha_c$ is taken as that value which maximizes (9.4), i.e. the mode of $f(\alpha_c|y)$. The resultant $\hat{\alpha}_c$, $c = 1, \ldots, m$, are called the "empirical Bayes estimates." Computation of the estimates is again achieved using numerical methods.

In the case where the response is say a claim size, the $\hat{\alpha}_c$ are the "experience" portions of the premium. As more data on a given risk is collected the experience portion of the premium will become more certain.

**Normal response distribution: mixed models.** For this model $g(\mu) = \mu$ and the response distribution is normal. This implies

$$y = x'\beta + z'\gamma + \epsilon, \qquad \gamma \sim N(0, G), \qquad \epsilon \sim N(0, \sigma^2), \qquad (9.5)$$

where the $\gamma$ and $\epsilon$ are independent. Here the draws of $\epsilon$ are different for each case, while draws of $\gamma$ are different across clusters. Model (9.5) is called the "mixed model." The likelihood of (9.5) follows from the multivariate normal distribution, and MLEs are readily computed. However the normal response distribution is typically inappropriate in insurance applications.

**Generalized linear mixed models (GLMMs).** This model assumes the response $y$ arises from a exponential family distribution with mean $\mu$, where (9.3) applies. This fully specifies a distribution, albeit complicated. The likelihood can be maximized with respect to $\beta$, $\phi$ and $G$, as discussed above in relation to the random intercept model. This involves burdensome numerical integration.

**SAS notes.**

- Mixed models (9.5) are implemented in `proc mixed`. The explanatory variables associated with random effects are specified in the `random` statement, together with cluster information.
- The GLMM is estimated using either `proc nlmixed` or `proc glimmix`. The latter procedure is, at time of writing, still experimental. The `glimmix` syntax is similar to that of `proc mixed` and `proc genmod`. However, in its current state it is limited in terms of memory and is not able to perform the analysis below, which is performed using `proc nlmixed`. Model specification in `nlmixed` is intricate compared with `genmod`, `mixed` and `glimmix`. For all three of these procedures, correlated data is entered in the same structure as in the mathematical model, i.e. a line or case corresponds to one observation within a cluster. A cluster identification variable is required. This is typically policy number or customer number.

**Vehicle insurance claims.** For the simulated three-year data set introduced on page 130, suppose the occurrence of a claim to be the response of interest. The random intercept model is:

$$y \sim B(1, \pi), \qquad \ln \frac{\pi}{1 - \pi} = \alpha + x'\beta, \qquad \alpha \sim N(0, \nu^2).$$

Parameter estimates are given in Table 9.2 – see code and output on page 183. The estimate of the variance of the random intercept is $\hat{\nu}^2 = 3.82$ ($p$-value $<0.0001$), indicating that the correlation of the occurrence of a claim over time

Table 9.2. *Logistic regression GLMM for vehicle insurance claims*

| Response variable | Occurrence of a claim |
|---|---|
| Response distribution | Bernoulli |
| Correlation structure | random intercept |
| Link | logit |

| Parameter | $\hat{\beta}$ | se | $e^{\hat{\beta}}$ | t | p-value |
|---|---|---|---|---|---|
| Intercept | −2.654 | 0.039 | 0.070 | −68.79 | <0.0001 |
| | | | | | |
| Driver's age | | | | | |
| 1 | 0.274 | 0.059 | 1.315 | 4.65 | <0.0001 |
| 2 | 0.008 | 0.047 | 1.009 | 0.18 | 0.8560 |
| 3 | 0.000 | . | 1.000 | . | . |
| 4 | −0.053 | 0.045 | 0.948 | −1.19 | 0.2331 |
| 5 | −0.275 | 0.051 | 0.760 | −5.41 | <0.0001 |
| 6 | −0.225 | 0.059 | 0.799 | −3.78 | 0.0002 |
| | | | | | |
| Vehicle value ($000's) | | | | | |
| <25 | 0.000 | . | 1.000 | . | . |
| 25–50 | 0.236 | 0.040 | 1.266 | 5.88 | <0.0001 |
| 50–75 | 0.087 | 0.114 | 1.091 | 0.77 | 0.4438 |
| 75–100 | −0.886 | 0.453 | 0.413 | −1.95 | 0.0507 |
| 100–125 | −0.613 | 0.696 | 0.542 | −0.88 | 0.3784 |
| >125 | −1.314 | 0.775 | 0.269 | −1.69 | 0.0902 |
| | | | | | |
| Time period | | | | | |
| 1 | −0.302 | 0.025 | 0.740 | −12.25 | <0.0001 |
| 2 | −0.172 | 0.024 | 0.842 | −7.08 | <0.0001 |
| 3 | 0.000 | . | 1.000 | . | . |
| | | | | | |
| Variance of random intercept | | | | | |
| $\hat{\nu}^2$ | 3.818 | 0.082 | | 46.52 | <0.0001 |

is significant. A $\hat{\nu}^2$ not significantly different from zero suggests the random effect has zero variance, implying no within-cluster correlation.

In practice some policies come into force after the start, and others terminate before the end of the three-year observation period. This is catered for by incorporating exposure into the model.

**Other random effects distributions.** The assumption of normal random effects in mixed models and GLMMs is adequate for most applications. However there are some situations where the assumption is inappropriate. Lee and Nelder (1996) and Lee and Nelder (2001) have developed hierarchical generalized linear models (HGLMs), which are GLMMs with random effects having non–normal distributions. HGLMs are implemented in Genstat. They are not covered in this text.

## 9.2 Specification of within-cluster correlation

In many situations it is convenient to spell out the within-cluster correlations explicitly, but to stay silent about the model generating the correlations. This constitutes a partial description of the distribution of the responses and hence one speaks of a "partially specified" or marginal model since although the distributions of the individual responses (the marginal distributions) are specified, the joint distribution of all the responses together is unspecified.

For partially specified models, estimation is organized so as to use only the specified parts of the model including the within-cluster correlations. The coefficients $\beta$ in the marginal model have the same interpretation as $\beta$ in models with independent observations.

Suppose responses in cluster $c$ have covariance matrix $\Sigma_c$. Then the covariance matrix of the entire sample is

$$\Sigma = \begin{pmatrix} \Sigma_1 & 0 & \cdots & 0 \\ 0 & \Sigma_2 & \cdots & 0 \\ \vdots & \vdots & \ddots & \vdots \\ 0 & 0 & \cdots & \Sigma_m \end{pmatrix},$$

where 0 denotes a block of zeros, of appropriate dimension. The off-diagonal blocks are zero since response outcomes in different clusters are uncorrelated. Cluster-specific covariance matrices are of the form $\Sigma_c = \phi S_c R_c S_c$ where $S_c$ is a diagonal matrix with diagonal entries $\sqrt{V(\mu_{ic})}$ as implied by the response distribution, and $R_c$ is a correlation matrix.

Each correlation matrix $R_c$ satisfies the usual conditions pertaining to correlation matrices, for example symmetry and diagonal entries of one. Further structure is imposed depending on the situation.

**Compound symmetric correlation.** Here the correlation between any two outcomes within a cluster is $\rho$, implying

$$R_c = \begin{pmatrix} 1 & \rho & \cdots & \rho \\ \rho & 1 & \cdots & \rho \\ \vdots & \vdots & \ddots & \vdots \\ \rho & \rho & \cdots & 1 \end{pmatrix}. \tag{9.6}$$

This correlation structure is also referred to as "exchangeable."

**Serial correlation.** Serial correlation refers to correlation between near terms in measurements made over time. Methods developed to deal with serial correlation can also be used in non-time series settings. The "AR(1)" correlation structure assumes the within-cluster correlations decay geometrically with the separation. For example, for cluster size $n_c = 4$:

$$R_c = \begin{pmatrix} 1 & \rho & \rho^2 & \rho^3 \\ \rho & 1 & \rho & \rho^2 \\ \rho^2 & \rho & 1 & \rho \\ \rho^3 & \rho^2 & \rho & 1 \end{pmatrix}. \tag{9.7}$$

The terminology of the above correlation structure refers to a time series generated by an autoregressive model of order one. The structure is often appropriate for longitudinal data such as repeated observations on policies over time.

**Unstructured correlation.** In this case each correlation is free to vary subject only to the usual correlation constraints – symmetry, positive definiteness and ones on the diagonal.

## 9.3 Generalized estimating equations

There is one situation when marginal models are in fact fully specified models. This is with a normal response and identity link. In this case the vector $y$ of all the responses is such that

$$y \sim \mathrm{N}(X\beta, \Sigma) \tag{9.8}$$

which fully describes the distribution, and hence can be used to form an explicit likelihood. Maximum likelihood estimates of $\beta$ are readily computed given the $R_c$ and $S_c$ and hence $\Sigma$. In particular the estimation equation for $\beta$ is

$$0 = X'W(y - \mu) \qquad \Leftrightarrow \qquad X'Wy = XWX\beta,$$

where $W = \phi^{-1}\Sigma^{-1}$.

In the case of non-normal responses, and hence partially specified models, the situation is more complicated. The "generalized estimated equations" (GEEs) provide a method for estimating $\beta$:

$$0 = X'WG(y - \mu) = \sum_c X_c'W_cG_c(y_c - \mu_c), \tag{9.9}$$

where $W$ and $G$ are matrices described in Section 5.5. The expression on the right breaks up the matrix expression into the parts corresponding to each cluster $c$, and with the indexed matrices and vectors corresponding to the parts of the corresponding matrix or vector.

In the uncorrelated case the matrices $W$ and $G$ are diagonal, the former containing reciprocals of $\{\dot{g}(\mu_i)\}^2 V(\mu_i)$ and the latter the $\dot{g}(\mu_i)$. Thus in the uncorrelated case $W_c$ and $G_c$ are diagonal. Note that $\phi W_c^{-1}$ has diagonal entries with the approximate variance of $g(y_i)$.

With the GEE approach $W_c$ is replaced by $(S_c R_c S_c)^{-1}$, where $R_c$ is the correlation matrix for cluster $c$ and $S_c$ is a diagonal matrix with entries $\dot{g}(\mu_{ic}) \sqrt{V(\mu_{ic})}$. Solving the estimation equations with these $W_c$ is the GEE method. A given $R_c$ is called the working correlation matrix which is structured as in (9.6), (9.7), or in any other appropriate way including unstructured. Note that $R_c = I$ returns to the uncorrelated situation.

A solution for $\beta$ to (9.9) is not a maximum likelihood solution since the equations (9.9) generally do not correspond to the derivative of any likelihood. However GEE solutions have been found to have good statistical properties (Diggle, Heagerty, Liang, and Zeger 2002). Since the GEE method is not based on a likelihood, likelihood-based statistics for model selection or goodness of fit are not available. There is no deviance, AIC or BIC corresponding to GEE estimated models.

**Hypothesis testing for GEE models.** As the usual deviance-based tests cannot be performed, score tests for the hypothesis $C\beta = 0$ based on the equations (9.9) are used. Analogous to the score test for GLMs (Section 5.8), the quantity

$$s(\tilde{\beta}) = \sum_c X'_c W_c G_c (y_c - \mu_c)$$

is used as a proxy for $\dot{\ell}(\tilde{\beta})$ in (5.14). The score statistic in this situation is

$$s'(\tilde{\beta})[\mathrm{Var}\{s(\tilde{\beta})\}]^{-1} s(\tilde{\beta}) \,,$$

where $\tilde{\beta}$ is the estimate of $\beta$ under the restrictions imposed by the hypothesis. A "sandwich estimator," robust to model misspecification, is used for the covariance matrix $\mathrm{Var}\{s(\tilde{\beta})\}$ (Williams 2000). If the hypothesis is true the score statistic has the $\chi^2_q$ distribution, where $q$ is the number of restrictions.

**SAS notes.**

- Model (9.8) is implemented in `proc mixed`. The correlation structure and cluster information are specified in the `repeated` statement. SAS provides correlation functions (9.6), (9.7), "unstructured" and many others.
- GEEs are implemented in `proc genmod`, using the `repeated` statement to specify the clusters and correlation structure. Type III score tests are available.

**Vehicle insurance.** Suppose the occurrence of a claim is modeled as a logistic regression with correlated observations

$$y \sim \mathrm{B}(1, \pi) \,, \qquad \ln \frac{\pi}{1 - \pi} = x'\beta \,, \tag{9.10}$$

where successive blocks of three responses are correlated with the $3 \times 3$ within-policy correlation matrix $R_c$.

Table 9.3. *Logistic regression GEE for vehicle insurance claims*

| Response variable | Occurrence of a claim |
| --- | --- |
| Response distribution | Bernoulli |
| Correlation structure | compound symmetric |
| Link | logit |

| Parameter | $\hat{\beta}$ | se | $e^{\hat{\beta}}$ | $z$ | $p$-value |
| --- | --- | --- | --- | --- | --- |
| Intercept | −1.684 | 0.025 | 0.186 | −68.29 | <0.0001 |
| | | | | | |
| Driver's age | | . | | | |
| 1 | 0.189 | 0.041 | 1.208 | 4.63 | <0.0001 |
| 2 | 0.005 | 0.033 | 1.005 | 0.15 | 0.8800 |
| 3 | 0.000 | . | 1.000 | . | . |
| 4 | −0.036 | 0.031 | 0.964 | −1.16 | 0.2455 |
| 5 | −0.195 | 0.036 | 0.823 | −5.47 | <0.0001 |
| 6 | −0.150 | 0.042 | 0.861 | −3.55 | 0.0004 |
| | | | | | |
| Vehicle value ($000's) | | | | | |
| <25 | 0.000 | . | 1.000 | . | . |
| 25–50 | 0.161 | 0.028 | 1.175 | 5.81 | <0.0001 |
| 50–75 | 0.059 | 0.079 | 1.061 | 0.75 | 0.4534 |
| 75–100 | −0.646 | 0.313 | 0.524 | −2.06 | 0.0391 |
| 100–125 | −0.237 | 0.581 | 0.789 | −0.41 | 0.6836 |
| >125 | −0.969 | 0.616 | 0.380 | −1.57 | 0.1157 |
| | | | | | |
| Time period | | | | | |
| 1 | −0.205 | 0.017 | 0.815 | −12.33 | <0.0001 |
| 2 | −0.116 | 0.016 | 0.890 | −7.2 | <0.0001 |
| 3 | 0.000 | . | 1.000 | . | . |
| | | | | | |
| Correlation $\hat{\rho}$ | 0.332 | | | | |

These data are longitudinal, suggesting an AR(1) correlation structure. This assumption is checked by fitting the model with unstructured correlation, and checking the pattern. The estimated unstructured correlation matrix is – see code and output on page 185:

$$\hat{R}_c = \begin{pmatrix} 1.000 & 0.327 & 0.326 \\ 0.327 & 1.000 & 0.343 \\ 0.326 & 0.343 & 1.000 \end{pmatrix}.$$

The estimate $\hat{R}_c$ suggests a compound symmetric correlation and it is this structure that is used in the model. Selection of explanatory variables is based on the Type III score statistics. Results are given in Table 9.3 – see code and output on page 185.

Parameters have the usual interpretation. For example, the effect of a driver being in age band 1 compared with age band 3, is a 20.8% increase in the odds of a claim ($e^{\hat{\beta}} = 1.208$). The incidence of claims has risen over time: the effect of time period 1 compared with period 3, is a reduction of 18.5% in the odds of a claim ($e^{\hat{\beta}} = 0.815$), while for period 2 there is a reduction of 11% ($e^{\hat{\beta}} = 0.890$). These are similar to estimates for the logistic regression GLMM.

### Exercise

9.1      Develop a model for the number of claims, in the simulated longitudinal vehicle insurance data set.

# 10

# Extensions to the generalized linear model

The early development of the GLM occurred in the 1970s and 80s. More recent research has focussed on relaxing the assumptions of the model including:

- **Response distribution.** The response distribution $f(y)$ is chosen from a broader class. For example, $f(y)$ has computable first and second derivatives.
- **Explanatory variable transformations.** Continuous explanatory variables are transformed with smooth functions such as smoothing splines.
- **Mean and dispersion models.** In addition to the model $g(\mu) = x'\beta$ for the mean, the dispersion parameter $\phi$ is also modeled in terms of explanatory variables $z$: $h(\phi) = z'\gamma$.
- **Location, scale and shape models.** Models for the mean, scale and up to two shape parameters, such as skewness and kurtosis, are specified.

These extensions are discussed in this chapter.

## 10.1 Generalized additive models

Generalized additive models (GAMs) model the effect of explanatory variables in terms of non-parametric functional forms. As with GLMs, the response distribution is from the exponential family and the mean of the response is related to the explanatory variables through a link. Explanatory variables appear as:

$$g(\mu) = \beta_0 + s_1(x_1) + \cdots + s_p(x_p) , \qquad (10.1)$$

where the $s_j$ are smooth functions of explanatory variables the $x_j$.

Examples of $s_j$ are scatterplot smoothers, such as splines or loess curves, or parametric terms such as $\beta_j x_j$ or $\beta_j x_j^2$. Specifying a scatterplot smoother avoids specification of an appropriate functional form. This is convenient when $g(\mu)$ is nonlinear in the explanatory variables. Categorical covariates are always specified in their original form, as sets of indicator variables.

**SAS notes.** GAMs are implemented in `proc gam`. This is an experimental procedure in version 9. Explanatory variables may be specified as a functional form, or a spline, loess or thin-plate spline. If a variable is specified as a smooth function $s_j(x_j)$, a linear term $x_j$ is automatically included. User-defined link functions are not implemented.

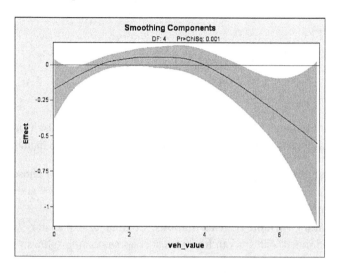

Fig. 10.1. Vehicle value component of fit, logistic regression GAM for vehicle claim

**Logistic regression GAM applied to vehicle insurance.** In Sections 7.3 and 7.4 a logistic regression is considered, where the response variable is the occurrence of a claim. The explanatory variables driver's age, area, vehicle body type and vehicle value are included in the final model, and exposure is adjusted for by using the modified link (7.5). The relationship of the log-odds of a claim with vehicle value appears nonlinear and hence vehicle value is banded. A similar regression, using a GAM with a spline smoother for vehicle value, and the other explanatory variables in their original form (since they are categorical), is demonstrated here. Responses are not adjusted for exposure. The fitted model is

$$\ln \frac{\hat{\pi}}{1 - \hat{\pi}} = -2.689 + 0.224x_1 + \cdots - 0.272x_{22} + 0.078x_{23} + s(x_{23})$$

where $x_1, \ldots, x_{22}$ are the indicator variables for driver's age, area and vehicle body type, and $x_{23}$ is vehicle value – see code and output on page 187. The spline term $s$ in vehicle value is depicted in Figure 10.1. As was evident in Section 7.3, the probability of a claim peaks around vehicle value \$40 000. The spline curve captures the nonlinear relationship which was previously noted.

**Use of GAMs.** GAM output does not include an explicit equation for the fitted value of the response. This is not necessarily a disadvantage. GAMs are useful for data exploration, in the initial stages of model building, when functional forms are not obvious. Analysts use GAM output to both suggest suitable transformations and to provide fitted values and predictions. GAM fits provide information for uncovering relationships, albeit not in the usual functional form format. References for the GAM are Hastie and Tibshirani (1990), Wood (2006) and Hastie and Tibshirani (1986).

## 10.2 Double generalized linear models

The exponential family response assumption of GLMs implies $\text{Var}(y) = \phi\,V(\mu)$, where $\mu$ is determined by $g(\mu) = x'\beta$ and $\phi$ is constant. Thus a model for the mean is implicitly a model for the variance or spread, up to the factor $\phi$. Combined mean and dispersion models break this nexus between the mean and variance by modeling the dispersion $\phi$. The double generalized linear model (DGLM) is the simplest mean and dispersion model. In addition to $g(\mu) = x'\beta$, the further equation $h(\phi) = z'\gamma$ is introduced, where $z$ denotes explanatory variables and $\gamma$ is a parameter vector. The vector $z$ can contain the same variables as in $x$. DGLMs were introduced by Smyth (1989). Smyth and Jørgensen (2002) use the DGLM for insurance claims. DGLMs are a special case of generalized additive models for location, scale and shape, which are discussed in the next section.

## 10.3 Generalized additive models for location, scale and shape

Rigby and Stasinopoulos (2005) introduced generalized additive models for location, scale and shape (GAMLSS). Response distributions in GAMLSS are not restricted to the exponential family: any distribution with computable first and second derivatives is permitted. With this approach, up to four response distribution parameters are modeled in terms of explanatory variables. The parameters are the mean and up to three scale/shape parameters.

For example suppose $\tau$ is one of the parameters such as the mean, dispersion, skewness or kurtosis. Then a model is specified of the form

$$g(\tau) = x_1'\beta + s(x_2) + x_3'\gamma$$

where $x_1$, $x_2$ and $x_3$ are vectors of explanatory variables, $\beta$ and $\gamma$ are fixed and random effects, respectively, and $s$ denotes a vector of smooth functions of each of the components in $x_2$.

The GAMLSS framework is very general, and encompasses all of the models described previously: normal linear models, GLMs, DGLMs, GAMs and

Table 10.1. *Fitting results for third party claims*

| Model | Response dist | $\ln \mu$ | Log of shape parameter | $\Delta$ | AIC |
|---|---|---|---|---|---|
| A | NB | ln(Accidents) | 1 | 2035.3 | 2041.3 |
| B | NB | ln(Accidents) + SD | 1 | 2005.3 | 2035.3 |
| C | NB | ln(Accidents) | SD | 1995.9 | 2025.9 |
| D | NB | ln(Accidents) + SD | SD | 1969.3 | 2023.3 |
| E | NB | ln(Accidents) | ln(Accidents) + SD | 1995.3 | 2027.3 |
| F | NB | ln(Accidents) + SD | ln(Accidents) + SD | 1967.6 | 2023.6 |
| G | PIG | ln(Accidents) | 1 | 2025.3 | 2031.3 |
| H | PIG | ln(Accidents) + SD | 1 | 1996.7 | 2026.7 |
| I | PIG | ln(Accidents) | SD | 1997.2 | 2027.2 |
| J | PIG | ln(Accidents) + SD | SD | 1964.7 | 2018.7 |
| K | PIG | ln(Accidents) | ln(Accidents) + SD | 1986.7 | 2030.0 |
| L | PIG | ln(Accidents) + SD | ln(Accidents) + SD | 1962.9 | 2018.9 |

GLMMs. Software for fitting GAMLSS is available as the R package `gamlss` (Stasinopoulos, Rigby, and Akantziliotou 2006).

**Third party claims.** A negative binomial regression for the number of third party claims in an area is given in Section 6.2. The model uses a log link and a constant shape parameter $\kappa$. A generalization is

$$y \sim \mathrm{NB}(\mu, \kappa), \qquad \ln \mu = \ln n + x'\beta, \qquad \ln \kappa = z'\gamma,$$

where $z$ is a vector of explanatory variables for $\kappa$ and $\gamma$ is the corresponding coefficient vector. If $z = 1$ then there is no variation in the dispersion. An alternative distribution for overdispersed counts is the Poisson-inverse Gaussian response $\mathrm{PIG}(\mu, \sigma)$ discussed in Section 2.9, where $\sigma$ is the shape parameter.

Table 10.1 displays deviances and AIC values for combinations of models for $\mu$ and the shape parameter. The explanatory variable SD denotes statistical division. Models A and B are negative binomial regression models (6.2). Model A is the same as (6.3). As noted in that section, according to AIC, model B is superior to A. The Poisson-inverse Gaussian GAMLSS regression, model J, is preferred. Hence $y \sim \mathrm{PIG}(\mu, \sigma)$ with

$$\ln \mu = \ln n + \beta_1 + \beta_2 \ln z + \beta_3 x_1 + \cdots + \beta_{14} x_{12},$$
$$\ln \sigma = \gamma_1 + \gamma_2 x_1 + \cdots + \gamma_{13} x_{12},$$

where $z$ is the number of accidents, and $x_1, \ldots, x_{12}$ are the indicator variables for statistical division – see code and output on page 189.

## 10.4 Zero-adjusted inverse Gaussian regression

The models for claim size in Chapter 8 are for positive claim sizes: they condition on a claim having been made. Analysis of claim size traditionally treats the occurrence of a claim and the amount of a claim, given that there is a claim, as separate models. The former is usually a logistic regression and the latter a model such as a gamma or inverse Gaussian regression. The results of these separate models are combined to produce predictions of expected claim sizes. This section and the next discuss models which unify the two features of the claims process.

Suppose $y$ is the claim size with $y \equiv 0$ if there is no claim. Then the distribution of claim size is mixed discrete–continuous. The probability of $y = 0$ is $1 - \pi$ while the probability associated with $y > 0$ is $\pi h(y)$ where $h(y)$ is the density of the distribution of (positive) claim size. Here $\pi$ is the probability of a non-zero claim. This setup does not fall within the GLM framework.

Take the discrete part of the model, that is the part that explains whether or not there is a claim, as Bernoulli $B(1, \pi)$, and suppose $h(y)$ to be inverse Gaussian $IG(\mu, \sigma^2)$. Allowing for exposure adjustment yields the response distribution

$$f(y) = \begin{cases} 1 - t\pi & \text{if } y = 0 \\ t\pi h(y) & \text{if } y > 0, \end{cases}$$

where $t$ is exposure. This resulting distribution is called the zero-adjusted inverse Gaussian (ZAIG) distribution (Heller, Stasinopoulos, and Rigby 2006) and

$$\mathrm{E}(y) = t\pi\mu, \qquad \mathrm{Var}(y) = t\pi\mu^2 \left(1 - t\pi + \mu\sigma^2\right).$$

Each of $\pi$, $\mu$ and $\sigma$ is made a function of explanatory variables. The explanatory variables can be different across the three parameters and explanatory variables affect the parameters in different ways.

The advantage of the ZAIG setup is that it models claim size, unconditional on a claim. The setup permits explanatory variables to explicitly affect each of the probability of a claim $\pi$, the mean claim size $\mu$, and the dispersion of claim size $\sigma$.

**Implementation.** The ZAIG model is implemented in the `gamlss` package. Quantiles of the estimated distribution can be computed.

**Vehicle insurance.** This example uses the ZAIG model with the logit, log and log links for $\pi$, $\mu$ and $\sigma^2$, respectively. The model is for claim size and yields estimates of the parameters for $\pi$, $\mu$ and $\sigma$ as shown in Tables 10.2 and 10.3. Model selection using the AIC results in the same sets of explanatory variables for $\mu$ (driver's age, gender and area) and $\pi$ (driver's age, area, vehicle

Table 10.2. *ZAIG model estimates for* $\pi$ *for vehicle claim sizes*

| Response variable | Claim size (including zeroes) |
|---|---|
| Response distribution | Zero-adjusted inverse Gaussian |
| Deviance | 109 609.7 |
| Degrees of freedom | 67 810 |
| Parameter | $\pi$ |
| Link | logit, adjusted for exposure |

|  | df | $\hat{\beta}$ | se | $e^{\hat{\beta}}$ | t | $p$-value |
|---|---|---|---|---|---|---|
| Intercept | 1 | −1.785 | 0.052 | 0.168 | −34.67 | 0.0000 |
|  |  |  |  |  |  |  |
| Driver's age | 5 |  |  |  |  |  |
| 1 | 1 | 0.288 | 0.063 | 1.333 | 4.59 | 0.0000 |
| 2 | 1 | 0.064 | 0.050 | 1.066 | 1.28 | 0.1991 |
| 3 | 0 | 0.000 | 0.000 | 1.000 | - | - |
| 4 | 1 | −0.036 | 0.048 | 0.965 | −0.75 | 0.4507 |
| 5 | 1 | −0.265 | 0.056 | 0.767 | −4.76 | 0.0000 |
| 6 | 1 | −0.255 | 0.067 | 0.775 | −3.81 | 0.0001 |
|  |  |  |  |  |  |  |
| Area | 5 |  |  |  |  |  |
| A | 1 | −0.036 | 0.045 | 0.965 | −0.79 | 0.4282 |
| B | 1 | 0.053 | 0.047 | 1.055 | 1.14 | 0.2560 |
| C | 0 | 0.000 | 0.000 | 1.000 | - | - |
| D | 1 | −0.138 | 0.058 | 0.871 | −2.36 | 0.0181 |
| E | 1 | −0.066 | 0.065 | 0.936 | −1.02 | 0.3073 |
| F | 1 | 0.021 | 0.076 | 1.021 | 0.27 | 0.7846 |
|  |  |  |  |  |  |  |
| Vehicle body | 12 |  |  |  |  |  |
| Bus | 1 | 1.136 | 0.449 | 3.115 | 2.53 | 0.0115 |
| Convertible | 1 | −0.371 | 0.642 | 0.690 | −0.58 | 0.5633 |
| Coupe | 1 | 0.433 | 0.148 | 1.542 | 2.92 | 0.0035 |
| Hatchback | 1 | −0.012 | 0.043 | 0.988 | −0.29 | 0.7737 |
| Hardtop | 1 | 0.099 | 0.105 | 1.104 | 0.94 | 0.3455 |
| Minicaravan | 1 | 0.596 | 0.328 | 1.815 | 1.82 | 0.0689 |
| Minibus | 1 | −0.111 | 0.172 | 0.895 | −0.65 | 0.5174 |
| Panel van | 1 | 0.019 | 0.145 | 1.020 | 0.13 | 0.8934 |
| Roadster | 1 | 0.070 | 0.801 | 1.072 | 0.09 | 0.9308 |
| Sedan | 0 | 0.000 | 0.000 | 1.000 | - | - |
| Station wagon | 1 | −0.019 | 0.050 | 0.981 | −0.38 | 0.7018 |
| Truck | 1 | −0.097 | 0.108 | 0.908 | −0.89 | 0.3718 |
| Utility | 1 | −0.246 | 0.076 | 0.782 | −3.23 | 0.0012 |
|  |  |  |  |  |  |  |
| Vehicle value ($000's) | 5 |  |  |  |  |  |
| <25 | 0 | 0.000 | 0.000 | 1.000 | - | - |
| 25–50 | 1 | 0.210 | 0.049 | 1.234 | 4.26 | 0.0000 |
| 50–75 | 1 | 0.137 | 0.124 | 1.146 | 1.10 | 0.2696 |
| 75–100 | 1 | −0.607 | 0.539 | 0.545 | −1.12 | 0.2606 |
| 100–125 | 1 | −0.290 | 0.773 | 0.748 | −0.38 | 0.7075 |
| >125 | 1 | −0.797 | 1.072 | 0.451 | −0.74 | 0.4571 |

Table 10.3. *ZAIG model estimates for $\mu$ and $\sigma$ for vehicle claim sizes*

|  | df | $\hat{\beta}$ | se | $e^{\hat{\beta}}$ | t | p-value |
|---|---|---|---|---|---|---|
| Parameter<br>Link |  | $\mu$<br>log |  |  |  |  |
| Intercept | 1 | 7.531 | 0.065 | 1864.723 | 116.31 | <0.0001 |
| Driver's age | 5 |  |  |  |  |  |
| 1 | 1 | 0.256 | 0.097 | 1.292 | 2.65 | 0.0080 |
| 2 | 1 | 0.086 | 0.074 | 1.090 | 1.17 | 0.2428 |
| 3 | 0 | 0.000 | 0.000 | 1.000 | - | - |
| 4 | 1 | −0.003 | 0.069 | 0.997 | −0.05 | 0.9624 |
| 5 | 1 | −0.129 | 0.079 | 0.879 | −1.64 | 0.1001 |
| 6 | 1 | −0.071 | 0.096 | 0.932 | −0.74 | 0.4618 |
| Gender | 1 |  |  |  |  |  |
| F | 1 | −0.156 | 0.050 | 1.169 | 3.15 | 0.0016 |
| M | 0 | 0.000 | 0.000 | 1.000 | - | - |
| Area | 5 |  |  |  |  |  |
| A | 1 | −0.073 | 0.068 | 0.930 | −1.08 | 0.2806 |
| B | 1 | −0.103 | 0.070 | 0.902 | −1.48 | 0.1387 |
| C | 0 | 0.000 | 0.000 | 1.000 | - | - |
| D | 1 | −0.098 | 0.081 | 0.907 | −1.21 | 0.2279 |
| E | 1 | 0.068 | 0.093 | 1.070 | 0.73 | 0.4646 |
| F | 1 | 0.281 | 0.114 | 1.325 | 2.47 | 0.0136 |
| Parameter<br>Link |  | $\sigma$<br>log |  |  |  |  |
| Intercept | 1 | −3.264 | 0.019 | 0.038 | −173.45 | 0.0000 |
| Area | 5 |  |  |  |  |  |
| A | 1 | −0.010 | 0.029 | 0.990 | −0.34 | 0.7309 |
| B | 1 | −0.005 | 0.030 | 0.995 | −0.17 | 0.8655 |
| C | 0 | 0.000 | 0.000 | 1.000 | - | - |
| D | 1 | −0.090 | 0.037 | 0.914 | −2.45 | 0.0143 |
| E | 1 | −0.116 | 0.041 | 0.891 | −2.85 | 0.0044 |
| F | 1 | −0.143 | 0.046 | 0.867 | −3.08 | 0.0020 |

body type and vehicle value) as found for the previously fitted inverse Gaussian (Section 8.2) and logistic regression (Section 7.4) models. The parameter estimates are similar to those derived from the inverse Gaussian and logistic fits. Area is chosen as the explanatory variable for $\sigma$ – see code and output on page 190.

Driver's age appears in the model equations for both $\pi$ and $\mu$. Area is in the model equations for $\pi, \mu$ and $\sigma$. Of interest is whether these explanatory variables have a similar effect on the occurrence of a claim, claim size and

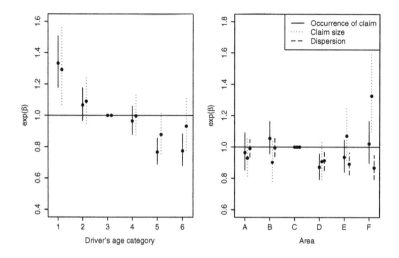

Fig. 10.2. Effect of age and area ($e^{\hat{\beta}}$ and 95% confidence interval) on occurrence of claim, claim size and dispersion

claim size dispersion (in the case of area). The left panel of Figure 10.2 shows the effect of driver's age on both the odds of a claim $\pi/(1 - \pi)$ and mean claim size $\mu$. Age band 1 (young drivers) increases, to a similar extent, the odds of a claim and the mean claim size. Age bands 2 and 4 have a similar effect to age band 3. Age bands 5 and 6 (older drivers) decrease both the odds of a claim and the mean claim size, with a greater effect on the odds of a claim. The right panel of Figure 10.2 shows the effect of area on $\pi/(1 - \pi)$, $\mu$ and $\sigma$. The effect on the odds of a claim, and mean claim size, is less clear. The single indication is that the mean claim size is higher in area F. However, area has quite a different effect on dispersion. The areas appear to fall into two distinct groups: A, B and C with higher dispersion, and D, E and F, with lower dispersion. A possible reason is urban/rural distinction, or demographic factors. Knowledge of the reason for the similarity will suggest sensible grouping of areas.

## 10.5 A mean and dispersion model for total claim size

The ZAIG model assumes either a claim or no claim on a policy and makes no allowance for multiple claims. This is a reasonable approximation if the probability of a claim is low. The following model is more sensible when multiple claims are likely.

Assume that the number of claims on a policy is $c$, where $c = 0, 1, ,\ldots$. Let $z_j$ be the size of the $j$th claim on the policy, so that the total claim size $y$ is

$$y = \begin{cases} 0 & \text{if } c = 0 \\ \sum_{j=1}^{c} z_j & \text{if } c > 0. \end{cases}$$

The distributions of $c$ and $z_j$ determine the resultant distribution of $y$. As the Tweedie and ZAIG distributions, this distribution has a probability mass at zero, which is the probability of no claims, and a continuous, right-skewed component for the positive total claim amount. This model allows for multiple claims.

If the distributions of $c$ and the $z_j$ are Poisson and gamma respectively, then the distribution of $y$ is Tweedie. As this is in the exponential family, a regression model based on the Tweedie response distribution is a GLM (Section 8.3). Different choices of $c$ and $z_j$ distributions permit greater flexibility in the distribution of $y$.

Heller, Stasinopoulos, Rigby, and de Jong (2007) implement the above model with the distribution of $c$ as either Poisson, zero-inflated Poisson or negative binomial; and the distribution of $z_j$ as either gamma or inverse Gaussian. The mean and dispersion parameters for the $c$ and $z_j$ distributions are modeled as functions of explanatory variables. The model falls outside the GLM framework, except with the Poisson–gamma setup. Software for fitting the mean and dispersion model for total claim size is available as the R package `rsm` (Stasinopoulos, Rigby, and Heller 2007).

## Exercises

10.1   Implement a GAM for the Swedish mortality data, for males, using smooth functions for age and year.

10.2   Implement a GAMLSS for the Swedish mortality data.

10.3   Investigate the use of a GAM for the third party claims data, using a smooth function for accidents (or log accidents).

10.4   In the Enterprise Miner data set, develop a statistical model for claim size, for all policies.

# Appendix 1

## Computer code and output

Computations are illustrated using SAS/STAT® (version 9.1). The statistical language R (version 2.4.1) (Ihaka and Gentleman 1996) is used where computations are not conveniently performed in SAS. R is downloadable from the R project website http://www.r-project.org/.

In SAS, proc genmod is used for the estimation of GLMs. The response distribution and link are specified in the dist= and link= options in the model statement. The default response distribution is the normal, and the default link is the canonical link, as given in Table 5.1.

### A1.1 Poisson regression

**Number of children: log link**

```
proc genmod data=act.birth;
model children = age / dist=poisson link=log type1 type3;
run;
```

```
                    The GENMOD Procedure

                     Model Information

             Data Set              ACT.BIRTH
             Distribution            Poisson
             Link Function               Log
             Dependent Variable     children

             Observations Used           141


          Criteria For Assessing Goodness Of Fit

    Criterion             DF         Value      Value/DF

    Deviance             139      165.0117        1.1871
    Scaled Deviance      139      165.0117        1.1871
    Pearson Chi-Square   139      173.3839        1.2474
    Scaled Pearson X2    139      173.3839        1.2474
    Log Likelihood               -113.3151
```

Algorithm converged.

Analysis Of Parameter Estimates

| Parameter | DF | Estimate | Standard Error | Wald 95% Confidence Limits | | Chi-Square | Pr>ChiSq |
|---|---|---|---|---|---|---|---|
| Intercept | 1 | -4.0895 | 0.7137 | -5.4883 | -2.6908 | 32.84 | <.0001 |
| age | 1 | 0.1129 | 0.0212 | 0.0714 | 0.1545 | 28.36 | <.0001 |
| Scale | 0 | 1.0000 | 0.0000 | 1.0000 | 1.0000 | | |

NOTE: The scale parameter was held fixed.

LR Statistics For Type 1 Analysis

| Source | Deviance | DF | Chi-Square | Pr > ChiSq |
|---|---|---|---|---|
| Intercept | 194.4201 | | | |
| age | 165.0117 | 1 | 29.41 | <.0001 |

LR Statistics For Type 3 Analysis

| Source | DF | Chi-Square | Pr > ChiSq |
|---|---|---|---|
| age | 1 | 29.41 | <.0001 |

## Number of children: identity link

```
proc genmod data=act.birth;
model children = age / dist=poisson link=id type1 type3;
run;
```

The GENMOD Procedure

Model Information

| | |
|---|---|
| Data Set | ACT.BIRTH |
| Distribution | Poisson |
| Link Function | Identity |
| Dependent Variable | children |
| Observations Used | 141 |

Criteria For Assessing Goodness Of Fit

| Criterion | DF | Value | Value/DF |
|---|---|---|---|
| Deviance | 139 | 171.4425 | 1.2334 |
| Scaled Deviance | 139 | 171.4425 | 1.2334 |
| Pearson Chi-Square | 139 | 143.6935 | 1.0338 |
| Scaled Pearson X2 | 139 | 143.6935 | 1.0338 |
| Log Likelihood | | -116.5304 | |

WARNING: The relative Hessian convergence criterion of 0.1003520726 is greater than the limit of 0.0001. The convergence is questionable.

Analysis Of Parameter Estimates

```
                       Standard Wald 95% Confidence Chi-
     Parameter  DF  Estimate  Error      Limits        Square  Pr>ChiSq

     Intercept  1   -0.9653   0.4600  -1.8669  -0.0637    4.40   0.0359
     age        1    0.0568   0.0155   0.0264   0.0872   13.39   0.0003
     Scale      0    1.0000   0.0000   1.0000   1.0000

     NOTE: The scale parameter was held fixed.


                    LR Statistics For Type 1 Analysis

                                             Chi-
          Source           Deviance    DF    Square    Pr > ChiSq

          Intercept        194.4201
          age              171.4425     1     22.98      <.0001


                    LR Statistics For Type 3 Analysis

                                        Chi-
            Source          DF          Square    Pr > ChiSq

            age             1           22.98      <.0001
```

### Diabetes deaths, categorical age

The data are set out as follows:

| Gender<br>gender | Age<br>age | Deaths<br>deaths | Population<br>popn | log(population)<br>l_popn | Age midpoint<br>agemidpt |
|---|---|---|---|---|---|
| Male | <25 | 3 | 1 141 100 | 13.95 | 20 |
| Male | 25–34 | 0 | 485 571 | 13.09 | 30 |
| Male | 35–44 | 12 | 504 312 | 13.13 | 40 |
| Male | z45–54 | 25 | 447 315 | 13.01 | 50 |
| Male | 55–64 | 61 | 330 902 | 12.71 | 60 |
| Male | 65–74 | 130 | 226 403 | 12.33 | 70 |
| Male | 75–84 | 192 | 130 527 | 11.78 | 80 |
| Male | 85+ | 102 | 29 785 | 10.30 | 90 |
| Female | <25 | 2 | 1 086 408 | 13.90 | 20 |
| Female | 25–34 | 1 | 489 948 | 13.10 | 30 |
| Female | 35–44 | 3 | 504 030 | 13.13 | 40 |
| Female | z45–54 | 11 | 445 763 | 13.01 | 50 |
| Female | 55–64 | 30 | 323 669 | 12.69 | 60 |
| Female | 65–74 | 63 | 241 488 | 12.39 | 70 |
| Female | 75–84 | 174 | 179 686 | 12.10 | 80 |
| Female | 85+ | 159 | 67 203 | 11.12 | 90 |

The base level for age, as chosen by SAS, is "<25." The level "45–54" is forced to be base by changing its coding to "z45–54."

```
proc genmod data=act.diabetes;
class gender age;
model deaths = gender age /
   dist=poisson offset=l_popn type1 type3;
run;
```

The GENMOD Procedure

Model Information

```
Data Set              ACT.DIABETES
Distribution          Poisson
Link Function         Log
Dependent Variable    Deaths     Deaths
Offset Variable       L_Popn     log( Popn )
```

```
Number of Observations Read        16
Number of Observations Used        16
```

[output omitted]

Criteria For Assessing Goodness Of Fit

| Criterion | DF | Value | Value/DF |
|---|---|---|---|
| Deviance | 7 | 10.8891 | 1.5556 |
| Scaled Deviance | 7 | 10.8891 | 1.5556 |
| Pearson Chi-Square | 7 | 10.3047 | 1.4721 |
| Scaled Pearson X2 | 7 | 10.3047 | 1.4721 |
| Log Likelihood | | 3602.6149 | |

Algorithm converged.

Analysis Of Parameter Estimates

| Parameter | | DF | Estimate | Standard Error | Wald 95% Confidence Limits | | Chi-Square | Pr>ChiSq |
|---|---|---|---|---|---|---|---|---|
| Intercept | | 1 | -9.8915 | 0.1684 | -10.2216 | -9.5615 | 3449.40 | <.0001 |
| Gender | Female | 1 | -0.5233 | 0.0653 | -0.6513 | -0.3954 | 64.27 | <.0001 |
| Gender | Male | 0 | 0.0000 | 0.0000 | 0.0000 | 0.0000 | . | . |
| Age | 25-34 | 1 | -3.6702 | 1.0138 | -5.6571 | -1.6832 | 13.11 | 0.0003 |
| Age | 35-44 | 1 | -0.9965 | 0.3073 | -1.5988 | -0.3942 | 10.51 | 0.0012 |
| Age | 55-64 | 1 | 1.2357 | 0.1969 | 0.8498 | 1.6216 | 39.39 | <.0001 |
| Age | 65-74 | 1 | 2.3343 | 0.1815 | 1.9785 | 2.6902 | 165.32 | <.0001 |
| Age | 85+ | 1 | 4.3055 | 0.1783 | 3.9560 | 4.6549 | 583.27 | <.0001 |
| Age | <25 | 1 | -2.8939 | 0.4773 | -3.8293 | -1.9584 | 36.77 | <.0001 |
| Age | z45-54 | 0 | 0.0000 | 0.0000 | 0.0000 | 0.0000 | . | . |
| Scale | | 0 | 1.0000 | 0.0000 | 1.0000 | 1.0000 | | |

NOTE: The scale parameter was held fixed.

LR Statistics For Type 1 Analysis

| Source | Deviance | DF | Chi-Square | Pr > ChiSq |
|---|---|---|---|---|
| Intercept | 3306.3834 | | | |
| Gender | 3298.3442 | 1 | 8.04 | 0.0046 |
| Age | 10.8891 | 7 | 3287.46 | <.0001 |

LR Statistics For Type 3 Analysis

| Source | DF | Chi-Square | Pr > ChiSq |
|---|---|---|---|
| Gender | 1 | 64.51 | <.0001 |
| Age | 7 | 3287.46 | <.0001 |

## Diabetes deaths, cubic age

In the model with cubic age, numerical problems occur when `agemidpt` is used. To remedy this, `agemidpt` is standardized, as described in Section 4.11:

```
proc means noprint data=act.diabetes;
/* extract minimum and maximum agemidpt; */
var agemidpt;
output out=stats (drop=_type_ _freq_)
   min=age1 max=age2 ;
run;

data diabetes;
set act.diabetes;
   if _n_=1 then set stats;
/* compute standardized age : */
   agestd =
     (agemidpt-0.5*(age1+age2))/(0.5*(age2-age1));
/* compute linear, quadratic and cubic age terms : */
array agepoly[3];
   agepoly[1]=agestd;
   do i=2 to 3;
   agepoly[i]=agepoly[i-1]*agestd;
   end; drop i;
   run;

proc genmod data=diabetes;
class gender;
model deaths = gender agepoly1 agepoly2 agepoly3  /
   dist=poisson offset=l_popn type1 type3;
run;
```

```
                        The GENMOD Procedure

                        Model Information

            Data Set              WORK.DIABETES
            Distribution              Poisson
            Link Function                 Log
            Dependent Variable         Deaths   Deaths
            Offset Variable            L_Popn   log( Popn )


                 Number of Observations Read        16
                 Number of Observations Used        16
```

[output omitted]

```
              Criteria For Assessing Goodness Of Fit

           Criterion              DF        Value       Value/DF

           Deviance               11      15.3336         1.3940
           Scaled Deviance        11      15.3336         1.3940
           Pearson Chi-Square     11      12.7083         1.1553
           Scaled Pearson X2      11      12.7083         1.1553
           Log Likelihood               3600.3927
```

```
Algorithm converged.
```

```
                         Analysis Of Parameter Estimates
```

|                        |        | DF | Estimate | Standard Error | Wald 95% Confidence Limits |         | Chi-Square | Pr>ChiSq |
| ---------------------- | ------ | -- | -------- | -------------- | -------- | -------- | ---------- | -------- |
| Intercept              |        | 1  | -9.2832  | 0.0876         | -9.4548  | -9.1115  | 11231.4    | <.0001   |
| Gender                 | Female | 1  | -0.5233  | 0.0653         | -0.6512  | -0.3953  | 64.26      | <.0001   |
| Gender                 | Male   | 0  | 0.0000   | 0.0000         | 0.0000   | 0.0000   | .          | .        |
| agepoly1               |        | 1  | 4.1780   | 0.1927         | 3.8004   | 4.5557   | 470.06     | <.0001   |
| agepoly2               |        | 1  | -0.0363  | 0.2487         | -0.5237  | 0.4510   | 0.02       | 0.8838   |
| agepoly3               |        | 1  | -0.4437  | 0.2710         | -0.9749  | 0.0876   | 2.68       | 0.1016   |
| Scale                  |        | 0  | 1.0000   | 0.0000         | 1.0000   | 1.0000   |            |          |

```
NOTE: The scale parameter was held fixed.
```

```
              LR Statistics For Type 1 Analysis
```

| Source    | Deviance  | DF | Chi-Square | Pr > ChiSq |
| --------- | --------- | -- | ---------- | ---------- |
| Intercept | 3306.3834 |    |            |            |
| Gender    | 3298.3442 | 1  | 8.04       | 0.0046     |
| agepoly1  | 22.8341   | 1  | 3275.51    | <.0001     |
| agepoly2  | 17.8776   | 1  | 4.96       | 0.0260     |
| agepoly3  | 15.3336   | 1  | 2.54       | 0.1107     |

```
              LR Statistics For Type 3 Analysis
```

| Source   | DF | Chi-Square | Pr > ChiSq |
| -------- | -- | ---------- | ---------- |
| Gender   | 1  | 64.50      | <.0001     |
| agepoly1 | 1  | 640.91     | <.0001     |
| agepoly2 | 1  | 0.02       | 0.8831     |
| agepoly3 | 1  | 2.54       | 0.1107     |

## Third party claims

```
proc genmod data=act.lgaclaims;
model claims = L_accidents /
  dist=poisson link=log type1 type3 offset=L_population;
run;
```

Only model fit statistics are shown.

```
                  The GENMOD Procedure

                  Model Information

        Data Set             ACT.LGACLAIMS
        Distribution               Poisson
        Link Function                  Log
        Dependent Variable          Claims    Claims
        Offset Variable       L_Population    log( Population )
        Observations Used              176
```

```
                    Criteria For Assessing Goodness Of Fit

        Criterion              DF         Value        Value/DF

        Deviance               174     15836.7282       91.0157
        Scaled Deviance        174     15836.7282       91.0157
        Pearson Chi-Square     174     17698.7159      101.7168
        Scaled Pearson X2      174     17698.7159      101.7168
        Log Likelihood                644365.6844

              [output omitted]
```

## A1.2  Negative binomial regression

### Third party claims

```
proc genmod data=act.lgaclaims;
model claims = L_accidents / dist=negbin link=log
   type1 type3 offset=L_population;
run;
```

```
                         The GENMOD Procedure

                         Model Information

        Data Set               ACT.LGACLAIMS
        Distribution          Negative Binomial
        Link Function              Log
        Dependent Variable        Claims        Claims
        Offset Variable         L_Population    log( Population )
        Observations Used          176


              Criteria For Assessing Goodness Of Fit

        Criterion              DF         Value        Value/DF

        Deviance               174      192.3342        1.1054
        Scaled Deviance        174      192.3342        1.1054
        Pearson Chi-Square     174      214.2632        1.2314
        Scaled Pearson X2      174      214.2632        1.2314
        Log Likelihood                651879.2752

        Algorithm converged.


                    Analysis Of Parameter Estimates

                          Standard Wald 95% Confidence  Chi-
        Parameter   DF Estimate  Error      Limits      Square  Pr > ChiSq

        Intercept    1  -6.9544  0.1623  -7.2725   -6.6364 1836.69  <.0001
        L_Accidents  1   0.2539  0.0254   0.2041    0.3036  100.04  <.0001
        Dispersion   1   0.1715  0.0197   0.1369    0.2149

NOTE: The negative binomial dispersion parameter was estimated by
      maximum likelihood.


                    LR Statistics For Type 1 Analysis
```

```
                    2*Log                 Chi-
    Source          Likelihood      DF    Square    Pr > ChiSq

    Intercept       1303674.84
    L_Accidents     1303758.55      1     83.71      <.0001
```

```
              LR Statistics For Type 3 Analysis

                                  Chi-
          Source          DF      Square    Pr > ChiSq

          L_Accidents     1       83.71      <.0001
```

## Swedish mortality, categorical age and year

```
proc genmod data=act.mortality;
class age(ref="50") year / param=ref;
model male_death = age year /
  dist= negbin offset = l_male_exp type1 type3;
run;
```

The parameter estimates table is omitted because of its length.

```
                     The GENMOD Procedure

                     Model Information

    Data Set                 ACT.MORTALITY
    Distribution         Negative Binomial
    Link Function                      Log
    Dependent Variable       Male_death    Male_death
    Offset Variable          L_male_exp
```

```
              Number of Observations Read      6105
              Number of Observations Used      5868
              Missing Values                    237
```

[output omitted]

```
              Criteria For Assessing Goodness Of Fit

          Criterion          DF         Value      Value/DF

          Deviance          5704      2838.3751      0.4976
          Scaled Deviance   5704      2838.3751      0.4976
          Pearson Chi-Square 5704     3085.0981      0.5409
          Scaled Pearson X2  5704     3085.0981      0.5409
          Log Likelihood            14093583.542
```

[output omitted]

```
              LR Statistics For Type 1 Analysis

                     2*Log                 Chi-
          Source     Likelihood      DF    Square    Pr > ChiSq

          Intercept  28158314.8
          Age        28184608.8      109   26294.0    <.0001
          Year       28187167.1      54    2558.32    <.0001
```

## Swedish mortality, polynomial age and year

The orthogonal polynomials are implemented using the `poly` function in R.

The negative binomial regression for mortality of Swedish males is illustrated for $p = 25$ and $q = 4$.

```
> mortality <- read.table("mortality.csv",header=T,sep=",")
> mortality <- mortality[,-c(3,5,7,9,11)]
> mortality <- na.omit(mortality)
> attach(mortality)
> library(MASS)
>
> model.final <- glm.nb(Male_death ~ poly(Age,25)+poly(Year,4)+
+ offset(L_male_exp))
There were 50 or more warnings (use warnings() to see the first 50)
> summary(model.final,correlation=F)

Call:
glm.nb(formula = Male_death ~ poly(Age, 25) + poly(Year, 4) +
   offset(L_male_exp), init.theta = 109.233848839689, link = log)

Deviance Residuals:
    Min       1Q    Median       3Q       Max
-7.48635  -0.70380  -0.06565   0.49930   6.64826

Coefficients:
                   Estimate Std. Error   z value Pr(>|z|)
(Intercept)       -4.631393   0.003142 -1474.125  < 2e-16 ***
poly(Age, 25)1   187.439346   0.365567   512.735  < 2e-16 ***
poly(Age, 25)2    29.783922   0.433956    68.634  < 2e-16 ***
poly(Age, 25)3   -18.497486   0.482899   -38.305  < 2e-16 ***
poly(Age, 25)4     3.982837   0.518784     7.677 1.63e-14 ***
poly(Age, 25)5   -10.185776   0.541931   -18.795  < 2e-16 ***
poly(Age, 25)6    12.858175   0.547718    23.476  < 2e-16 ***
poly(Age, 25)7   -13.401140   0.535787   -25.012  < 2e-16 ***
poly(Age, 25)8     9.466237   0.512428    18.473  < 2e-16 ***
poly(Age, 25)9    -3.384275   0.485044    -6.977 3.01e-12 ***
poly(Age, 25)10    0.769338   0.460041     1.672  0.09446 .
poly(Age, 25)11   -0.022258   0.446198    -0.050  0.96022
poly(Age, 25)12    3.529284   0.444062     7.948 1.90e-15 ***
poly(Age, 25)13   -4.339621   0.454158    -9.555  < 2e-16 ***
poly(Age, 25)14    7.567058   0.469808    16.107  < 2e-16 ***
poly(Age, 25)15   -4.989211   0.484704   -10.293  < 2e-16 ***
poly(Age, 25)16    5.202372   0.495475    10.500  < 2e-16 ***
poly(Age, 25)17   -0.925532   0.499463    -1.853  0.06387 .
poly(Age, 25)18    1.164163   0.495399     2.350  0.01878 *
poly(Age, 25)19    0.976063   0.475295     2.054  0.04001 *
poly(Age, 25)20    0.825494   0.450439     1.833  0.06686 .
poly(Age, 25)21   -0.782478   0.401932    -1.947  0.05156 .
poly(Age, 25)22    1.930786   0.355691     5.428 5.69e-08 ***
poly(Age, 25)23   -1.608996   0.299282    -5.376 7.61e-08 ***
poly(Age, 25)24    1.224794   0.225750     5.425 5.78e-08 ***
poly(Age, 25)25   -0.555632   0.210648    -2.638  0.00835 **
poly(Year, 4)1   -13.591997   0.130638  -104.043  < 2e-16 ***
poly(Year, 4)2    -3.932468   0.129566   -30.351  < 2e-16 ***
poly(Year, 4)3    -0.909476   0.129561    -7.020 2.22e-12 ***
poly(Year, 4)4     1.387264   0.129437    10.718  < 2e-16 ***
---
Signif. codes:  0 '***' 0.001 '**' 0.01 '*' 0.05 '.' 0.1 ' ' 1

(Dispersion parameter for Negative Binomial(109.2338) family
 taken to be 1)

    Null deviance: 1662580.8  on 5867  degrees of freedom
```

```
Residual deviance:      7721.1  on 5838  degrees of freedom
AIC: 53902

Number of Fisher Scoring iterations: 1

             Theta:  109.23
         Std. Err.:  3.71

  2 x log-likelihood:  -53840.27
```

The $\hat{\beta}$s and their standard errors are well behaved, indicating no numerical problems.

## A1.3  Quasi-likelihood regression

```
proc genmod data=act.lgaclaims;
model claims = L_accidents / dist=poisson dscale
  link=log type1 type3 offset=L_population;
run;
```

```
                   The GENMOD Procedure

                    Model Information

         Data Set              ACT.LGACLAIMS
         Distribution               Poisson
         Link Function                  Log
         Dependent Variable          Claims  Claims
         Offset Variable       L_Population  log( Population )
         Observations Used              176


         Criteria For Assessing Goodness Of Fit

      Criterion              DF        Value      Value/DF

      Deviance              174   15836.7282       91.0157
      Scaled Deviance       174     174.0000        1.0000
      Pearson Chi-Square    174   17698.7159      101.7168
      Scaled Pearson X2     174     194.4579        1.1176
      Log Likelihood             7079.7218

      Algorithm converged.

           Analysis Of Parameter Estimates

                       Standard  Wald 95% Confidence Chi-
   Parameter   DF  Estimate  Error     Limits         Square Pr>ChiSq

   Intercept    1   -7.0938  0.2575  -7.5985   -6.5891  758.87  <.0001
   L_Accidents  1    0.2591  0.0322   0.1960    0.3222   64.71  <.0001
   Scale        0    9.5402  0.0000   9.5402    9.5402

NOTE: The scale parameter was estimated by the square root of DEVIANCE/DOF.


              LR Statistics For Type 1 Analysis
                                               .
                                             Chi-
   Source        Deviance  Num DF Den DF F Value Pr > F  Square  Pr>ChiSq
```

```
Intercept    22392.5975
L_Accidents  15836.7282    1     174     72.03   <.0001   72.03  <.0001
```

```
                    LR Statistics For Type 3 Analysis

                                                    Chi-
    Source       Num DF  Den DF   F Value   Pr > F   Square   Pr>ChiSq

    L_Accidents     1      174     72.03   <.0001    72.03     <.0001
```

## A1.4 Logistic regression

Logistic regression is implemented in `proc genmod` using `dist=bin` (or `binomial`). For this response distribution, SAS accepts a response variable having any two distinct values (not necessarily 0 and 1). Its default is to model the probability of the lower value, so if the coding is 0/1, $\pi$ will be the probability that $y = 0$, which is not generally desired. To change this to $\pi = P(y = 1)$, the `descending` option is specified in the `proc` statement.

Two models from Section 7.3 are presented: that with a quadratic form of vehicle value and with vehicle value banded.

### Vehicle insurance: quadratic vehicle value

```
proc genmod data=act.car descending;
model clm =  veh_value veh_value*veh_value /
   dist=bin type1 type3;
run;
```

```
                    The GENMOD Procedure

                      Model Information

            Data Set              ACT.CAR
            Distribution          Binomial
            Link Function           Logit
            Dependent Variable        clm


        Number of Observations Read      67856
        Number of Observations Used      67856
        Number of Events                  4624
        Number of Trials                 67856


                    Response Profile

            Ordered              Total
            Value     clm      Frequency

               1       1          4624
               2       0         63232

PROC GENMOD is modeling the probability that clm='1'.


            Criteria For Assessing Goodness Of Fit
```

```
Criterion                     DF          Value      Value/DF

Deviance                    68E3     33712.9206        0.4969
Scaled Deviance             68E3     33712.9206        0.4969
Pearson Chi-Square          68E3     67923.1655        1.0010
Scaled Pearson X2           68E3     67923.1655        1.0010
Log Likelihood                      -16856.4603
```

Algorithm converged.

```
                     Analysis Of Parameter Estimates

                          Standard Wald 95% Confidence   Chi-
Parameter            DF  Estimate  Error      Limits       Square Pr>ChiSq

Intercept             1   -2.8926  0.0440  -2.9789   -2.8062 4312.09   <.0001
veh_value             1    0.2196  0.0358   0.1495    0.2897   37.69   <.0001
veh_value*veh_value   1   -0.0260  0.0059  -0.0376   -0.0144   19.38   <.0001
Scale                 0    1.0000  0.0000   1.0000    1.0000
```

NOTE: The scale parameter was held fixed.

```
                   LR Statistics For Type 1 Analysis

                                                Chi-
Source                     Deviance      DF     Square   Pr > ChiSq

Intercept                 33766.7978
veh_value                 33745.1178      1      21.68     <.0001
veh_value*veh_value       33712.9206      1      32.20     <.0001
```

```
                   LR Statistics For Type 3 Analysis

                                        Chi-
Source                       DF        Square   Pr > ChiSq

veh_value                     1         52.57     <.0001
veh_value*veh_value           1         32.20     <.0001
```

**Vehicle insurance: banded vehicle value**

The variable valuecat has been computed according to Table 7.2. Band 1
is specified as the base level.

```
proc genmod data=act.car descending;
class valuecat (ref="1")/ param=ref;
model clm =  valuecat / dist=bin type1 type3;
run;
```

```
                     The GENMOD Procedure

                     Model Information

              Data Set              ACT.CAR
              Distribution          Binomial
              Link Function           Logit
              Dependent Variable        clm


         Number of Observations Read       67856
         Number of Observations Used       67856
```

```
              Number of Events              4624
              Number of Trials            67856
```

[output omitted]
### Response Profile

```
            Ordered                     Total
              Value      clm          Frequency

                1        1              4624
                2        0             63232
```

PROC GENMOD is modeling the probability that clm='1'.

### Criteria For Assessing Goodness Of Fit

| Criterion | DF | Value | Value/DF |
|---|---|---|---|
| Deviance | 68E3 | 33744.0322 | 0.4973 |
| Scaled Deviance | 68E3 | 33744.0322 | 0.4973 |
| Pearson Chi-Square | 68E3 | 67855.9988 | 1.0001 |
| Scaled Pearson X2 | 68E3 | 67855.9988 | 1.0001 |
| Log Likelihood | | -16872.0161 | |

Algorithm converged.

### Analysis Of Parameter Estimates

| Parameter | | DF | Estimate | Standard Error | Wald 95% Confidence Limits | | Chi-Square | Pr>ChiSq |
|---|---|---|---|---|---|---|---|---|
| Intercept | | 1 | -2.6475 | 0.0172 | -2.6811 | -2.6139 | 23799.7 | <.0001 |
| valuecat | 2 | 1 | 0.1737 | 0.0389 | 0.0974 | 0.2500 | 19.93 | <.0001 |
| valuecat | 3 | 1 | 0.1020 | 0.1096 | -0.1129 | 0.3168 | 0.87 | 0.3523 |
| valuecat | 4 | 1 | -0.5714 | 0.5102 | -1.5713 | 0.4286 | 1.25 | 0.2627 |
| valuecat | 5 | 1 | -0.3970 | 0.7240 | -1.8159 | 1.0219 | 0.30 | 0.5834 |
| valuecat | 6 | 1 | -0.8182 | 1.0156 | -2.8088 | 1.1724 | 0.65 | 0.4205 |
| Scale | | 0 | 1.0000 | 0.0000 | 1.0000 | 1.0000 | | |

NOTE: The scale parameter was held fixed.

### LR Statistics For Type 1 Analysis

| Source | Deviance | DF | Chi-Square | Pr > ChiSq |
|---|---|---|---|---|
| Intercept | 33766.7978 | | | |
| valuecat | 33744.0322 | 5 | 22.77 | 0.0004 |

### LR Statistics For Type 3 Analysis

| Source | DF | Chi-Square | Pr > ChiSq |
|---|---|---|---|
| valuecat | 5 | 22.77 | 0.0004 |

## Vehicle insurance: full model, adjusting for exposure

The `fwdlink` and `invlink` statements give the non-standard link and inverse link functions (7.5). They make use of the internal SAS variables:

$$\_MEAN\_ = \pi^* , \qquad \_XBETA\_ = x'\beta .$$

```
proc genmod data=act.car descending;
class agecat area veh_body valuecat(ref="1") / param=ref;
model clm = agecat area veh_body valuecat /
    dist=bin type3;
fwdlink
    link=log((_MEAN_/exposure)/(1-(_MEAN_/exposure)));
invlink
    ilink=exposure*exp(_XBETA_)/(1+exp(_XBETA_));
run;
```

The GENMOD Procedure

Model Information

| Data Set | ACT.CAR |
|---|---|
| Distribution | Binomial |
| Link Function | User |
| Dependent Variable | clm |

| Number of Observations Read | 67856 |
|---|---|
| Number of Observations Used | 67856 |
| Number of Events | 4624 |
| Number of Trials | 67856 |

[output omitted]

Response Profile

| Ordered Value | clm | Total Frequency |
|---|---|---|
| 1 | 1 | 4624 |
| 2 | 0 | 63232 |

PROC GENMOD is modeling the probability that clm='1'.

Criteria For Assessing Goodness Of Fit

| Criterion | DF | Value | Value/DF |
|---|---|---|---|
| Deviance | 68E3 | 32493.5297 | 0.4791 |
| Scaled Deviance | 68E3 | 32493.5297 | 0.4791 |
| Pearson Chi-Square | 68E3 | 96677.4022 | 1.4253 |
| Scaled Pearson X2 | 68E3 | 96677.4022 | 1.4253 |
| Log Likelihood | | -16246.7648 | |

Algorithm converged.

Analysis Of Parameter Estimates

| Parameter | | DF | Estimate | Standard Error | Wald 95% Confidence Limits | | Chi-Square | Pr>ChiSq |
|---|---|---|---|---|---|---|---|---|
| Intercept | | 1 | -1.7496 | 0.0486 | -1.8448 | -1.6544 | 1297.98 | <.0001 |
| agecat | 1 | 1 | 0.2876 | 0.0623 | 0.1656 | 0.4097 | 21.35 | <.0001 |
| agecat | 2 | 1 | 0.0643 | 0.0500 | -0.0336 | 0.1623 | 1.66 | 0.1978 |
| agecat | 4 | 1 | -0.0360 | 0.0476 | -0.1292 | 0.0572 | 0.57 | 0.4492 |
| agecat | 5 | 1 | -0.2650 | 0.0555 | -0.3738 | -0.1562 | 22.77 | <.0001 |
| agecat | 6 | 1 | -0.2550 | 0.0668 | -0.3860 | -0.1240 | 14.56 | 0.0001 |
| area | A | 1 | -0.0358 | 0.0451 | -0.1242 | 0.0526 | 0.63 | 0.4272 |
| area | B | 1 | 0.0534 | 0.0468 | -0.0384 | 0.1451 | 1.30 | 0.2543 |
| area | D | 1 | -0.1381 | 0.0583 | -0.2524 | -0.0239 | 5.62 | 0.0178 |
| area | E | 1 | -0.0664 | 0.0647 | -0.1932 | 0.0605 | 1.05 | 0.3052 |
| area | F | 1 | 0.0209 | 0.0761 | -0.1282 | 0.1700 | 0.08 | 0.7839 |

```
veh_body    BUS     1    1.1361    0.4557    0.2430    2.0292    6.22    0.0127
veh_body    CONVT   1   -0.3709    0.6399   -1.6250    0.8833    0.34    0.5622
veh_body    COUPE   1    0.4333    0.1474    0.1444    0.7223    8.64    0.0033
veh_body    HBACK   1   -0.0124    0.0430   -0.0966    0.0718    0.08    0.7729
veh_body    HDTOP   1    0.0990    0.1046   -0.1060    0.3039    0.90    0.3439
veh_body    MCARA   1    0.5960    0.3235   -0.0380    1.2301    3.39    0.0654
veh_body    MIBUS   1   -0.1112    0.1717   -0.4477    0.2254    0.42    0.5173
veh_body    PANVN   1    0.0194    0.1443   -0.2634    0.3023    0.02    0.8930
veh_body    RDSTR   1    0.0696    0.8161   -1.5298    1.6691    0.01    0.9320
veh_body    STNWG   1   -0.0191    0.0499   -0.1168    0.0786    0.15    0.7013
veh_body    TRUCK   1   -0.0967    0.1081   -0.3085    0.1151    0.80    0.3709
veh_body    UTE     1   -0.2456    0.0759   -0.3942   -0.0969   10.48    0.0012
valuecat    2       1    0.2102    0.0493    0.1136    0.3067   18.19   <.0001
valuecat    3       1    0.1365    0.1237   -0.1059    0.3789    1.22    0.2697
valuecat    4       1   -0.6067    0.5411   -1.6672    0.4539    1.26    0.2622
valuecat    5       1   -0.2900    0.7714   -1.8020    1.2220    0.14    0.7070
valuecat    6       1   -0.7972    1.0623   -2.8792    1.2848    0.56    0.4530
Scale               0    1.0000    0.0000    1.0000    1.0000
```

NOTE: The scale parameter was held fixed.

```
                LR Statistics For Type 3 Analysis

                                        Chi-
            Source              DF    Square    Pr > ChiSq

            agecat              5     87.10       <.0001
            area                5     11.43       0.0435
            veh_body           12     32.98       0.0010
            valuecat            5     20.78       0.0009
```

## Vehicle insurance: logistic regression on grouped data

When performing logistic regression on grouped data, two variables appear on the left hand side of the `model` equation, separated by a slash: the first is the number of events $y$ (in this case `claims`) and the second the total number $n$ in the group (`number`).

```
proc genmod data=act.car_grouped;
class agecat area veh_body valuecat(ref="1") / param=ref;
model claims/number = agecat area veh_body valuecat /
   dist=bin type3;
run;
```

```
                    The GENMOD Procedure

                    Model Information

            Data Set               ACT.CAR_GROUPED
            Distribution                  Binomial
            Link Function                    Logit
            Response Variable (Events)      claims
            Response Variable (Trials)      Number


            Number of Observations Read      929
            Number of Observations Used      929
            Number of Events                4624
            Number of Trials               67856

    [output omitted]

            Criteria For Assessing Goodness Of Fit
```

```
Criterion                    DF        Value      Value/DF


Deviance                    901      868.3800       0.9638
Scaled Deviance             901      868.3800       0.9638
Pearson Chi-Square          901      896.2585       0.9947
Scaled Pearson X2           901      896.2585       0.9947
Log Likelihood                    -16812.1782

      Algorithm converged.
```

                    Analysis Of Parameter Estimates

| Parameter | | DF | Estimate | Standard Error | Wald 95% Confidence Limits | | Chi-Square | Pr>ChiSq |
|---|---|---|---|---|---|---|---|---|
| Intercept | | 1 | -2.5880 | 0.0451 | -2.6764 | -2.4996 | 3292.09 | <.0001 |
| agecat | 1 | 1 | 0.2296 | 0.0568 | 0.1182 | 0.3410 | 16.31 | <.0001 |
| agecat | 2 | 1 | 0.0261 | 0.0462 | -0.0645 | 0.1167 | 0.32 | 0.5723 |
| agecat | 4 | 1 | -0.0318 | 0.0442 | -0.1185 | 0.0548 | 0.52 | 0.4713 |
| agecat | 5 | 1 | -0.2216 | 0.0521 | -0.3238 | -0.1194 | 18.05 | <.0001 |
| agecat | 6 | 1 | -0.2324 | 0.0629 | -0.3556 | -0.1092 | 13.67 | 0.0002 |
| area | A | 1 | -0.0371 | 0.0419 | -0.1192 | 0.0450 | 0.79 | 0.3755 |
| area | B | 1 | 0.0593 | 0.0434 | -0.0257 | 0.1444 | 1.87 | 0.1715 |
| area | D | 1 | -0.1280 | 0.0544 | -0.2347 | -0.0213 | 5.53 | 0.0187 |
| area | E | 1 | -0.0529 | 0.0602 | -0.1710 | 0.0651 | 0.77 | 0.3795 |
| area | F | 1 | 0.0677 | 0.0703 | -0.0701 | 0.2054 | 0.93 | 0.3356 |
| veh_body | BUS | 1 | 1.0774 | 0.3725 | 0.3474 | 1.8074 | 8.37 | 0.0038 |
| veh_body | CONVT | 1 | -0.4904 | 0.6049 | -1.6759 | 0.6951 | 0.66 | 0.4175 |
| veh_body | COUPE | 1 | 0.2525 | 0.1305 | -0.0033 | 0.5083 | 3.74 | 0.0530 |
| veh_body | HBACK | 1 | -0.0143 | 0.0400 | -0.0928 | 0.0641 | 0.13 | 0.7204 |
| veh_body | HDTOP | 1 | 0.1584 | 0.0967 | -0.0310 | 0.3479 | 2.69 | 0.1012 |
| veh_body | MCARA | 1 | 0.5576 | 0.2859 | -0.0027 | 1.1180 | 3.80 | 0.0511 |
| veh_body | MIBUS | 1 | -0.1651 | 0.1600 | -0.4786 | 0.1484 | 1.07 | 0.3019 |
| veh_body | PANVN | 1 | 0.1782 | 0.1356 | -0.0876 | 0.4440 | 1.73 | 0.1887 |
| veh_body | RDSTR | 1 | -0.0497 | 0.7377 | -1.4955 | 1.3962 | 0.00 | 0.9463 |
| veh_body | STNWG | 1 | -0.0088 | 0.0462 | -0.0993 | 0.0817 | 0.04 | 0.8489 |
| veh_body | TRUCK | 1 | -0.0583 | 0.1008 | -0.2558 | 0.1391 | 0.34 | 0.5626 |
| veh_body | UTE | 1 | -0.2500 | 0.0711 | -0.3894 | -0.1107 | 12.37 | 0.0004 |
| valuecat | 2 | 1 | 0.1732 | 0.0453 | 0.0844 | 0.2620 | 14.61 | 0.0001 |
| valuecat | 3 | 1 | 0.0842 | 0.1135 | -0.1383 | 0.3068 | 0.55 | 0.4582 |
| valuecat | 4 | 1 | -0.5515 | 0.5160 | -1.5628 | 0.4599 | 1.14 | 0.2852 |
| valuecat | 5 | 1 | -0.3434 | 0.7326 | -1.7794 | 1.0925 | 0.22 | 0.6392 |
| valuecat | 6 | 1 | -0.7784 | 1.0222 | -2.7820 | 1.2251 | 0.58 | 0.4463 |
| Scale | | 0 | 1.0000 | 0.0000 | 1.0000 | 1.0000 | | |

NOTE: The scale parameter was held fixed.

                  LR Statistics For Type 3 Analysis

| Source | DF | Chi-Square | Pr > ChiSq |
|---|---|---|---|
| agecat | 5 | 67.75 | <.0001 |
| area | 5 | 13.86 | 0.0165 |
| veh_body | 12 | 36.36 | 0.0003 |
| valuecat | 5 | 17.02 | 0.0045 |

These estimates are different to those in the previous section, because no adjustment for exposure has been made. The following code, which computes estimates based on individual policy-level data with no exposure adjustment, produces estimates identical to those above:

```
proc genmod data=act.car descending;
```

```
class agecat area veh_body valuecat(ref="1") / param=ref;
model clm = agecat  area veh_body valuecat /
  dist=bin type3;
run;
```

(Output not shown.)

## proc logistic

For logistic regression unadjusted for exposure, proc logistic may be used. This produces specialized logistic regression output which is not provided by proc genmod.

```
proc logistic data=act.car descending;
class agecat area veh_body valuecat(ref="1") / param=ref;
model clm = agecat  area veh_body valuecat /
  ctable pprob=0.08 outroc=act.outlogistic;
run;
```

                    The LOGISTIC Procedure

                    Model Information

        Data Set                        ACT.CAR
        Response Variable               clm
        Number of Response Levels       2
        Model                           binary logit
        Optimization Technique          Fisher's scoring


        Number of Observations Read       67856
        Number of Observations Used       67856


                    Response Profile

        Ordered                         Total
         Value      clm              Frequency

           1         1                   4624
           2         0                  63232

     Probability modeled is clm='1'.

     [output omitted]

                Model Convergence Status

        Convergence criterion (GCONV=1E-8) satisfied.

                 Model Fit Statistics

                                Intercept
                    Intercept        and
        Criterion        Only   Covariates

        AIC         33768.798    33680.356
        SC          33777.923    33935.860
        -2 Log L    33766.798    33624.356


        Testing Global Null Hypothesis: BETA=0
```
```

| Test | Chi-Square | DF | Pr > ChiSq |
|------|-----------|-----|-----------|
| Likelihood Ratio | 142.4414 | 27 | <.0001 |
| Score | 146.4057 | 27 | <.0001 |
| Wald | 144.2066 | 27 | <.0001 |

### Type 3 Analysis of Effects

| Effect | DF | Wald Chi-Square | Pr > ChiSq |
|--------|-----|-----------|-----------|
| agecat | 5 | 67.8204 | <.0001 |
| area | 5 | 13.7564 | 0.0172 |
| veh_body | 12 | 38.2438 | 0.0001 |
| valuecat | 5 | 16.7858 | 0.0049 |

### Analysis of Maximum Likelihood Estimates

| Parameter | | DF | Estimate | Standard Error | Wald Chi-Square | Pr > ChiSq |
|-----------|---|-----|----------|----------------|-----------------|------------|
| Intercept | | 1 | -2.5880 | 0.0451 | 3292.1026 | <.0001 |
| agecat | 1 | 1 | 0.2296 | 0.0568 | 16.3138 | <.0001 |
| agecat | 2 | 1 | 0.0261 | 0.0462 | 0.3188 | 0.5723 |
| agecat | 4 | 1 | -0.0318 | 0.0442 | 0.5190 | 0.4713 |
| agecat | 5 | 1 | -0.2216 | 0.0521 | 18.0535 | <.0001 |
| agecat | 6 | 1 | -0.2324 | 0.0629 | 13.6701 | 0.0002 |
| area | A | 1 | 0.0371 | 0.0419 | 0.7854 | 0.3755 |
| area | B | 1 | 0.0593 | 0.0434 | 1.8699 | 0.1715 |
| area | D | 1 | -0.1280 | 0.0544 | 5.5279 | 0.0187 |
| area | E | 1 | -0.0529 | 0.0602 | 0.7721 | 0.3796 |
| area | F | 1 | 0.0677 | 0.0703 | 0.9270 | 0.3356 |
| veh_body | BUS | 1 | 1.0808 | 0.3721 | 8.4382 | 0.0037 |
| veh_body | CONVT | 1 | -0.4903 | 0.6048 | 0.6572 | 0.4175 |
| veh_body | COUPE | 1 | 0.2525 | 0.1305 | 3.7428 | 0.0530 |
| veh_body | HBACK | 1 | -0.0143 | 0.0400 | 0.1281 | 0.7204 |
| veh_body | HDTOP | 1 | 0.1584 | 0.0967 | 2.6872 | 0.1012 |
| veh_body | MCARA | 1 | 0.5577 | 0.2859 | 3.8048 | 0.0511 |
| veh_body | MIBUS | 1 | -0.1651 | 0.1600 | 1.0658 | 0.3019 |
| veh_body | PANVN | 1 | 0.1782 | 0.1356 | 1.7274 | 0.1887 |
| veh_body | RDSTR | 1 | -0.0497 | 0.7377 | 0.0045 | 0.9463 |
| veh_body | STNWG | 1 | -0.00880 | 0.0462 | 0.0363 | 0.8489 |
| veh_body | TRUCK | 1 | -0.0583 | 0.1008 | 0.3353 | 0.5626 |
| veh_body | UTE | 1 | -0.2500 | 0.0711 | 12.3662 | 0.0004 |
| valuecat | 2 | 1 | 0.1732 | 0.0453 | 14.6111 | 0.0001 |
| valuecat | 3 | 1 | 0.0842 | 0.1135 | 0.5502 | 0.4582 |
| valuecat | 4 | 1 | -0.5514 | 0.5160 | 1.1421 | 0.2852 |
| valuecat | 5 | 1 | -0.3434 | 0.7326 | 0.2198 | 0.6392 |
| valuecat | 6 | 1 | -0.7779 | 1.0220 | 0.5794 | 0.4465 |

### Odds Ratio Estimates

| Effect | | | Point Estimate | 95% Wald Confidence Limits | |
|--------|---|---|----------------|----------------------------|---|
| agecat | 1 | vs 10 | 1.258 | 1.125 | 1.406 |
| agecat | 2 | vs 10 | 1.026 | 0.938 | 1.124 |
| agecat | 4 | vs 10 | 0.969 | 0.888 | 1.056 |
| agecat | 5 | vs 10 | 0.801 | 0.723 | 0.887 |
| agecat | 6 | vs 10 | 0.793 | 0.701 | 0.897 |
| area | A vs Z | | 0.964 | 0.888 | 1.046 |
| area | B vs Z | | 1.061 | 0.975 | 1.155 |
| area | D vs Z | | 0.880 | 0.791 | 0.979 |

```
area      E vs Z                    0.948      0.843      1.067
area      F vs Z                    1.070      0.932      1.228
veh_body BUS   vs ZSEDA             2.947      1.421      6.111
veh_body CONVT vs ZSEDA            0.612      0.187      2.004
veh_body COUPE vs ZSEDA            1.287      0.997      1.662
veh_body HBACK vs ZSEDA            0.986      0.911      1.066
veh_body HDTOP vs ZSEDA            1.172      0.969      1.416
veh_body MCARA vs ZSEDA            1.747      0.997      3.059
veh_body MIBUS vs ZSEDA            0.848      0.620      1.160
veh_body PANVN vs ZSEDA            1.195      0.916      1.559
veh_body RDSTR vs ZSEDA            0.952      0.224      4.040
veh_body STNWG vs ZSEDA            0.991      0.905      1.085
veh_body TRUCK vs ZSEDA            0.943      0.774      1.149
veh_body UTE   vs ZSEDA            0.779      0.677      0.895
valuecat 2 vs 1                    1.189      1.088      1.300
valuecat 3 vs 1                    1.088      0.871      1.359
valuecat 4 vs 1                    0.576      0.210      1.584
valuecat 5 vs 1                    0.709      0.169      2.982
valuecat 6 vs 1                    0.459      0.062      3.404


      Association of Predicted Probabilities and Observed Responses

           Percent Concordant       51.8     Somers' D    0.097
           Percent Discordant       42.2     Gamma        0.103
           Percent Tied              6.0     Tau-a        0.012
           Pairs              292384768     c            0.548


                          Classification Table

              Correct      Incorrect              Percentages
   Prob           Non-          Non-              Sensi- Speci- False  False
   Level  Event  Event   Event  Event  Correct  tivity ficity  POS    NEG

   0.080    872  54193    9039   3752     81.1    18.9   85.7  91.2    6.5
```

- Parameter estimates are identical to those obtained from `proc genmod`.

- The AUC of the ROC curve of this model is the value $c = 0.548$ in the table "Association of Predicted Probabilities and Observed Responses."

- The classification table (Table A1.1) is obtained by specifying `ctable` in the `model` statement; `pprob=0.08` specifies a cutoff probability of 0.08.

Table A1.1. *Classification table, unadjusted model, cutoff probability = 0.08*

|  |  | Predicted claim | | |
|---|---|---|---|---|
|  |  | No | Yes | Total |
| Actual | No | 54 193 | 9039 | 63 232 |
| Claim | Yes | 3752 | 872 | 4624 |
| | Total | 57 945 | 9911 | 67 856 |

- The `outroc=act.outlogistic` option specifies the output file for the data from which the ROC curve may be plotted.

- The param=ref option in the class statement specifies dummy variables to be set up in the same way as in proc genmod. (The default is different from this.)

**ROC curves and AUC**

When fitting the exposure-adjusted model, one needs to use proc genmod rather than proc logistic, because the latter does not allow user-specified link functions. In this case, macros to compute the ROC curves and AUC, are used. The macro roc.sas is downloadable from the SAS website
http://support.sas.com/ctx/samples/index.jsp?sid=520.
The following code assumes that roc.sas has been downloaded to the directory c:\yourpath.

```
/* Vehicle claims, adjusting for exposure */

%include "c:\yourpath\roc.sas";
proc genmod data=act.car descending;
class agecat area veh_body valuecat(ref="1") / param=ref;
model clm = agecat  area veh_body valuecat /
  dist=bin type3;
fwdlink
  link=log((_MEAN_/exposure)/(1-(_MEAN_/exposure)));
invlink
  ilink=exposure*exp(_XBETA_)/(1+exp(_XBETA_));
output out=act.outadjcar p=fittedadj;
run;

%roc(data=act.outadjcar,var=fittedadj,response=clm)
```

```
[proc genmod output omitted]

              ROC Curve Areas and 95% Confidence Intervals

                 ROC Area Std Error Confidence Limits

          fittedadj  0.6621    0.0038    0.6546    0.6697
```

The macro rocplot.sas is used to plot the ROC curves. This is downloadable from
http://support.sas.com/ctx/samples/index.jsp?sid=521

**Note.** Figure 7.3 was produced using R.

## A1.5  Ordinal regression

**Proportional odds model**

As the data are expressed in grouped format, with frequencies given in the variable number, the weight statement effectively replicates each line of data number times.

```
proc logistic data=act.injury;
class agecat sex roaduserclass / param=ref;
model degree = roaduserclass agecat sex agecat*sex;
weight number;
run;
```

The LOGISTIC Procedure
Model Information

| | | |
|---|---|---|
| Data Set | ACT.INJURY | |
| Response Variable | Degree | Degree |
| Number of Response Levels | 3 | |
| Weight Variable | Number | Number |
| Model | cumulative logit | |
| Optimization Technique | Fisher's scoring | |

| | |
|---|---|
| Number of Observations Read | 209 |
| Number of Observations Used | 209 |
| Sum of Weights Read | 76341 |
| Sum of Weights Used | 76341 |

Response Profile

| Ordered Value | Degree | Total Frequency | Total Weight |
|---|---|---|---|
| 1 | 1 | 77 | 44296.000 |
| 2 | 2 | 79 | 31369.000 |
| 3 | 3 | 53 | 676.000 |

Probabilities modeled are cumulated over the lower Ordered Values.

[output omitted]

Model Convergence Status

Convergence criterion (GCONV=1E-8) satisfied.

Score Test for the Proportional Odds Assumption

| Chi-Square | DF | Pr > ChiSq |
|---|---|---|
| 374.1260 | 16 | <.0001 |

Model Fit Statistics

| Criterion | Intercept Only | Intercept and Covariates |
|---|---|---|
| AIC | 110415.17 | 107739.37 |
| SC | 110421.85 | 107799.53 |
| -2 Log L | 110411.17 | 107703.37 |

Testing Global Null Hypothesis: BETA=0

| Test | Chi-Square | DF | Pr > ChiSq |
|---|---|---|---|
| Likelihood Ratio | 2707.7993 | 16 | <.0001 |

```
          Score                    2637.3229        16        <.0001
          Wald                     2085.4793        16        <.0001
```

                     Type 3 Analysis of Effects

```
                                         Wald
          Effect              DF    Chi-Square    Pr > ChiSq

          roaduserclass        3     1897.9398       <.0001
          agecat               6      116.2267       <.0001
          Sex                  1       26.4531       <.0001
          agecat*Sex           6       24.3524       0.0004
```

              Analysis of Maximum Likelihood Estimates

```
                                    Standard      Wald
Parameter          DF   Estimate     Error    Chi-Square  Pr > ChiSq

Intercept     1     1     0.4704    0.0212      494.0941     <.0001
Intercept     2     1     5.0492    0.0451    12518.4920     <.0001
roaduserclass 2     1    -0.1506    0.0269       31.2251     <.0001
roaduserclass 4     1    -0.2967    0.0365       66.1039     <.0001
roaduserclass 6     1    -2.4492    0.0568     1858.7794     <.0001
agecat        1     1     0.1789    0.0323       30.7282     <.0001
agecat        2     1     0.1122    0.0321       12.2275     0.0005
agecat        3     1     0.0581    0.0364        2.5456     0.1106
agecat        5     1    -0.0550    0.0300        3.3696     0.0664
agecat        6     1    -0.0699    0.0331        4.4677     0.0345
agecat        7     1    -0.1505    0.0344       19.0894     <.0001
Sex           F     1    -0.1719    0.0334       26.4531     <.0001
agecat*Sex    1  F  1    -0.1290    0.0531        5.8974     0.0152
agecat*Sex    2  F  1    -0.1179    0.0522        5.1061     0.0238
agecat*Sex    3  F  1    -0.0419    0.0601        0.4865     0.4855
agecat*Sex    5  F  1    -0.0284    0.0487        0.3398     0.5600
agecat*Sex    6  F  1    -0.0184    0.0556        0.1091     0.7412
agecat*Sex    7  F  1     0.1483    0.0595        6.2165     0.0127
```

                         Odds Ratio Estimates

```
                               Point        95% Wald
          Effect              Estimate   Confidence Limits

   roaduserclass 2  vs 10      0.860      0.816      0.907
   roaduserclass 4  vs 10      0.743      0.692      0.798
   roaduserclass 6  vs 10      0.086      0.077      0.097
```

       Association of Predicted Probabilities and Observed Responses

```
          Percent Concordant    46.5    Somers' D    -.033
          Percent Discordant    49.8    Gamma        -.034
          Percent Tied           3.8    Tau-a        -.022
          Pairs                14351    c            0.484
```

## Partial proportional odds model

For a detailed explanation of this method of restructuring and estimation for the partial proportional odds model, see Chapter 15 of Stokes, Davis, and Koch (2000).

The data need to be case-by-case, rather than grouped, so each line of data is written `number` times to the new data file `injury2`:

```
data injury2;
set act.injury;
do i=1 to number;output;end;
drop i;
run;
```

The following restructuring is then necessary:

```
data injury2;
set injury2;
id=_n_;
do; if degree>2 then y=1; else y=0; degreej=2;output;end;
do; if degree>1 then y=1; else y=0; degreej=1;output;end;
run;
```

The newly created variable `degreej` is category level $j$. Interaction terms with `degreej` allow different $\beta$s across the levels, i.e. non-proportional odds for those explanatory variables. The model with non-proportional odds for age, sex, road user class and age by sex interaction is estimated:

```
proc genmod data=injury2;
class agecat roaduserclass sex degreej id;
model y = agecat sex roaduserclass agecat*sex degreej
   agecat*degreej sex*degreej roaduserclass*degreej
   agecat*sex*degreej / dist=bin link=logit type3;
repeated subject=id / type=un;
run;
```

The interactions with `degreej` are the elements of $\alpha_j$ in Section 7.8. Omitting the rest of the output, we examine the Type 3 tests for their significance:

```
              Score Statistics For Type 3 GEE Analysis
```

| Source | DF | Chi-Square | Pr > ChiSq |
|---|---|---|---|
| agecat | 6 | 20.68 | 0.0021 |
| Sex | 1 | 0.95 | 0.3309 |
| roaduserclass | 3 | 152.20 | <.0001 |
| agecat*Sex | 6 | 7.10 | 0.3119 |
| degreej | 1 | 3954.54 | <.0001 |
| agecat*degreej | 6 | 14.00 | 0.0296 |
| Sex*degreej | 1 | 28.56 | <.0001 |
| roaduserclas*degreej | 3 | 204.81 | <.0001 |
| agecat*Sex*degreej | 6 | 7.00 | 0.3210 |

The hypothesis of proportional odds is rejected for age ($p$-value = 0.0296), sex ($p$-value $<0.0001$) and road user class ($p$-value $<0.0001$), but is not rejected for age by sex interaction ($p$-value = 0.3210). The model is now re-estimated with proportional odds for age by sex (i.e. omitting `agecat*Sex*degreej`), and allowing non-proportional odds for the remaining variables:

```
proc genmod data=injury2;
class agecat roaduserclass sex degreej id;
model y = agecat sex roaduserclass agecat*sex degreej
  agecat*degreej sex*degreej roaduserclass*degreej
  / dist=bin link=logit type3;
repeated subject=id / type=un;
run;
```

The GENMOD Procedure

Model Information

| | |
|---|---|
| Data Set | WORK.INJURY2 |
| Distribution | Binomial |
| Link Function | Logit |
| Dependent Variable | y |

| | |
|---|---|
| Number of Observations Read | 152682 |
| Number of Observations Used | 152682 |
| Number of Events | 119961 |
| Number of Trials | 152682 |

[output omitted]

Criteria For Assessing Goodness Of Fit

| Criterion | DF | Value | Value/DF |
|---|---|---|---|
| Deviance | 15E4 | 108512.9559 | 0.7108 |
| Scaled Deviance | 15E4 | 108512.9559 | 0.7108 |
| Pearson Chi-Square | 15E4 | 152540.9516 | 0.9993 |
| Scaled Pearson X2 | 15E4 | 152540.9516 | 0.9993 |
| Log Likelihood | | -54256.4780 | |

Algorithm converged.

GEE Model Information

| | |
|---|---|
| Correlation Structure | Unstructured |
| Subject Effect | id (76341 levels) |
| Number of Clusters | 76341 |
| Correlation Matrix Dimension | 2 |
| Maximum Cluster Size | 2 |
| Minimum Cluster Size | 2 |

Algorithm converged.

Analysis Of GEE Parameter Estimates
Empirical Standard Error Estimates

| Parameter | | Estimate | Standard Error | 95% Confidence Limits | | Z | Pr > \|Z\| |
|---|---|---|---|---|---|---|---|
| Intercept | | 5.0919 | 0.1015 | 4.8929 | 5.2908 | 50.17 | <.0001 |
| agecat | 1 | -0.1749 | 0.1420 | -0.4532 | 0.1034 | -1.23 | 0.2181 |
| agecat | 2 | -0.0003 | 0.1435 | -0.2816 | 0.2809 | -0.00 | 0.9982 |
| agecat | 3 | -0.0013 | 0.1618 | -0.3184 | 0.3157 | -0.01 | 0.9935 |
| agecat | 5 | -0.0720 | 0.1279 | -0.3227 | 0.1786 | -0.56 | 0.5732 |
| agecat | 6 | -0.2958 | 0.1342 | -0.5588 | -0.0327 | -2.20 | 0.0275 |
| agecat | 7 | -0.6855 | 0.1352 | -0.9504 | -0.4206 | -5.07 | <.0001 |
| agecat | 10 | 0.0000 | 0.0000 | 0.0000 | 0.0000 | . | . |
| Sex | F | 0.2798 | 0.1014 | 0.0811 | 0.4786 | 2.76 | 0.0058 |
| Sex | M | 0.0000 | 0.0000 | 0.0000 | 0.0000 | . | . |
| roaduserclass | 2 | -0.6811 | 0.1206 | -0.9174 | -0.4448 | -5.65 | <.0001 |

| | | | | | | | | |
|---|---|---|---|---|---|---|---|---|
| roaduserclass | 4 | | -1.4765 | 0.1173 | -1.7065 | -1.2465 | -12.58 | <.0001 |
| roaduserclass | 6 | | -1.4665 | 0.1417 | -1.7443 | -1.1887 | -10.35 | <.0001 |
| roaduserclass | 10 | | 0.0000 | 0.0000 | 0.0000 | 0.0000 | . | . |
| agecat*Sex | 1 | F | -0.1331 | 0.0532 | -0.2374 | -0.0287 | -2.50 | 0.0124 |
| agecat*Sex | 1 | M | 0.0000 | 0.0000 | 0.0000 | 0.0000 | . | . |
| agecat*Sex | 2 | F | -0.1216 | 0.0524 | -0.2243 | -0.0189 | -2.32 | 0.0203 |
| agecat*Sex | 2 | M | 0.0000 | 0.0000 | 0.0000 | 0.0000 | . | . |
| agecat*Sex | 3 | F | -0.0439 | 0.0603 | -0.1622 | 0.0743 | -0.73 | 0.4664 |
| agecat*Sex | 3 | M | 0.0000 | 0.0000 | 0.0000 | 0.0000 | . | . |
| agecat*Sex | 5 | F | -0.0290 | 0.0489 | -0.1248 | 0.0668 | -0.59 | 0.5530 |
| agecat*Sex | 5 | M | 0.0000 | 0.0000 | 0.0000 | 0.0000 | . | . |
| agecat*Sex | 6 | F | -0.0210 | 0.0558 | -0.1303 | 0.0884 | -0.38 | 0.7069 |
| agecat*Sex | 6 | M | 0.0000 | 0.0000 | 0.0000 | 0.0000 | . | . |
| agecat*Sex | 7 | F | 0.1414 | 0.0595 | 0.0247 | 0.2581 | 2.38 | 0.0175 |
| agecat*Sex | 7 | M | 0.0000 | 0.0000 | 0.0000 | 0.0000 | . | . |
| agecat*Sex | 10 | F | 0.0000 | 0.0000 | 0.0000 | 0.0000 | . | . |
| agecat*Sex | 10 | M | 0.0000 | 0.0000 | 0.0000 | 0.0000 | . | . |
| degreej | 1 | | -4.6233 | 0.1010 | -4.8213 | -4.4254 | -45.77 | <.0001 |
| degreej | 2 | | 0.0000 | 0.0000 | 0.0000 | 0.0000 | . | . |
| agecat*degreej | 1 | 1 | 0.3614 | 0.1406 | 0.0858 | 0.6371 | 2.57 | 0.0102 |
| agecat*degreej | 1 | 2 | 0.0000 | 0.0000 | 0.0000 | 0.0000 | . | . |
| agecat*degreej | 2 | 1 | 0.1166 | 0.1423 | -0.1624 | 0.3956 | 0.82 | 0.4127 |
| agecat*degreej | 2 | 2 | 0.0000 | 0.0000 | 0.0000 | 0.0000 | . | . |
| agecat*degreej | 3 | 1 | 0.0603 | 0.1600 | -0.2533 | 0.3739 | 0.38 | 0.7062 |
| agecat*degreej | 3 | 2 | 0.0000 | 0.0000 | 0.0000 | 0.0000 | . | . |
| agecat*degreej | 5 | 1 | 0.0166 | 0.1271 | -0.2324 | 0.2657 | 0.13 | 0.8959 |
| agecat*degreej | 5 | 2 | 0.0000 | 0.0000 | 0.0000 | 0.0000 | . | . |
| agecat*degreej | 6 | 1 | 0.2307 | 0.1334 | -0.0308 | 0.4922 | 1.73 | 0.0838 |
| agecat*degreej | 6 | 2 | 0.0000 | 0.0000 | 0.0000 | 0.0000 | . | . |
| agecat*degreej | 7 | 1 | 0.5481 | 0.1340 | 0.2855 | 0.8107 | 4.09 | <.0001 |
| agecat*degreej | 7 | 2 | 0.0000 | 0.0000 | 0.0000 | 0.0000 | . | . |
| agecat*degreej | 10 | 1 | 0.0000 | 0.0000 | 0.0000 | 0.0000 | . | . |
| agecat*degreej | 10 | 2 | 0.0000 | 0.0000 | 0.0000 | 0.0000 | . | . |
| Sex*degreej | F | 1 | -0.4553 | 0.0967 | -0.6448 | -0.2658 | -4.71 | <.0001 |
| Sex*degreej | F | 2 | 0.0000 | 0.0000 | 0.0000 | 0.0000 | . | . |
| Sex*degreej | M | 1 | 0.0000 | 0.0000 | 0.0000 | 0.0000 | . | . |
| Sex*degreej | M | 2 | 0.0000 | 0.0000 | 0.0000 | 0.0000 | . | . |
| roaduserclas*degreej | 2 | 1 | 0.5407 | 0.1201 | 0.3053 | 0.7761 | 4.50 | <.0001 |
| roaduserclas*degreej | 2 | 2 | 0.0000 | 0.0000 | 0.0000 | 0.0000 | . | . |
| roaduserclas*degreej | 4 | 1 | 1.2209 | 0.1168 | 0.9920 | 1.4498 | 10.45 | <.0001 |
| roaduserclas*degreej | 4 | 2 | 0.0000 | 0.0000 | 0.0000 | 0.0000 | . | . |
| roaduserclas*degreej | 6 | 1 | -1.3998 | 0.1580 | -1.7094 | -1.0902 | -8.86 | <.0001 |
| roaduserclas*degreej | 6 | 2 | 0.0000 | 0.0000 | 0.0000 | 0.0000 | . | . |
| roaduserclas*degreej | 10 | 1 | 0.0000 | 0.0000 | 0.0000 | 0.0000 | . | . |
| roaduserclas*degreej | 10 | 2 | 0.0000 | 0.0000 | 0.0000 | 0.0000 | . | . |

Score Statistics For Type 3 GEE Analysis

| Source | DF | Chi-Square | Pr > ChiSq |
|---|---|---|---|
| agecat | 6 | 26.00 | 0.0002 |
| Sex | 1 | 0.21 | 0.6492 |
| roaduserclass | 3 | 151.07 | <.0001 |
| agecat*Sex | 6 | 24.19 | 0.0005 |
| degreej | 1 | 3963.29 | <.0001 |
| agecat*degreej | 6 | 20.93 | 0.0019 |
| Sex*degreej | 1 | 24.37 | <.0001 |
| roaduserclas*degreej | 3 | 204.45 | <.0001 |

The coefficients for the two model equations (7.8) are obtained by recognizing that degreej=$j$, so that the coefficients for the non-casualty model equation ($j = 1$) need to include the degreej interaction terms, whereas the coefficients for the injury equation ($j = 2$, base level for `degreej`) do not. For example:

- The intercept for the non-casualty equation is $\hat{\theta}_1 = 5.0919 - 4.6233 = 0.4686$; for the injury equation it is $\hat{\theta}_2 = 5.0919$.
- The coefficient for road user class = 2 (light truck driver) in the non-casualty equation is $\hat{\beta} = -0.6811 + 0.5407 = -0.1404$; for the injury equation it is $\hat{\beta} = -0.6811$.

## A1.6 Nominal regression

This data set is not available on the book's website. Because its information is at individual respondent level, it is subject to data privacy considerations and access to it is controlled by the Australian Bureau of Statistics (ABS). Readers wishing to obtain the data for analysis should apply to the ABS for Confidentialised Unit Record File (CURF) access; instructions on the application process are given on the ABS website: `www.abs.gov.au`.

The codes for private health insurance status are:

| | | | |
|---|---|---|---|
| 0 | not applicable | 3 | ancillary only |
| 1 | hospital and ancillary | 4 | unknown |
| 2 | hospital only | 5 | none |

```
proc logistic data=nhs.nhs95;
class agegroup sex empstat seifaqse inc / param=ref;
 model instype (ref=last) = agegroup sex  empstat
   seifaqse inc /  link=glogit;
where instype <> 0 & instype <> 4 & empstat <> 0 &
   seifaqse <> 0 ;
run;
```

The LOGISTIC Procedure

Model Information

| | |
|---|---|
| Data Set | NHS.NHS95 |
| Response Variable | instype |
| Number of Response Levels | 4 |
| Model | generalized logit |
| Optimization Technique | Fisher's scoring |

| | |
|---|---|
| Number of Observations Read | 17980 |
| Number of Observations Used | 13851 |

Response Profile

| Ordered Value | instype | Total Frequency |
|---|---|---|
| 1 | 1 | 4338 |
| 2 | 2 | 780 |

```
        3      3                           769
        4      5                          7964
```

Logits modeled use instype='5' as the reference category.

NOTE: 4129 observations were deleted due to missing values for the
response or explanatory variables.

[output omitted]

### Model Convergence Status

Convergence criterion (GCONV=1E-8) satisfied.

### Model Fit Statistics

| Criterion | Intercept Only | Intercept and Covariates |
|---|---|---|
| AIC | 27827.549 | 25612.265 |
| SC | 27850.157 | 25906.173 |
| -2 Log L | 27821.549 | 25534.265 |

### Testing Global Null Hypothesis: BETA=0

| Test | Chi-Square | DF | Pr > ChiSq |
|---|---|---|---|
| Likelihood Ratio | 2287.2840 | 36 | <.0001 |
| Score | 2147.9065 | 36 | <.0001 |
| Wald | 1859.5277 | 36 | <.0001 |

### Type 3 Analysis of Effects

| Effect | DF | Wald Chi-Square | Pr > ChiSq |
|---|---|---|---|
| agegroup | 6 | 532.5752 | <.0001 |
| sex | 3 | 131.0052 | <.0001 |
| empstat | 6 | 210.1074 | <.0001 |
| seifaqse | 12 | 437.1163 | <.0001 |
| inc | 9 | 374.1719 | <.0001 |

### Analysis of Maximum Likelihood Estimates

| Parameter | | instype | DF | Estimate | Standard Error | Wald Chi-Square | Pr>ChiSq |
|---|---|---|---|---|---|---|---|
| Intercept | | 1 | 1 | -1.7362 | 0.0736 | 556.9768 | <.0001 |
| Intercept | | 2 | 1 | -3.7249 | 0.1587 | 550.9891 | <.0001 |
| Intercept | | 3 | 1 | -2.7718 | 0.1278 | 470.3297 | <.0001 |
| agegroup | 2 | 1 | 1 | 0.6183 | 0.0468 | 174.4084 | <.0001 |
| agegroup | 2 | 2 | 1 | 0.5355 | 0.0941 | 32.3590 | <.0001 |
| agegroup | 2 | 3 | 1 | 0.7484 | 0.0853 | 77.0560 | <.0001 |
| agegroup | 3 | 1 | 1 | 1.1284 | 0.0569 | 393.6878 | <.0001 |
| agegroup | 3 | 2 | 1 | 1.2621 | 0.1025 | 151.5620 | <.0001 |
| agegroup | 3 | 3 | 1 | 0.5319 | 0.1174 | 20.5222 | <.0001 |
| sex | 1 | 1 | 1 | -0.4905 | 0.0442 | 123.0164 | <.0001 |
| sex | 1 | 2 | 1 | -0.4154 | 0.0840 | 24.4591 | <.0001 |
| sex | 1 | 3 | 1 | -0.2943 | 0.0814 | 13.0626 | 0.0003 |
| empstat | 2 | 1 | 1 | -1.3552 | 0.1473 | 84.6931 | <.0001 |
| empstat | 2 | 2 | 1 | -0.7484 | 0.2555 | 8.5811 | 0.0034 |
| empstat | 2 | 3 | 1 | -0.6696 | 0.2087 | 10.2970 | 0.0013 |
| empstat | 3 | 1 | 1 | -0.7163 | 0.0648 | 122.3595 | <.0001 |

| empstat | 3 | 2 | 1 | -0.2348 | 0.1161 | 4.0908 | 0.0431 |
|---------|---|---|---|---------|--------|--------|--------|
| empstat | 3 | 3 | 1 | -0.8759 | 0.1303 | 45.1575 | <.0001 |
| seifaqse | 2 | 1 | 1 | 0.5015 | 0.0743 | 45.5599 | <.0001 |
| seifaqse | 2 | 2 | 1 | 0.5763 | 0.1618 | 12.6922 | 0.0004 |
| seifaqse | 2 | 3 | 1 | 0.2249 | 0.1282 | 3.0781 | 0.0794 |
| seifaqse | 3 | 1 | 1 | 0.6961 | 0.0726 | 91.8409 | <.0001 |
| seifaqse | 3 | 2 | 1 | 0.7409 | 0.1582 | 21.9325 | <.0001 |
| seifaqse | 3 | 3 | 1 | 0.2651 | 0.1277 | 4.3069 | 0.0380 |
| seifaqse | 4 | 1 | 1 | 0.7082 | 0.0701 | 101.9793 | <.0001 |
| seifaqse | 4 | 2 | 1 | 1.0586 | 0.1475 | 51.5379 | <.0001 |
| seifaqse | 4 | 3 | 1 | 0.2722 | 0.1229 | 4.9081 | 0.0267 |
| seifaqse | 5 | 1 | 1 | 1.2449 | 0.0693 | 322.3867 | <.0001 |
| seifaqse | 5 | 2 | 1 | 1.5746 | 0.1439 | 119.7047 | <.0001 |
| seifaqse | 5 | 3 | 1 | 0.4435 | 0.1251 | 12.5673 | 0.0004 |
| inc | 2 | 1 | 1 | 0.3499 | 0.0544 | 41.3514 | <.0001 |
| inc | 2 | 2 | 1 | 0.2625 | 0.1070 | 6.0142 | 0.0142 |
| inc | 2 | 3 | 1 | 0.2189 | 0.0978 | 5.0165 | 0.0251 |
| inc | 3 | 1 | 1 | 0.9492 | 0.0688 | 190.1922 | <.0001 |
| inc | 3 | 2 | 1 | 0.7290 | 0.1322 | 30.4289 | <.0001 |
| inc | 3 | 3 | 1 | 0.4052 | 0.1281 | 10.0012 | 0.0016 |
| inc | 4 | 1 | 1 | 1.3010 | 0.0816 | 254.2517 | <.0001 |
| inc | 4 | 2 | 1 | 1.2071 | 0.1438 | 70.4568 | <.0001 |
| inc | 4 | 3 | 1 | 0.0649 | 0.1793 | 0.1310 | 0.7174 |

Odds Ratio Estimates

| Effect | | | instype | Point Estimate | 95% Wald Confidence Limits | |
|--------|---|---|---------|----------------|------------|---|
| agegroup | 2 vs 99 | | 1 | 1.856 | 1.693 | 2.034 |
| agegroup | 2 vs 99 | | 2 | 1.708 | 1.420 | 2.054 |
| agegroup | 2 vs 99 | | 3 | 2.114 | 1.788 | 2.498 |
| agegroup | 3 vs 99 | | 1 | 3.091 | 2.765 | 3.455 |
| agegroup | 3 vs 99 | | 2 | 3.533 | 2.890 | 4.319 |
| agegroup | 3 vs 99 | | 3 | 1.702 | 1.352 | 2.142 |
| sex | 1 vs 2 | | 1 | 0.612 | 0.561 | 0.668 |
| sex | 1 vs 2 | | 2 | 0.660 | 0.560 | 0.778 |
| sex | 1 vs 2 | | 3 | 0.745 | 0.635 | 0.874 |
| empstat | 2 vs 99 | | 1 | 0.258 | 0.193 | 0.344 |
| empstat | 2 vs 99 | | 2 | 0.473 | 0.287 | 0.781 |
| empstat | 2 vs 99 | | 3 | 0.512 | 0.340 | 0.771 |
| empstat | 3 vs 99 | | 1 | 0.489 | 0.430 | 0.555 |
| empstat | 3 vs 99 | | 2 | 0.791 | 0.630 | 0.993 |
| empstat | 3 vs 99 | | 3 | 0.416 | 0.323 | 0.538 |
| seifaqse | 2 vs 99 | | 1 | 1.651 | 1.427 | 1.910 |
| seifaqse | 2 vs 99 | | 2 | 1.779 | 1.296 | 2.443 |
| seifaqse | 2 vs 99 | | 3 | 1.252 | 0.974 | 1.610 |
| seifaqse | 3 vs 99 | | 1 | 2.006 | 1.740 | 2.313 |
| seifaqse | 3 vs 99 | | 2 | 2.098 | 1.539 | 2.860 |
| seifaqse | 3 vs 99 | | 3 | 1.304 | 1.015 | 1.674 |
| seifaqse | 4 vs 99 | | 1 | 2.030 | 1.770 | 2.330 |
| seifaqse | 4 vs 99 | | 2 | 2.882 | 2.159 | 3.848 |
| seifaqse | 4 vs 99 | | 3 | 1.313 | 1.032 | 1.670 |
| seifaqse | 5 vs 99 | | 1 | 3.473 | 3.031 | 3.978 |
| seifaqse | 5 vs 99 | | 2 | 4.829 | 3.642 | 6.402 |
| seifaqse | 5 vs 99 | | 3 | 1.558 | 1.219 | 1.991 |
| inc | 2 vs 99 | | 1 | 1.419 | 1.275 | 1.579 |
| inc | 2 vs 99 | | 2 | 1.300 | 1.054 | 1.604 |
| inc | 2 vs 99 | | 3 | 1.245 | 1.028 | 1.508 |
| inc | 3 vs 99 | | 1 | 2.584 | 2.258 | 2.957 |
| inc | 3 vs 99 | | 2 | 2.073 | 1.600 | 2.686 |
| inc | 3 vs 99 | | 3 | 1.500 | 1.167 | 1.928 |
| inc | 4 vs 99 | | 1 | 3.673 | 3.130 | 4.310 |
| inc | 4 vs 99 | | 2 | 3.344 | 2.522 | 4.432 |
| inc | 4 vs 99 | | 3 | 1.067 | 0.751 | 1.516 |

## A1.7 Gamma regression

### Vehicle insurance

The analysis is restricted to positive claim costs only with the `where` statement:

```
proc genmod data=act.car;
class agecat(ref='3') gender area veh_body / param=ref;
model claimcst0 = agecat gender agecat*gender area
  veh_body / dist=gamma link=log type3;
where claimcst0>0;
run;
```

Only model fit statistics are shown.

```
                    The GENMOD Procedure

                    Model Information

              Data Set                ACT.CAR
              Distribution              Gamma
              Link Function               Log
              Dependent Variable    claimcst0


         Number of Observations Read       4624
         Number of Observations Used       4624
```

[output omitted]

```
          Criteria For Assessing Goodness Of Fit

     Criterion              DF        Value      Value/DF

     Deviance              4595    7172.4590       1.5609
     Scaled Deviance       4595    5517.2969       1.2007
     Pearson Chi-Square    4595   13069.9608       2.8444
     Scaled Pearson X2     4595   10053.8538       2.1880
     Log Likelihood              -39584.1410
```

[output omitted]

### Personal injury insurance, no adjustment for quickly settled claims

```
proc genmod data=persinj;
class legrep (ref="0") / param=ref;
model total = op_time legrep op_time*legrep
    / dist=gamma link=log type1 type3 ;
run;
```

```
                    The GENMOD Procedure

                    Model Information

       Data Set        WORK.PERSINJ
       Distribution          Gamma
       Link Function           Log
       Dependent Variable    TOTAL     TOTAL


        Number of Observations Read       22036
```

```
Number of Observations Used        22036
```

Class Level Information

| Class | Value | Design Variables |
|-------|-------|------------------|
| LEGREP | 0 | 0 |
|        | 1 | 1 |

Criteria For Assessing Goodness Of Fit

| Criterion | DF | Value | Value/DF |
|-----------|-----|-------|----------|
| Deviance | 22E3 | 25411.6917 | 1.1534 |
| Scaled Deviance | 22E3 | 25436.1756 | 1.1545 |
| Pearson Chi-Square | 22E3 | 53582.4354 | 2.4320 |
| Scaled Pearson X2 | 22E3 | 53634.0615 | 2.4344 |
| Log Likelihood |  | -245326.0735 |  |

Algorithm converged.

Analysis Of Parameter Estimates

| Parameter | | DF | Estimate | Standard Error | Wald 95% Confidence Limits | | Chi-Square | Pr>ChiSq |
|-----------|---|-----|----------|----------|-------|-------|--------|----------|
| Intercept | | 1 | 8.2118 | 0.0220 | 8.1687 | 8.2549 | 139276 | <.0001 |
| OP_TIME | | 1 | 0.0383 | 0.0004 | 0.0375 | 0.0392 | 7991.30 | <.0001 |
| LEGREP | 1 | 1 | 0.4668 | 0.0279 | 0.4121 | 0.5215 | 279.36 | <.0001 |
| OP_TIME*LEGREP | 1 | 1 | -0.0050 | 0.0005 | -0.0060 | -0.0040 | 88.24 | <.0001 |
| Scale | | 1 | 1.0010 | 0.0084 | 0.9846 | 1.0176 | | |

NOTE: The scale parameter was estimated by maximum likelihood.

LR Statistics For Type 1 Analysis

| Source | 2*Log Likelihood | DF | Chi-Square | Pr > ChiSq |
|--------|------------------|-----|------------|------------|
| Intercept | -505065.18 | | | |
| OP_TIME | -491019.17 | 1 | 14046.0 | <.0001 |
| LEGREP | -490740.42 | 1 | 278.75 | <.0001 |
| OP_TIME*LEGREP | -490652.15 | 1 | 88.27 | <.0001 |

LR Statistics For Type 3 Analysis

| Source | DF | Chi-Square | Pr > ChiSq |
|--------|-----|------------|------------|
| OP_TIME | 1 | 6811.20 | <.0001 |
| LEGREP | 1 | 271.17 | <.0001 |
| OP_TIME*LEGREP | 1 | 88.27 | <.0001 |

## Personal injury insurance, with adjustment for quickly settled claims

```
data persinj;
set act.persinj;
if op_time<=5 then fast=1; else fast=0;
```

```
run;

proc genmod data=persinj;
class legrep (ref="0") fast / param=ref;
model total =
     op_time legrep fast
     op_time*legrep  fast*op_time fast*legrep
     fast*op_time*legrep /
     dist=gamma link=log type1 type3;
run;
```

Output for this model is not shown.

## Runoff triangle

```
data runoff;
set act.runoff;
if y<0 then y=1;  /* replace negative value by 1 */
if devyear=1 then devyear=99;
   /* make devyear=1 the base level for devyear */
if accyear=1 then accyear=99;
   /* make accyear=1 the base level for accyear */
run;

proc genmod data=runoff;
class devyear accyear;
model y = devyear accyear /
    dist=gamma link=log type1 type3;
run;
```

The GENMOD Procedure

Model Information

|  |  |
|---|---|
| Data Set | WORK.RUNOFF |
| Distribution | Gamma |
| Link Function | Log |
| Dependent Variable | Y |

Number of Observations Read          55
Number of Observations Used          55

Class Level Information

| Class | Levels | Values |
|---|---|---|
| accyear | 10 | 2 3 4 5 6 7 8 9 10 99 |
| devyear | 10 | 2 3 4 5 6 7 8 9 10 99 |

Criteria For Assessing Goodness Of Fit

| Criterion | DF | Value | Value/DF |
|---|---|---|---|
| Deviance | 36 | 31.7196 | 0.8811 |
| Scaled Deviance | 36 | 59.7443 | 1.6596 |
| Pearson Chi-Square | 36 | 15.9213 | 0.4423 |
| Scaled Pearson X2 | 36 | 29.9880 | 0.8330 |
| Log Likelihood |  | -475.8061 |  |

Algorithm converged.

Analysis Of Parameter Estimates

| Parameter | | DF | Estimate | Standard Error | Wald 95% Confidence Limits | | Chi-Square | Pr>ChiSq |
|---|---|---|---|---|---|---|---|---|
| Intercept | | 1 | 7.7406 | 0.3373 | 7.0796 | 8.4017 | 526.72 | <.0001 |
| accyear | 2 | 1 | -0.1999 | 0.3914 | -0.9671 | 0.5673 | 0.26 | 0.6096 |
| accyear | 3 | 1 | 0.0894 | 0.3624 | -0.6210 | 0.7998 | 0.06 | 0.8052 |
| accyear | 4 | 1 | 0.3173 | 0.3771 | -0.4218 | 1.0563 | 0.71 | 0.4001 |
| accyear | 5 | 1 | 0.1528 | 0.4232 | -0.6767 | 0.9824 | 0.13 | 0.7180 |
| accyear | 6 | 1 | -0.1727 | 0.4400 | -1.0350 | 0.6896 | 0.15 | 0.6946 |
| accyear | 7 | 1 | -0.3594 | 0.4848 | -1.3095 | 0.5908 | 0.55 | 0.4585 |
| accyear | 8 | 1 | -0.0035 | 0.5241 | -1.0306 | 1.0236 | 0.00 | 0.9947 |
| accyear | 9 | 1 | -0.0913 | 0.6004 | -1.2681 | 1.0855 | 0.02 | 0.8791 |
| accyear | 10 | 1 | -0.1087 | 0.8029 | -1.6824 | 1.4650 | 0.02 | 0.8923 |
| accyear | 99 | 0 | 0.0000 | 0.0000 | 0.0000 | 0.0000 | . | . |
| devyear | 2 | 1 | 0.7530 | 0.3612 | 0.0451 | 1.4608 | 4.35 | 0.0371 |
| devyear | 3 | 1 | 0.7580 | 0.3875 | -0.0016 | 1.5175 | 3.83 | 0.0505 |
| devyear | 4 | 1 | 0.3246 | 0.4005 | -0.4603 | 1.1096 | 0.66 | 0.4176 |
| devyear | 5 | 1 | 0.1604 | 0.4117 | -0.6465 | 0.9673 | 0.15 | 0.6968 |
| devyear | 6 | 1 | -0.1228 | 0.4273 | -0.9602 | 0.7146 | 0.08 | 0.7739 |
| devyear | 7 | 1 | -1.0752 | 0.4597 | -1.9762 | -0.1742 | 5.47 | 0.0193 |
| devyear | 8 | 1 | -1.2522 | 0.5173 | -2.2661 | -0.2384 | 5.86 | 0.0155 |
| devyear | 9 | 1 | -1.8722 | 0.6446 | -3.1357 | -0.6087 | 8.43 | 0.0037 |
| devyear | 10 | 1 | -2.5931 | 0.8029 | -4.1668 | -1.0194 | 10.43 | 0.0012 |
| devyear | 99 | 0 | 0.0000 | 0.0000 | 0.0000 | 0.0000 | . | . |
| Scale | | 1 | 1.8835 | 0.3323 | 1.3329 | 2.6615 | | |

NOTE: The scale parameter was estimated by maximum likelihood.

LR Statistics For Type 1 Analysis

| Source | 2*Log Likelihood | DF | Chi-Square | Pr > ChiSq |
|---|---|---|---|---|
| Intercept | -987.7723 | | | |
| accyear | -981.2526 | 9 | 6.52 | 0.6870 |
| devyear | -951.6122 | 9 | 29.64 | 0.0005 |

LR Statistics For Type 3 Analysis

| Source | DF | Chi-Square | Pr > ChiSq |
|---|---|---|---|
| accyear | 9 | 3.30 | 0.9513 |
| devyear | 9 | 29.64 | 0.0005 |

## A1.8 Inverse Gaussian regression

```
proc genmod data=act.car;
class agecat gender area / param=ref;
model claimcst0 = agecat gender area  /
   dist=ig link=log type3;
estimate 'areadiffs' area 0 0 0 1 -1 0 ;
where claimcst0>0;
run;
```

The GENMOD Procedure

```
                        Model Information

            Data Set                           ACT.CAR
            Distribution            Inverse Gaussian
            Link Function                          Log
            Dependent Variable              claimcst0


            Number of Observations Read         4624
            Number of Observations Used         4624
```

[output omitted]

```
            Criteria For Assessing Goodness Of Fit

        Criterion              DF           Value        Value/DF

        Deviance             4612          6.3765          0.0014
        Scaled Deviance      4612       4624.0031          1.0026
        Pearson Chi-Square   4612          6.7533          0.0015
        Scaled Pearson X2    4612       4897.2321          1.0618
        Log Likelihood                -38568.1596
```

Algorithm converged.

```
                    Analysis Of Parameter Estimates

                          Standard  Wald 95% Confidence  Chi-
    Parameter    DF   Estimate    Error       Limits      Square  Pr>ChiSq

    Intercept     1     7.6830    0.0734    7.5391    7.8269   10946.8   <.0001
    agecat    1   1     0.2511    0.0976    0.0599    0.4423      6.62    0.0101
    agecat    2   1     0.0927    0.0748   -0.0539    0.2393      1.53    0.2154
    agecat    4   1    -0.0053    0.0700   -0.1425    0.1319      0.01    0.9394
    agecat    5   1    -0.1213    0.0798   -0.2776    0.0351      2.31    0.1285
    agecat    6   1    -0.0675    0.0979   -0.2594    0.1243      0.48    0.4903
    gender    F   1    -0.1528    0.0505   -0.2519   -0.0538      9.14    0.0025
    area      A   1    -0.0729    0.0663   -0.2029    0.0571      1.21    0.2718
    area      B   1    -0.1026    0.0685   -0.2369    0.0316      2.24    0.1341
    area      D   1    -0.0978    0.0848   -0.2640    0.0684      1.33    0.2488
    area      E   1     0.0695    0.0991   -0.1247    0.2637      0.49    0.4831
    area      F   1     0.2825    0.1255    0.0365    0.5285      5.07    0.0244
    Scale         1     0.0371    0.0004    0.0364    0.0379
```

NOTE: The scale parameter was estimated by maximum likelihood.

```
                LR Statistics For Type 3 Analysis

                                    Chi-
        Source             DF      Square    Pr > ChiSq

        agecat              5       17.24        0.0041
        gender              1        9.35        0.0022
        area                5       14.97        0.0105
```

```
                    Contrast Estimate Results

                     Standard                        Chi-
    Label      Estimate   Error   Alpha  Confidence Limits  Square  Pr>ChiSq

    areadiffs   -0.2130  0.1466   0.05  -0.5002    0.0743    2.11    0.1462
```

## A1.9  Logistic regression GLMM

The GLMM is estimated using `proc nlmixed`. The syntax is more basic than that of `proc genmod`, which means that more effort has to be put into specifying the model.

As `proc nlmixed` does not have a `class` statement, indicator variables for the categorical variables have to be created:

```
data claimslong;
set act.claimslong;

/* age1,...,age6 are the indicator variables
for agecat */
if agecat=1 then age1=1;else age1=0;
if agecat=2 then age2=1;else age2=0;
if agecat=4 then age4=1;else age4=0;
if agecat=5 then age5=1;else age5=0;
if agecat=6 then age6=1;else age6=0;

/* value2,...,value6 are the indicator variables
for valuecat */
if valuecat=2 then value2=1;else value2=0;
if valuecat=3 then value3=1;else value3=0;
if valuecat=4 then value4=1;else value4=0;
if valuecat=5 then value5=1;else value5=0;
if valuecat=6 then value6=1;else value6=0;

/* period1 and period2 are the indicator variables
for period */
if period=1 then period1=1;else period1=0;
if period=2 then period2=1;else period2=0;

run;
```

The linear predictor $\alpha + x'\beta$ and the probability of occurrence $\pi$ have to be computed explicitly. The `random` statement specifies the distribution of the random effect `alpha`, and the variable which identifies the clusters (`subject=policyid`).

```
proc nlmixed data=claimslong;

/* nu2 is the variance of the random intercept.
Constrain nu2 to be positive with the
bounds statement: */
bounds nu2>0;

/* Compute the linear predictor z : */
zage = beta1age*age1 + beta2age*age2 + beta4age*age4 +
  beta5age*age5 + beta6age*age6;
zvalue = beta2value*value2 + beta3value*value3 +
  beta4value*value4 + beta5value*value5 +
  beta6value*value6;
zperiod = beta1period*period1 + beta2period*period2;
```

```
z = alpha + beta0 + zage + zvalue + zperiod ;
/* alpha is the random intercept */

/* Compute the probability p : */
expz = exp(z);
p = expz/(1+expz);

/* Specify the model : */
model claim ~ binary(p);
random alpha ~ normal(0,nu2) subject=policyid;
run;
```

The NLMIXED Procedure
Specifications

| | |
|---|---|
| Data Set | WORK.CLAIMSLONG |
| Dependent Variable | claim |
| Distribution for Dependent Variable | Binary |
| Random Effects | alpha |
| Distribution for Random Effects | Normal |
| Subject Variable | policyID |
| Optimization Technique | Dual Quasi-Newton |
| Integration Method | Adaptive Gaussian Quadrature |

Dimensions

| | |
|---|---|
| Observations Used | 120000 |
| Observations Not Used | 0 |
| Total Observations | 120000 |
| Subjects | 40000 |
| Max Obs Per Subject | 3 |
| Parameters | 14 |
| Quadrature Points | 5 |

[output omitted]

NOTE: GCONV convergence criterion satisfied.

Fit Statistics

| | |
|---|---|
| -2 Log Likelihood | 89672 |
| AIC (smaller is better) | 89700 |
| AICC (smaller is better) | 89700 |
| BIC (smaller is better) | 89820 |

Parameter Estimates

| Parameter | Estimate | Standard Error | DF | t Value | Pr > \|t\| | Alpha | Lower | Upper | Gradient |
|---|---|---|---|---|---|---|---|---|---|
| nu2 | 3.8175 | 0.08207 | 4E4 | 46.52 | <.0001 | 0.05 | 3.6566 | 3.9783 | 0.002377 |
| beta1age | 0.2738 | 0.05893 | 4E4 | 4.65 | <.0001 | 0.05 | 0.1583 | 0.3893 | 0.007508 |
| beta2age | 0.008467 | 0.04665 | 4E4 | 0.18 | 0.8560 | 0.05 | -0.08297 | 0.09991 | 0.000096 |
| beta4age | -0.05306 | 0.04450 | 4E4 | -1.19 | 0.2331 | 0.05 | -0.1403 | 0.03416 | -0.00344 |
| beta5age | -0.2748 | 0.05078 | 4E4 | -5.41 | <.0001 | 0.05 | -0.3744 | -0.1753 | -0.00568 |
| beta6age | -0.2247 | 0.05949 | 4E4 | -3.78 | 0.0002 | 0.05 | -0.3413 | -0.1081 | 0.006262 |
| beta2value | 0.2355 | 0.04003 | 4E4 | 5.88 | <.0001 | 0.05 | 0.1570 | 0.3139 | 0.006118 |
| beta3value | 0.08725 | 0.1139 | 4E4 | 0.77 | 0.4438 | 0.05 | -0.1361 | 0.3106 | -0.0003 |
| beta4value | -0.8855 | 0.4532 | 4E4 | -1.95 | 0.0507 | 0.05 | -1.7737 | 0.002751 | 0.002956 |
| beta5value | -0.6133 | 0.6963 | 4E4 | -0.88 | 0.3784 | 0.05 | -1.9780 | 0.7514 | -0.17003 |
| beta6value | -1.3139 | 0.7754 | 4E4 | -1.69 | 0.0902 | 0.05 | -2.8337 | 0.2059 | 0.11466 |
| beta1period | -0.3015 | 0.02461 | 4E4 | -12.25 | <.0001 | 0.05 | -0.3497 | -0.2532 | 0.008229 |
| beta2period | -0.1715 | 0.02423 | 4E4 | -7.08 | <.0001 | 0.05 | -0.2190 | -0.1240 | -0.01007 |
| beta0 | -2.6541 | 0.03858 | 4E4 | -68.79 | <.0001 | 0.05 | -2.7297 | -2.5784 | 0.00377 |

There was no problem with convergence in this example; however, the SAS manual recommends the specification of parameter starting values, using the `parms` statement. If this statement is not included, the default starting values are 1 for all parameters.

## A1.10 Logistic regression GEE

GEEs are implemented in `proc genmod`. The model is specified as one would specify a GLM, and the clustering information and correlation structure are given in the `repeated` statement.

```
proc genmod data=act.claimslong descending;
class agecat valuecat policyid period;
model claim =  agecat valuecat period / dist=bin type3;
repeated subject=policyid / type=un within=period corrw;
run;
```

The `repeated` statement gives the following information:

- The name of the variable identifying clusters (or subjects) is `policyid`;
- The type of correlation structure is `un` (unstructured);
- `within=period` specifies the name of the variable (`period`) which gives the times at which the observations were taken. This is essential if some observations are missing, so that the software is able to line up the observations at their correct times. In this data set, there are no missing times but it is a good habit to always specify the `within=` variable.
- `corrw` is the estimated within-subject correlation matrix $\hat{R}$ to be printed out.

```
                    [output omitted]

                Working Correlation Matrix

                Col1        Col2        Col3

        Row1    1.0000      0.3265      0.3256
        Row2    0.3265      1.0000      0.3431
        Row3    0.3256      0.3431      1.0000
```

The working correlation matrix suggests a compound symmetric correlation structure. The model is re-estimated with `type=cs`:

```
proc genmod data=act.claimslong descending;
class agecat valuecat policyid period;
model claim =  agecat valuecat period / dist=bin type3;
repeated subject=policyid / type=cs within=period corrw;
run;
```

The "Criteria For Assessing Goodness Of Fit" and "Analysis Of Initial Parameter Estimates" (not shown here) relate to the model which ignores the correlation, i.e. these are estimates for the model with independent observations, and should therefore be ignored. Relevant output starts from "GEE Model Information".

```
                        The GENMOD Procedure

                        Model Information

            Data Set                    ACT.CLAIMSLONG
            Distribution                      Binomial
            Link Function                        Logit
            Dependent Variable                   claim


        Number of Observations Read        120000
        Number of Observations Used        120000
        Number of Events                    17130
        Number of Trials                   120000

    [output omitted]
                        Response Profile

                Ordered                     Total
                  Value      claim       Frequency

                      1        1             17130
                      2        0            102870

    PROC GENMOD is modeling the probability that claim='1'.

        [output omitted]

                        GEE Model Information

        Correlation Structure                     Exchangeable
        Within-Subject Effect               period (3 levels)
        Subject Effect            policyID (40000 levels)
        Number of Clusters                               40000
        Correlation Matrix Dimension                         3
        Maximum Cluster Size                                 3
        Minimum Cluster Size                                 3

         Algorithm converged.

                    Working Correlation Matrix

                        Col1        Col2        Col3

                Row1    1.0000      0.3317      0.3317
                Row2    0.3317      1.0000      0.3317
                Row3    0.3317      0.3317      1.0000

                    Exchangeable Working
                          Correlation

                Correlation      0.3316776334


                    Analysis Of GEE Parameter Estimates
                    Empirical Standard Error Estimates
```

| Parameter | | Estimate | Standard Error | 95% Confidence Limits | | Z | Pr > \|Z\| |
|---|---|---|---|---|---|---|---|
| Intercept | | -1.6837 | 0.0247 | -1.7320 | -1.6354 | -68.29 | <.0001 |
| agecat | 1 | 0.1889 | 0.0408 | 0.1089 | 0.2689 | 4.63 | <.0001 |
| agecat | 2 | 0.0049 | 0.0325 | -0.0589 | 0.0687 | 0.15 | 0.8800 |
| agecat | 4 | -0.0362 | 0.0311 | -0.0972 | 0.0249 | -1.16 | 0.2455 |
| agecat | 5 | -0.1952 | 0.0357 | -0.2651 | -0.1253 | -5.47 | <.0001 |
| agecat | 6 | -0.1497 | 0.0422 | -0.2325 | -0.0670 | -3.55 | 0.0004 |
| agecat | 10 | 0.0000 | 0.0000 | 0.0000 | 0.0000 | . | . |
| valuecat | 2 | 0.1613 | 0.0278 | 0.1069 | 0.2157 | 5.81 | <.0001 |
| valuecat | 3 | 0.0594 | 0.0792 | -0.0959 | 0.2147 | 0.75 | 0.4534 |
| valuecat | 4 | -0.6456 | 0.3129 | -1.2588 | -0.0324 | -2.06 | 0.0391 |
| valuecat | 5 | -0.2368 | 0.5811 | -1.3757 | 0.9021 | -0.41 | 0.6836 |
| valuecat | 6 | -0.9688 | 0.6159 | -2.1759 | 0.2383 | -1.57 | 0.1157 |
| valuecat | 9 | 0.0000 | 0.0000 | 0.0000 | 0.0000 | . | . |
| period | 1 | -0.2051 | 0.0166 | -0.2377 | -0.1725 | -12.33 | <.0001 |
| period | 2 | -0.1161 | 0.0161 | -0.1476 | -0.0845 | -7.20 | <.0001 |
| period | 3 | 0.0000 | 0.0000 | 0.0000 | 0.0000 | . | . |

Score Statistics For Type 3 GEE Analysis

| Source | DF | Chi-Square | Pr > ChiSq |
|---|---|---|---|
| agecat | 5 | 88.83 | <.0001 |
| valuecat | 5 | 44.07 | <.0001 |
| period | 2 | 152.71 | <.0001 |

## A1.11 Logistic regression GAM

The variables agecat, area and veh_body are entered into the model as
linear (or parametric) terms (param), and vehicle value (veh_value) in the
form of a spline smoother, with five degrees of freedom. When a smoother is
specified for a variable, a linear term is automatically included in the model,
leaving one less degree of freedom for the spline than that specified in the
model equation. Loess and thin-plate spline smoothers may also be specified.

```
ods html; ods graphics on;
proc gam data=act.car;
class agecat area veh_body;
model clm =
   param(agecat area veh_body) spline(veh_value,df=5) /
   dist=binomial;
run;
ods graphics off; ods html close;
```

The GAM Procedure
Dependent Variable: clm
Regression Model Component(s): agecat area veh_body
Smoothing Model Component(s): spline(veh_value)

Summary of Input Data Set

| | |
|---|---|
| Number of Observations | 67856 |
| Number of Missing Observations | 0 |
| Distribution | Binomial |
| Link Function | Logit |

[output omitted]

### Iteration Summary and Fit Statistics

| | |
|---|---|
| Number of local score iterations | 7 |
| Local score convergence criterion | 6.136141E-11 |
| Final Number of Backfitting Iterations | 1 |
| Final Backfitting Criterion | 3.616223E-10 |
| The Deviance of the Final Estimate | 33588.205198 |

The local score algorithm converged.

### Regression Model Analysis
### Parameter Estimates

| Parameter | Parameter Estimate | Standard Error | t Value | Pr > \|t\| |
|---|---|---|---|---|
| Intercept | -2.68861 | 0.05072 | -53.01 | <.0001 |
| agecat 1 | 0.22395 | 0.05687 | 3.94 | <.0001 |
| agecat 2 | 0.02502 | 0.04623 | 0.54 | 0.5884 |
| agecat 4 | -0.03019 | 0.04422 | -0.68 | 0.4948 |
| agecat 5 | -0.22096 | 0.05216 | -4.24 | <.0001 |
| agecat 6 | -0.22239 | 0.06290 | -3.54 | 0.0004 |
| agecat 10 | 0 | . | . | . |
| area A | -0.03852 | 0.04190 | -0.92 | 0.3579 |
| area B | 0.05997 | 0.04340 | 1.38 | 0.1671 |
| area D | -0.12921 | 0.05446 | -2.37 | 0.0177 |
| area E | -0.05811 | 0.06025 | -0.96 | 0.3349 |
| area F | 0.05279 | 0.07028 | 0.75 | 0.4526 |
| area Z | 0 | . | . | . |
| veh_body BUS | 1.12071 | 0.37314 | 3.00 | 0.0027 |
| veh_body CONVT | -0.50409 | 0.59456 | -0.85 | 0.3965 |
| veh_body COUPE | 0.27326 | 0.13027 | 2.10 | 0.0359 |
| veh_body HBACK | 0.01199 | 0.04019 | 0.30 | 0.7655 |
| veh_body HDTOP | 0.11485 | 0.09657 | 1.19 | 0.2343 |
| veh_body MCARA | 0.51035 | 0.28603 | 1.78 | 0.0744 |
| veh_body MIBUS | -0.19226 | 0.15998 | -1.20 | 0.2295 |
| veh_body PANVN | 0.17884 | 0.13568 | 1.32 | 0.1875 |
| veh_body RDSTR | -0.04963 | 0.73780 | -0.07 | 0.9464 |
| veh_body STNWG | -0.04648 | 0.04546 | -1.02 | 0.3066 |
| veh_body TRUCK | -0.07890 | 0.10031 | -0.79 | 0.4315 |
| veh_body UTE | -0.27245 | 0.07085 | -3.85 | 0.0001 |
| veh_body ZSEDA | 0 | . | . | . |
| Linear(veh_value) | 0.07787 | 0.01538 | 5.06 | <.0001 |

### Smoothing Model Analysis
### Fit Summary for Smoothing Components

| Component | Smoothing Parameter | DF | GCV | Num Unique Obs |
|---|---|---|---|---|
| Spline(veh_value) | 1.000000 | 4.000006 | 58.175037 | 986 |

### Smoothing Model Analysis
### Analysis of Deviance

| Source | DF | Sum of Squares | Chi-Square | Pr > ChiSq |
|---|---|---|---|---|
| Spline(veh_value) | 4.00001 | 35.478850 | 35.4788 | <.0001 |

## A1.12 GAMLSS

The `gamlss` function is in the `gamlss` package in R, which may be down-loaded from the R project website. It is advisable to read the `gamlss` manual before attempting to implement these models. The code and output for model J in Table 10.1 is shown.

```
> lga <- read.table("LGAclaims.csv",header=T,sep=",")
> library(gamlss)
> pig4 <- gamlss(Claims~log(Accidents)+factor(SD)+offset(L_Population),
+   sigma.formula=~factor(SD),family=PIG,data=lga)
GAMLSS-RS iteration 1: Global Deviance = 2210.573

[output omitted]

> summary(pig4)
*******************************************************************
Family:  c("PIG", "Poisson.Inverse.Gaussian")
Call:  gamlss(formula = Claims ~ log(Accidents) + factor(SD) +
  offset(L_Population), sigma.formula = ~factor(SD), family = PIG,
  data = lga)
Fitting method: RS()


-----------------------------------------------------------------
Mu link function:  log
Mu Coefficients:
                Estimate  Std. Error    t value   Pr(>|t|)
(Intercept)    -6.537675     0.27112  -24.11320  1.773e-55
log(Accidents)  0.201406     0.03250    6.19799  4.561e-09
factor(SD)2    -0.153483     0.08864   -1.73150  8.527e-02
factor(SD)3    -0.051802     0.12120   -0.42739  6.697e-01
factor(SD)4    -0.148795     0.14398   -1.03342  3.029e-01
factor(SD)5    -0.230067     0.16488   -1.39538  1.648e-01
factor(SD)6    -0.002986     0.11324   -0.02637  9.790e-01
factor(SD)7    -0.485661     0.13773   -3.52630  5.483e-04
factor(SD)8    -0.007098     0.21589   -0.03288  9.738e-01
factor(SD)9    -0.095860     0.12337   -0.77704  4.383e-01
factor(SD)10    0.087249     0.15299    0.57030  5.693e-01
factor(SD)11   -0.040958     0.15689   -0.26107  7.944e-01
factor(SD)12   -0.304194     0.22271   -1.36587  1.739e-01
factor(SD)13    0.471325     0.45175    1.04334  2.983e-01


-----------------------------------------------------------------
Sigma link function:  log
Sigma Coefficients:
               Estimate  Std. Error   t value   Pr(>|t|)
(Intercept)   -1.77794      0.2822   -6.30052  2.657e-09
factor(SD)2   -2.34620      1.1508   -2.03875  4.309e-02
factor(SD)3   -0.70713      0.7047   -1.00339  3.172e-01
factor(SD)4   -0.88079      1.2543   -0.70224  4.835e-01
factor(SD)5   -0.31828      0.9284   -0.34283  7.322e-01
factor(SD)6   -1.30941      0.9026   -1.45063  1.488e-01
factor(SD)7   -0.53341      0.6023   -0.88557  3.772e-01
factor(SD)8   -0.94154      5.3857   -0.17482  8.614e-01
factor(SD)9   -0.88677      0.5005   -1.77166  7.832e-02
factor(SD)10   0.36351      0.5546    0.65542  5.131e-01
factor(SD)11   0.02318      0.5142    0.04508  9.641e-01
factor(SD)12   1.18910      0.4692    2.53452  1.220e-02
factor(SD)13   1.38858      0.9921    1.39960  1.635e-01


-----------------------------------------------------------------
No. of observations in the fit:  176
Degrees of Freedom for the fit:  27
      Residual Deg. of Freedom:  149
                    at cycle:  20
```

```
Global Deviance:     1964.729
            AIC:     2018.729
            SBC:     2104.332
*****************************************************************
```

## A1.13  Zero-adjusted inverse Gaussian regression

See remarks about `gamlss` on page 189. In order to implement the adjustment for exposure (`nu.link="own"`), the file `own-link-functions-ZAIG.R` needs to be run. This is available from the companion website.

```
### Change base levels for vehicle body and area
> veh_ref<-c("SEDAN",levels(veh_body)[-10])
> area_ref<-c("C","A","B","D","E","F")
> model1 <- gamlss(claimcst0 ~ C(factor(agecat),base=3)+
  gender+factor(area,levels=area_ref),
  + sigma.fo=~+factor(area,levels=area_ref),
  nu.fo = ~C(factor(agecat),base=3) + factor(area,levels=area_ref) +
  factor(veh_body,levels=veh_ref) + factor(valuecat),
  family=ZAIG(nu.link="own"),data=car)
GAMLSS-RS iteration 1: Global Deviance = 109609.8
GAMLSS-RS iteration 2: Global Deviance = 109609.7
GAMLSS-RS iteration 3: Global Deviance = 109609.7
>
> summary(model1)
*****************************************************************
Family:  c("ZAIG", "Zero adjusted IG")
Call:  gamlss(formula = claimcst0 ~ C(factor(agecat), base = 3) +
  gender + factor(area, levels = area_ref),
  sigma.formula = ~+factor (area,levels = area_ref),
  nu.formula = ~C(factor(agecat), base = 3) + factor(area, levels =
  area_ref) + factor(veh_body, levels = veh_ref) + factor(valuecat),

  family = ZAIG(nu.link = "own"), data = car)
Fitting method: RS()


-----------------------------------------------------------------
Mu link function:  log
Mu Coefficients:
```

|                                | Estimate  | Std. Error | t value   | Pr(>\|t\|) |
|--------------------------------|-----------|------------|-----------|------------|
| (Intercept)                    | 7.530868  | 0.06475    | 116.31157 | 0.000000   |
| C(factor(agecat), base = 3)1   | 0.256466  | 0.09663    | 2.65417   | 0.007952   |
| C(factor(agecat), base = 3)2   | 0.086311  | 0.07389    | 1.16815   | 0.242751   |
| C(factor(agecat), base = 3)4   | -0.003264 | 0.06918    | -0.04718  | 0.962367   |
| C(factor(agecat), base = 3)5   | -0.129357 | 0.07868    | -1.64418  | 0.100144   |
| C(factor(agecat), base = 3)6   | -0.070668 | 0.09602    | -0.73596  | 0.461758   |
| genderM                        | 0.156137  | 0.04961    | 3.14730   | 0.001649   |
| factor(area, levels = area_ref)A | -0.072992 | 0.06765  | -1.07901  | 0.280588   |
| factor(area, levels = area_ref)B | -0.102934 | 0.06951  | -1.48083  | 0.138658   |
| factor(area, levels = area_ref)D | -0.097635 | 0.08097  | -1.20574  | 0.227921   |
| factor(area, levels = area_ref)E | 0.067865 | 0.09281   | 0.73125   | 0.464629   |
| factor(area, levels = area_ref)F | 0.281411 | 0.11402   | 2.46807   | 0.013587   |

```
-----------------------------------------------------------------
Sigma link function:  log
Sigma Coefficients:
```

|                                | Estimate  | Std. Error | t value   | Pr(>\|t\|) |
|--------------------------------|-----------|------------|-----------|------------|
| (Intercept)                    | -3.264020 | 0.01882    | -173.4544 | 0.000000   |
| factor(area, levels = area_ref)A | -0.009818 | 0.02855  | -0.3439   | 0.730896   |
| factor(area, levels = area_ref)B | -0.005001 | 0.02953  | -0.1693   | 0.865546   |
| factor(area, levels = area_ref)D | -0.090445 | 0.03691  | -2.4506   | 0.014266   |
| factor(area, levels = area_ref)E | -0.115772 | 0.04061  | -2.8506   | 0.004365   |
| factor(area, levels = area_ref)F | -0.142623 | 0.04626  | -3.0832   | 0.002049   |

```
------------------------------------------------------------------
Nu link function:  own
Nu Coefficients:
```

|  | Estimate | Std. Error | t value | Pr(>\|t\|) |
|---|---|---|---|---|
| (Intercept) | -1.74963 | 0.04875 | -35.89094 | 1.792e-279 |
| C(factor(agecat), base = 3)1 | 0.28764 | 0.06264 | 4.59204 | 4.397e-06 |
| C(factor(agecat), base = 3)2 | 0.06435 | 0.05011 | 1.28423 | 1.991e-01 |
| C(factor(agecat), base = 3)4 | -0.03599 | 0.04772 | -0.75421 | 4.507e-01 |
| C(factor(agecat), base = 3)5 | -0.26499 | 0.05567 | -4.76009 | 1.939e-06 |
| C(factor(agecat), base = 3)6 | -0.25499 | 0.06694 | -3.80940 | 1.394e-04 |
| factor(area, levels = area_ref)A | -0.03580 | 0.04519 | -0.79221 | 4.282e-01 |
| factor(area, levels = area_ref)B | 0.05338 | 0.04699 | 1.13597 | 2.560e-01 |
| factor(area, levels = area_ref)D | -0.13814 | 0.05846 | -2.36306 | 1.813e-02 |
| factor(area, levels = area_ref)E | -0.06636 | 0.06500 | -1.02085 | 3.073e-01 |
| factor(area, levels = area_ref)F | 0.02086 | 0.07633 | 0.27328 | 7.846e-01 |
| factor(veh_body, levels = veh_ref)BUS | 1.13610 | 0.44940 | 2.52801 | 1.147e-02 |
| factor(veh_body, levels = veh_ref)CONVT | -0.37088 | 0.64170 | -0.57797 | 5.633e-01 |
| factor(veh_body, levels = veh_ref)COUPE | 0.43332 | 0.14843 | 2.91934 | 3.509e-03 |
| factor(veh_body, levels = veh_ref)HBACK | -0.01240 | 0.04314 | -0.28755 | 7.737e-01 |
| factor(veh_body, levels = veh_ref)HDTOP | 0.09898 | 0.10493 | 0.94329 | 3.455e-01 |
| factor(veh_body, levels = veh_ref)MCARA | 0.59604 | 0.32765 | 1.81914 | 6.889e-02 |
| factor(veh_body, levels = veh_ref)MIBUS | -0.11119 | 0.17178 | -0.64729 | 5.174e-01 |
| factor(veh_body, levels = veh_ref)PANVN | 0.01942 | 0.14484 | 0.13404 | 8.934e-01 |
| factor(veh_body, levels = veh_ref)RDSTR | 0.06960 | 0.80143 | 0.08685 | 9.308e-01 |
| factor(veh_body, levels = veh_ref)STNWG | -0.01913 | 0.04995 | -0.38289 | 7.018e-01 |
| factor(veh_body, levels = veh_ref)TRUCK | -0.09668 | 0.10824 | -0.89320 | 3.718e-01 |
| factor(veh_body, levels = veh_ref)UTE | -0.24555 | 0.07599 | -3.23150 | 1.232e-03 |
| factor(valuecat)2 | 0.21017 | 0.04936 | 4.25814 | 2.064e-05 |
| factor(valuecat)3 | 0.13652 | 0.12367 | 1.10390 | 2.696e-01 |
| factor(valuecat)4 | -0.60666 | 0.53927 | -1.12495 | 2.606e-01 |
| factor(valuecat)5 | -0.29002 | 0.77299 | -0.37519 | 7.075e-01 |
| factor(valuecat)6 | -0.79717 | 1.07207 | -0.74358 | 4.571e-01 |

```
------------------------------------------------------------------
No. of observations in the fit:  67856
Degrees of Freedom for the fit:  46

        Residual Deg. of Freedom:  67810
                    at cycle:  3

Global Deviance:      109609.7
           AIC:      109701.7
           SBC:      110121.5
******************************************************************
```

# Bibliography

Arbous, A. G. and J. Kerrich (1951). Accident statistics and the concept of accident-proneness. *Biometrics 7*, 340–432.

Australian Bureau of Statistics (1996). *National Health Survey User's Guide 4363.0*. Canberra: Australian Bureau of Statistics.

Cameron, A. C. and P. K. Trivedi (1998). *Regression Analysis of Count Data*. Cambridge: Cambridge University Press.

Chambers, J. M. and T. J. Hastie (1991). *Statistical Models in S*. Boca Raton, FL, USA: CRC Press, Inc.

Collett, D. (2003). *Modelling Binary Data* (Second edn). Boca Raton, FL: Chapman and Hall/CRC.

Diggle, P. J., P. Heagerty, K. Y. Liang, and S. L. Zeger (2002). *Analysis of Longitudinal Data* (Second edn). New York: Oxford University Press.

Dobson, A. J. (2002). *An Introduction to Generalized Linear Models* (Second edn). Florida: Chapman and Hall/CRC.

England, P. and R. Verrall (2002). Stochastic claims reserving in general insurance. *Journal of the Institute of Actuaries 129*, 1–76.

Fahrmeir, L. and G. Tutz (2001). *Multivariate Statistical Modelling Based on Generalized Linear Models* (Second edn). New York: Springer Verlag.

Friendly, M. (2000). *Visualizing Categorical Data*. Cary, NC: SAS Press.

Goldstein, H. (2003). *Multilevel Statistical Models* (3rd edn). London: Edward Arnold.

Greenwood, M. and G. U. Yule (1920). An inquiry into the nature of frequency distributions representative of multiple happenings, with particular reference to the occurrence of multiple attacks of disease or of repeated accidents. *Journal of the Royal Statistical Society 83*, 255–279.

Hastie, T. J. and R. J. Tibshirani (1986). Generalized additive models. *Statistical Science 1*, 297–318.

Hastie, T. J. and R. J. Tibshirani (1990). *Generalized Additive Models*. Boca Raton, FL: Chapman and Hall/CRC.

Heller, G. Z., D. M. Stasinopoulos, and R. A. Rigby (2006). The zero-adjusted inverse Gaussian distribution as a model for insurance data. *Proceedings of the International Workshop on Statistical Modelling, Galway*, 226–233.

Heller, G. Z., D. M. Stasinopoulos, R. A. Rigby, and P. de Jong (2007). Mean and dispersion modelling for policy claims costs. *Scandinavian Actuarial Journal*. 2007(4).

Hogg, R. V. and S. A. Klugman (1984). *Loss Distributions*. New York: Wiley.

Hosmer, D. W. and S. Lemeshow (1999). *Applied Survival Analysis*. New York: John Wiley.

Human Mortality Database (2007). http://www.mortality.org. (Accessed 13 May 2007).

Ihaka, R. and R. Gentleman (1996). R: A language for data analysis and graphics. *Journal of Computational and Graphical Statistics 5*(3), 299–314.

Jørgensen, B. and M. de Souza (1994). Fitting Tweedie's compound Poisson model to insurance claims data. *Scandinavian Actuarial Journal, 1* 69–93.

Leader, L. R. (1994). Births at the Royal Hospital for Women, Paddington, personal communication.

Lee, Y. and J. A. Nelder (1996). Hierarchical generalized linear models. *Journal of the Royal Statistical Society (B) 58*, 619–678.

Lee, Y. and J. A. Nelder (2001). Hierarchical generalised linear models: A synthesis of generalised linear models, random-effect models and structured dispersions. *Biometrika 88*, 987–1006.

Lemaire, J. (1991). Negative binomial or Poisson-inverse Gaussian? *ASTIN Bulletin 21*, 167–168.

Lindsey, J. K. (1997). *Applying Generalized Linear Models*. New York: Springer.

Lundberg, O. (1940). *On Random Processes and their Application to Sickness and Accident Statistics*. Uppsala: Almqvist and Wiksells.

McCullagh, P. and J. A. Nelder (1989). *Generalized Linear Models* (Second edn). New York: Chapman and Hall.

Nelder, J. A. and R. W. M. Wedderburn (1972). Generalized linear models. *Journal of the Royal Statistical Society, Series A 135(3)*, 370–384.

Newbold, E. (1927). Practical applications of the statistics of repeated events, particularly to industrial accidents. *Journal of the Royal Statistical Society 90*, 487–547.

Peterson, B. and F. E. Harrell (1990). Partial proportional odds models for ordinal response variables. *Applied Statistics 39*(2), 205–217.

Rigby, R. A. and D. M. Stasinopoulos (2005). Generalized additive models for location, scale and shape. *Applied Statistics 54*(3), 507–554.

Roads and Traffic Authority (2004). *Road Traffic Crashes in New South Wales*. Sydney: Roads and Traffic Authority.

Seal, H. (1982). Mixed Poisson – an ideal distribution of claim numbers? *Insurance: Mathematics and Economics 8*, 35–46.

Smyth, G. K. (1989). Generalized linear models with varying dispersion. *Journal of the Royal Statistical Society (B) 51*, 47–60.

Smyth, G. K. and B. Jørgensen (2002). Fitting Tweedie's compound Poisson model to insurance claims data: dispersion modelling. *ASTIN Bulletin 32*, 143–157.

Stasinopoulos, D. M., R. A. Rigby, and C. Akantziliotou (2006). gamlss: A collection of functions to fit Generalized Additive Models for Location, Scale and Shape, R package version 1.1-0. *http://www.londonmet.ac.uk/gamlss/*.

Stasinopoulos, D. M., R. A. Rigby, and G. Z. Heller (2007). The rsm package in R. *www.londonmet.ac.uk/gamlss/*.

Stokes, M. E., C. S. Davis, and G. G. Koch (2000). *Categorical Data Analysis Using the SAS System* (Second edn). Cary, NC: SAS Institute Inc.

Williams, R. L. (2000). A note on robust variance estimation for cluster-correlated data. *Biometrics 56*, 645–646.

Willmot, G. E. (1987). The Poisson-inverse Gaussian distribution as an alternative to the negative binomial. *Scandinavian Actuarial Journal 87*, 113–127.

Wood, S. N. (2006). *Generalized Additive Models: An Introduction with R*. Chapman and Hall/CRC.

# Index

9 780521 879149